THE HIDDEN COST

OF MONEY

THE HIDDEN COST OF MONEY

How Financial Forces Shape
Our Lives & the World Around Us

By SEB BUNNEY

ACKNOWLEDGMENTS

From the absolute bottom of my heart, I would like to thank the individuals who have been instrumental in shaping this book from mere ideas into the work that now rests in your hands. That includes:

- My mum, Janine, whose invaluable feedback, and unwavering support have been a guiding light throughout this journey.
- Daz, my best friend, and partner in crime, for generously sharing his thoughts and ideas, enriching the narrative.
- Angela, whose insightful observations have helped fill gaps and enhance the clarity of explanations.
- Anna Sobieniak Design, for her talent and assistance in creating the captivating cover design.
- Leo, for his candid honesty and constructive feedback, urging me to refine the book after the first draft.
- Daniel Prince, for graciously crafting the foreword and whose thoughtful words have supported the reader's journey beyond measure.
- Dalia, for her fantastic early feedback, providing essential insights during the book's early stages.
- Haley Weaver, the editor, whose profound thoughts regarding the narrative flow have been truly invaluable.

I am also equally appreciative to James, Mike, Kudzai, and Jonathan, each of whom offered valuable insights at different stages of the book's development.

Lastly, I would like to thank Jeff Booth, Preston Pysh, Gabor Maté, Alex Gladstein, Greg Foss, Michael Saylor, and Satoshi, whose incredible work and shared knowledge have and continue to play a significant role in helping me piece together the complex puzzle that is our world.

This book would not be what it is today without the support, encouragement, and inspiration provided by these wonderful friends, family members, and individuals. From the bottom of my heart, thank you.

TABLE OF CONTENTS

FOREWORD

The Hidden Cost of Money.
Huh?
Hidden?
What's hidden?
Sure, you instinctively know that it costs something to produce money, the design, the ink and printing of the paper, the natural resources used to make coins, managing the supply chains downstream of the mines and paper mills, and the eventual distribution of the physical notes and coins into circulation. This is all an enormous task and one that incurs lots of tangible and easy-to-see costs.

So, what is the author and the title of this book hinting at?

What are the costs that are being hidden from us, and why am I only hearing about this now?

What have been the social, environmental, and political impacts on a local and global scale?

Are the people in charge of and perpetuating these hidden costs aware of the long-term unintended consequences to humanity and the world at large?

As you've probably already experienced through the "cost of living crisis," you will see a continual withering away of your purchasing power if we continue along this current economic path.

This isn't a drill.

Your money, which has been diligently saved from tiresome work, has been and will continue to be gradually siphoned off in a seemingly unceasing list of rising costs and new expenses, trapping you in a cycle, affecting your judgment, and disconnecting you from your core values.

The fact that you are likely reading this whilst exhausted on a commute to a job you dislike but have to perform just to keep food on the table should be a cause for concern.

> *"If you do not change direction, you may end up where you are heading."* —Lao Tzu

So, how do you turn this ship around?

Work harder and longer hours, compete with your colleagues at all costs to get ahead, climb that corporate ladder, get that promotion, make it into that corner office, get that five-bedroom house and BMW on finance, then lever up and make smart investments in the stock markets.

Right guys?

Well, that's the conventional advice you would get from many of the flapping-head "self-help gurus" out there. But there is another way, a much simpler way, and it all starts here, with this book in your hands.

You can only fix a problem if you know what the problem is.

This book has been thoughtfully written to take you on a journey through the history of money and how our species uses money as a form of communication. Seb Bunney explains how this vital communication channel has been captured, producing a myriad of unintended consequences and shaping society in unexpected ways.

Seb's passion and unique skillset is educating others, and he boasts a wide variety of teaching experiences. His career has taken him from leading mountain biking expeditions through the back mountains of British Colombia to co-founding Looking Glass

Education, an online education platform designed to remove the veil of complexity shrouding our monetary and economic systems.

With this book, *The Hidden Cost of Money*, Seb will expose the reality of our current economic path and then offer you a potential solution that you might find quite surprising.

Then, it will be up to you, dear reader, to decide which path to take.

I hope to see you on the other side, where Seb, myself and many others wait to welcome you.

"This is your last chance. After this, there is no turning back. You take the blue pill – the story ends, you wake up in your bed and believe whatever you want to believe. You take the red pill – you stay in Wonderland, and I show you how deep the rabbit hole goes. Remember, all I'm offering is the truth – nothing more."
—Morpheus.

Daniel Prince - Author of *Choose Life*.
Host of *The Once Bitten Podcast*.
SW France.
September 2023

PREFACE

I grew up in what I believed to be a typical household. When I was five years old, my parents separated as they found themselves no longer meeting each other's needs.

Following the separation, my mother, in search of happiness and a new start, moved my two brothers and me halfway across the world, not once, but twice. As we navigated this challenging time, I unknowingly took on the role of my mother's emotional support, regularly prioritizing her needs above my own.

Throughout this period, my connection with my father was sporadic at best. And to compound matters, we struggled to see eye-to-eye. I frequently felt brushed aside when I brought up my passions and pursuits, as they largely didn't align with my father's values of academia and financial security. It was disheartening to feel like my dreams weren't taken seriously, and I frequently questioned whether I was on the right path. I longed for the kind of fatherly support I saw in other families, but the reality of our relationship often fell short.

That said, I was incredibly fortunate to have a supportive mother. One who actively promoted my love for sports and assisted me when I wanted to leave traditional schooling to pursue a career in mountain bike coaching. However, her top priority was to put food on the table and a roof over our heads, which didn't always come easily as a single mum, let alone leave much wiggle room for funding non-essentials or quality time for herself or my brothers and me.

Between a father who rarely endorsed my love for the outdoors and a mother desperately trying to get by while caring for three children, my developmental years often left me in need of greater support. I didn't know who I was, what my needs were, or how to understand my own emotions. I turned to my peers to fill the gap left by my parents, but as a result, I learned to suppress how I felt in an effort to conform and fit in.

But I did not give up striving to find my authentic self— my personality, values, and spirit, regardless of the external pressures to act otherwise.

Looking back, I feel incredibly fortunate to have had the childhood I did. My brothers and I had food on the table, clothes on our backs, and a roof over our heads. We were safe and cared for, but as I grew into young adulthood, I couldn't help wondering how the particulars of my upbringing had shaped me.

Following a challenging breakup and 23 years of looking outward in an attempt to fit in and meet the needs of others, I was in a difficult emotional state. It was at this moment that I finally set out to answer some burning questions:

- Who am I?
- What are my needs and boundaries?
- How can I explore my authentic self without a sense of shame?

As I struggled to answer these questions, I realized that many of my peers—*from a range of backgrounds*—were facing similar crises of identity. I began to question whether, rather than an individual issue as I had originally assumed, there was a larger impediment to living authentically.

It wasn't until I started to wonder what was behind this widespread hurdle to authenticity that I realized I had already been flirting with the answer for many years.

When I started coaching mountain biking in my late teens, I was enamoured with my job. Yet, despite my adoration, I felt an unease in the pit of my stomach. I was struggling to get by. Food and rent engulfed most of my paycheque, and even when I looked at some of the world-renowned coaches I was working with, they, too, were in a similar position. They had little to their name, lacked housing security, and many were overcome with credit card debt.

I am not going to lie. This scared me! I regularly questioned myself and the career path I had taken. I didn't want to abandon my vocation, but I recognized that I had to do something about my financial situation if I wanted to live my best life.

From then on, I started devouring every course, book, and podcast on investing I could get my hands on, all to prolong my much-loved mountain biking career.

But I quickly realized something was wrong. When I considered the tried-and-true advice for how to live a financially sound life, I realized that following the old guard's wisdom would not be enough. It was becoming harder and harder to get ahead. For a house my parents would've paid $80,000 for, I would have to fork out $800,000.

"How can anyone afford financial security?" I thought to myself. I wasn't trying to get rich. I just wanted to live a stable and fulfilling life. Ultimately, this line of questioning led me to the realization:

Everything is downstream of money.

This revelation, stemming from my exploration of finance, ignited within me an entirely new line of thinking concerning money's profound influence on our environment and, therefore, who we are.

When our money no longer meets the needs of its users nor reflects what society values, everyone and everything feels the effects. The challenges I encountered during my upbringing, the overwhelming pressure to conform, my mother's limited availability and energy, and my father's relentless pursuit of financial security all originated from our complex relationship with money. I can attempt to disregard its influence and prioritize other areas of life, but the reality remains: money will inevitably leave its mark on me, regardless of my personal inclinations.

All in all, embarking on my journey to seek answers, I could have never anticipated that my pursuit of self-discovery would evolve into a decade-long commitment to ingesting every book on money, monetary policy, macroeconomics, parenting, and psychology that crossed my path. This unexpected adventure has not only provided deep personal insights but also granted me the humbling opportunity to share my thoughts at global financial conferences and on respected podcasts, write for international platforms, and connect with some of the most inspiring minds. This path ultimately led me to this moment, writing this book connecting money and our societal challenges.

And so here we are. When life gives you lemons, write a book on the rising cost of lemonade.

Leveraging my background as a mountain bike instructor, business owner, investor, aspiring therapist, dedicated educator, and perpetual learner, I believe I offer a unique outlook on money. While I do not want to disregard the value traditional academia has added to our understanding of this powerful tool that underpins society, I feel they've missed, arguably, the most crucial aspect of all: relatability. A jargon-heavy, data-rich approach to money makes it hard for everyday folk to connect with. Therefore, given my background, it's my intention to explain and expand on money from multiple—*non-traditional*—perspectives, aiming to make it more relatable and understandable for everyone.

For some, this idea that everything is downstream of money might seem foreign, but for others, it hits close to home. Regardless of where you fall on this spectrum, the incentives emanating from our monetary system have far-reaching consequences that most definitely alter how we show up and interact in this world.

MONEY IS MORE THAN JUST A MEDIUM OF EXCHANGE

Why Money Is the Ultimate Form of Expression

*"Self-expression must pass into communication for its
fulfillment." —Pearl S. Buck*

....

D o you ever feel like you're treading water, struggling to keep
up with the rising tide of expenses? From groceries to housing
to transportation, your cost of living continues to climb while
your wages struggle to keep up.

Deep down, you know something just isn't right. You've
pushed yourself to the limit, hoping that a little more grind would
bring you closer to your goals. However, despite your tireless
efforts, it doesn't seem to get any easier. Life still seems like an
uphill battle, with few lasting rewards to show for all your hard
work.

It's a frustrating and often isolating feeling. But the truth
is, not only are you not alone in this struggle, but the problem is
not with you. The problems we face are with our money!

Bit by bit, our purchasing power has been withering away.
And this erosion has far-reaching effects on our lives and the

lives of those around us. The necessities many of us have taken for granted—*a roof over our heads, a reliable car, a full stomach*—are becoming harder to afford. In turn, simple luxuries like occasional travel or a daily latte become more of a pipe dream.

In the not-too-distant past, a sole breadwinner could afford a spacious home in the suburbs and still have enough disposable income to sustain their household. Unfortunately, as we have all seen, those days are long gone. Today, millennials (born between 1981 and 1996) have reached their prime home-buying age, yet despite making up nearly 22% of the population, they represent just 4% of the current housing market. And that's not because millennials aren't diligent savers.[1,2] By comparison, when baby boomers (born between 1946 and 1964) were of a similar age, they owned upwards of 35% of the housing market.

Or take vehicles, for instance. In 1970, your standard American could buy a brand-new average-priced car for 45% of their income.[3,4] Today, that ratio has more than doubled to 106%.[5,6]

As you crack open these pages, I invite you to consider how money has impacted your own journey and those around you.

- Have you ever had to sacrifice something important to you because of financial constraints?
- Has the pressure to "earn a living" ever affected your mental and physical health?
- Have financial pressures ever meant that money has become a source of conflict between you and the people you care about?

And perhaps most importantly, what kind of ripple effects might this decline in purchasing power have on you, those you care about, and society as a whole if it were to persist or increase? Most of us will have some confronting answers to at least one, if not all, of these questions.

But does it have to be this way? The answer is a resounding NO. The gradual erosion of our collective purchasing power is not an inevitable part of life. Rather, it results from how our governments and central banks govern money.

Given money's remarkable (often negative) capacity to shape our lives and influence our perspectives on the world, it's no wonder that throughout history and even today, many people view money with suspicion or even disdain. We're all familiar with sayings that warn against the corrupting influence of money:

"Money doesn't buy happiness."
"Money is the root of all evil."
"It's rude to talk about money."

These statements speak to the potential and power of money, physically, socially, and psychologically. However, money holds a broader significance than just facilitating exchange. Money, like language, is a powerful medium of expression, providing insight into people's values and priorities. How we spend our money sheds light on the very essence of what we hold dear.

Therefore, while money itself may not directly buy happiness, the extent to which it supports expression undeniably influences our perception of it. Does our money hold value over time, and can we spend our money where we see fit? For this reason, it is often overlooked that money is inherently amoral— neither good nor bad. *That said, this doesn't mean there aren't superior or inferior forms of money.* Our perception usually gravitates towards the unfavourable due to the unintended consequences of money in its current form, combined with its built-in limitations that hinder our ability to express ourselves.

So, while at first glance, money may seem like a simple tool, a middleman between people and their true desires, let's look at what makes money a potent form of expression.

Time, as it is finite and irreversible, is arguably our most prized possession. We only have so much time in our lives, let alone in our day. Because of the scarcity of time, we ought to be incredibly conscious about how we choose to spend it. Some of us may wish to prioritize activities like baking and crafts, while others prefer sports and music. Although where we would like to spend our time differs from person to person, one thing is certain. Most of us have more we would like to do than we will ever have time for.

Considering the scarcity of time and the infinite demand for it, the choices we make as human beings regarding how we invest our time and what we are willing to exchange for it hold tremendous significance. Our allocation of time serves as a direct reflection of our priorities, values, and aspirations. Therefore, by examining how we distribute our time, we can gain valuable insights into our individual and collective preferences, societal values, and the things people attach meaning to.

Fortunately, we have the means to monitor how individuals choose to allocate their time: Money! Money acts as a medium of expression, offering insights into the choices people make with their time.

When we work, we are renumerated for our time spent in the form of money. For us to obtain money, we must expend time. In this way, you can think of money as a method of storing time, time that can later be spent on whatever it is we want:

- Obtaining housing in a community or location where we feel a sense of belonging.
- Acquiring food that aligns with our tastes.
- Experiencing enjoyable and entertaining activities.
- Purchasing aesthetically pleasing objects to personalize our living spaces or enhance our appearances.
- Investing in education for ourselves or our children
...among numerous other examples.

But as with anything, money can be corrupted.

Some forms of money, such as physical coins and bills, struggle to maintain value, while certain digital currencies impose usage restrictions. For instance, in China, restrictions are placed on domestic households to prevent capital flight abroad by limiting their ability to invest.[7] These constraints not only distort our sense of priorities but also obstruct our capacity to allocate our time in alignment with our core values, thus impinging on our ability to express ourselves authentically.

Moreover, when a significant portion of our time is consumed by working 60 hours a week just to afford the essentials, it leaves little time for connecting with family, preparing enjoyable meals, or engaging in community volunteering. The diminishing purchasing power of our time raises questions about our capacity to prioritize long-term goals when immediate needs demand a considerable share of our limited resources. If your money is losing value from one day to the next, are you incentivized to save for the future? Of course not. You might as well purchase what you can while you can!

With this in mind, in the current state of affairs, we cannot accurately assess what it is that people value. Our visibility is limited to what currency controls and monetary intervention dictates, preventing us from gaining a comprehensive understanding of true societal values. Therefore, money that enables us to express what we value accurately is crucial to effective decision-making, the precursor for economic prosperity. Without such money, accurately assessing society's needs to thrive becomes a formidable challenge, as we remain unaware of what people truly value.

When our money is free of limitations, intervention, and constraints, it can more precisely reflect what society values, enabling us to better invest our time, energy, and resources in productive pursuits that align with our goals and create value for ourselves and others.

Many modern economists have spread stale maxims about how the world works. You may have heard that:

- Inflation, or the continual rise of prices, is a natural and unavoidable phenomenon.
- Monetary intervention, such as government bailouts and other forms of financial assistance, is necessary to prevent economic pressures and ensure stability.
- Endless economic growth and consumption are both possible and desirable.

Yet in following this wisdom, wealth inequality continues to expand, and mounting health issues, social tension, and financial instability are becoming the norm. These trends should give us cause for concern.

As tempting as it may seem to continue along this well-trodden path of monetary intervention, maybe we should step back and ask ourselves:

Are we building a monetary system that allows us to thrive and adapt to our changing conditions?

OR

Is our monetary system inadvertently setting us up for failure by undermining our decision-making and altering our sense of what truly matters?

In this book, I want to take you, the reader, on a journey into the depths of our monetary system, exploring the incentives that emanate from our money and how they impact who we are and how we act. Along the way, we'll discuss how money in its current form adversely affects almost every aspect of society, including:

Social & Environmental Impacts
- The deterioration of the family unit
- The decline of altruism and the rise of consumerism, meaninglessness, and apathy
- The overconsumption of our planet's resources

Economic Consequences
- The climbing cost of living
- Elevated risk-taking and unproductive business practices

Political Implications
- The infringement of free speech and human rights
- The rise of government overreach

My intention is to challenge the conventional belief that money is a wild, uncontrollable force that requires taming by the government and central banks and, instead, illustrate how it is the government that has created the "beast" that is our current monetary system.

By better understanding the difficulties and far-reaching effects of our money, we can not only better assess our changing circumstances, but we also have the power to build a more sustainable, equitable, and just society. And don't worry. This won't be a dry lecture on economics. Instead, we'll explore real-world examples, and as we approach the end of the book, I'll leave you with some food for thought— the possibility of an alternative monetary system that realigns incentives and fosters truth, integrity, and freedom of expression.

With this in mind, I want to invite you on a journey of exploration into how something as counterintuitive as money can profoundly impact our lives, from our personal authenticity to the health of our planet. Everything is downstream of money. If we are misguided in our approach, the consequences won't just be a few lost coins in the couch cushions.

AUTHORS NOTE

Before diving in, I preface these ideas with five important points.

First, the monetary system we have inherited from those before us incentivizes certain behaviours. Throughout this book, we will explore these incentives and how they influence the actions of everyone involved in our economic system.

While I will sometimes use examples that may paint the government in an unfavourable light, I want to stress that I believe that we are all doing the best given the information we've got, so my intention is not to criticize individuals but rather to shed light on the underlying incentives that influence certain behaviours and shape our decision-making processes.

Additionally, although I primarily use the United States for my examples, it's important to note that the monetary incentive structures we will explore currently exist to some degree in every country.

Second, it is worth noting that while the Federal Reserve Banks in the United States and many other central banks globally are private corporations owned by shareholders, they are also an extension of the government. In the US, the seven-member Federal Reserve Board of Governors is nominated by the President and confirmed by the Senate, giving the government significant influence over the Fed's decision-making and policy direction.[8]

Throughout the book, I will use "government" as a catch-all term that includes the central banks since they work in concert with one another.

For those unfamiliar with the term central bank, you can think of it as a national bank that offers financial and banking services to its country's government and commercial banking system, including your local bank. What gives a central bank its power is that it is granted exclusive control over the production and distribution of a nation's money and credit. With this in mind, a central bank is responsible for crafting and implementing monetary policies as well as regulating member banks. In modern economies, the central bank is seen as playing a critical role in ensuring economic stability and facilitating the growth of the financial sector.

Third, the byproducts we have and will discuss over the following chapters are by no means an exhaustive list but rather a high-level overview to raise awareness of money's hidden influence on society.

Fourth, I'd like to acknowledge that this book may evoke strong emotions and prompt you to question the stability of our economy. This might be unsettling for some readers, but I encourage you to persevere with the book. While there are no easy solutions to the challenges I'm presenting—*every course of action involves trade-offs, drawbacks, and pitfalls*—facing the truth is enlightening. Only by examining the structure and incentives that underpin our monetary system can we make more informed decisions about the best path forward for ourselves and our economy.

Finally, before we face some confronting truths, I'd like to note that I wholeheartedly believe that **the future is bright!** We not only have options, which I will shed light on in the latter chapters, but also countless inspiring individuals who tirelessly strive to build a more prosperous, equitable, and just monetary system that meets the varied needs of its participants. So, without further ado, I hope you find value and insight in this book.

CHAPTER 1

A BRIEF HISTORY OF MONEY

How Intervention Has Shaped the Money We Use

"It ain't what you don't know that gets you into trouble. It's what you know for sure that just ain't so."
—*Mark Twain*

....

Consider David, a passionate individual who consistently directs his savings toward acquiring outdoor gear, such as camping equipment. The farmer whose livelihood is transformed by an unprecedented surge in demand for ethically sourced, locally produced, grass-fed beef. A boycott where conscientious consumers unite in their refusal to support manufacturers that disregard ethical practices. Or a nation whose economy plummets due to a global rejection of natural resources extracted under inhumane conditions.

In each of these scenarios, what valuable insights can we gain from analyzing the money flow, or lack thereof?

By monitoring the movement of money, be it on an individual or macroeconomic level, we can uncover profound insights into the underlying values driving personal expenditure or, in a broader context, our shared societal values. Take, for example, David's spending habits which reveal his deep appreciation for nature and the outdoors. Similarly, the surging demand for grass-fed beef not only reflects changing dietary preferences but also underscores the growing significance of ethical, locally sourced products. However, this revelation comes with a crucial caveat: only under specific monetary conditions can money truly serve as an authentic reflection of who we are, our unwavering priorities, and the very essence of what we hold dear.

When it comes to romantic relationships, no matter how much time or effort we invest, without establishing effective lines of communication, our understanding of our partner's needs becomes distorted, and vice versa. This breakdown in comprehension ultimately dooms the connection, as we lack the capacity to discern the necessary steps for progress. That said, just as how a breakdown in communication can spell the end of a relationship, numerous societal challenges arise when an ineffective monetary system impedes our ability to convey our needs and values.

Open lines of monetary communication mean we can allocate our capital according to our beliefs. When declining purchasing power, capital controls, spending limits, or purchasing restrictions hinder our capacity to direct capital where we see fit, money's ability to mirror our societal values begins to erode. Under such circumstances, our capacity to express ourselves monetarily becomes inhibited, suppressing the truth. Consequently, the economy experiences cascading effects, including loss of authenticity, wealth inequality, needless consumption, and environmental degradation, among others. Much like how emotional expression is integral to emotional maturity, freedom of monetary expression is vital for a sustainable and functioning economy.

For both relationships and societies to endure, let alone thrive, we must cultivate genuine self-expression in alignment with our beliefs. This allows us to perceive reality as it truly is, or at the very least, as closely aligned with reality as possible, aiding us in offering value.

Remember, everything is downstream of money. If we want humanity to flourish, we must ensure truth and integrity underpin our money.

With all this in mind, let's delve into the heart of our economy—*our monetary system*—to uncover how it has gone astray, hindering our ability to express ourselves truthfully and precisely.

OUR MONETARY SYSTEM

Picture yourself embarking on a journey from New York's JFK Airport to Tokyo's Narita International Airport. Spanning over 14 hours, this flight covers 10,871 kilometres. Now, imagine the pilot miscalculates his trajectory by a mere 1º during takeoff. Though seemingly insignificant, you'd discover yourself hundreds of kilometres off-course from Tokyo by the time you intended to arrive. You're now over the Sea of Japan or the Pacific Ocean, with dwindling fuel reserves. Much like we rely on faith and trust in our pilot's skills, flight instruments, and navigation systems, we must also bestow substantial faith and trust in the layers of our monetary system:

- We place our trust in central bankers, hoping they possess the expertise and knowledge necessary to navigate the complexities of a macroeconomic environment and make decisions for the betterment of society.
- We must rely on commercial banks to access our money whenever we make a withdrawal.
- We place great trust in our money, hoping it incentivizes positive and productive behaviour.

- We rely on the stability and continued usability of the currency we earn as income to fulfill our desires and meet our essential needs.
- We must put our faith in those in positions of power, trusting that they have the best interests of the economy and the people at heart.

Just like the pilot example above, in any of these situations, if the individuals or institutions in question were to fall short, the consequences could be catastrophic.

So, is our monetary system and its participants deserving of the considerable trust we grant them? Let's take a closer look at the history and current state of our monetary system to explore whether it's truly worthy of our confidence.

The 4 Factors of Production

Our economy may seem complex and overwhelming at first glance, with numerous moving parts and intricate systems. However, with a closer examination, it becomes clear that everything within our economy can be distilled into four key areas: land, labour, enterprise, and capital. These four areas are known as the four factors of production, which, combined, form the building blocks of all goods and services. Understanding them, therefore, is essential to understanding how our economy functions.

Let's take a look at the four factors of production and explore how each one plays a crucial role in the functioning of our economy.

Land

First, we have the factor of land, which encompasses all types of land, including everything from agricultural land to commercial real estate. However, and more importantly, it includes all our natural resources, such as oil, gold, lumber, and minerals. Anything involving land use or requiring extraction from our natural environment falls under the land factor.

Labour

Second, there is the factor of labour, which is the mental and physical effort the population expends to bring goods or services to the market. This includes everyone from construction workers and restaurant staff to receptionists and manufacturing plant employees. Demographics, like age composition or education levels, greatly impact the productivity of the labour workforce.

Capital

Third, we have the factor of capital. Capital is the lifeblood of most businesses, providing the necessary funds to purchase equipment and infrastructure required to manufacture goods and provide services. Capital goods can include machinery, vehicles, tools, and other physical assets necessary to produce goods and services efficiently. Without capital, businesses struggle to survive, unable to meet their expenses, purchase materials, pay for production, or invest in the equipment needed to improve productivity and expand operations. As such, the availability and accessibility of capital play a critical role in the health and growth of the economy.

Enterprise

Last, we have the factor of enterprise or entrepreneurship, which utilizes the other three factors to create innovative products and services that generate profit and increase productivity. Enterprise is the catalyst that brings the factors together with purpose. As Luis Portes, a professor of economics at Montclair State University, explains: "Entrepreneurial activity is the engine of innovation that brings new ways of organizing land, capital and labour to produce new goods and services." In short, enterprise plays a critical role in a nation's economic growth and development.

With an understanding of the four factors of production, we can start to piece together the incentives that underlie our economy. But... have you ever noticed that although there are four factors that make up our economy, we only ever seem to hear about one in particular. That is the factor of capital. There are far more news stories, such as:

"Fed announces massive cash injection to relieve U.S. debt market."[9]

"Biden, McCarthy reach agreement ... to raise debt ceiling as default looms."[10]

"Stimulus Checks Substantially Reduced Hardship, Study Shows."[11]

Yet far and few between about how:

"We need to have more children to boost labour capacity!"

"Increase our ability to extract more natural resources."

"Bet on technological change to fix our issues."

If you're wondering, "Why does capital command this attention?" You're not alone! When times get tough, we can think of each of these factors as a lever that can be pulled to increase productivity and reduce economic stress. For instance, pulling the "land" lever can involve redirecting efforts toward obtaining more natural resources or improving agricultural productivity.

However, this approach has several challenges, such as:

- There is no guarantee that we will discover new resources or experience a significant increase in land productivity within the desired timeframe.
- The process of promoting land use and increasing resource production can take a long time. For example, it takes roughly five years to build a new solar farm and between 1 to 10 years to build a gold mine.[12,13] Even after completion, there is only a small chance it will be a productive site.

- Regulations aimed at minimizing environmental impact have made it increasingly difficult to start new projects related to traditional energy production. In fact, some countries are even buying out farmers to meet their climate goals, such as the Netherlands, the second-largest agricultural exporter globally.[14] As a result, pulling the "land" lever has become less effective and less profitable than it has been historically.

Another option could be to direct our attention to the "labour" lever. By implementing austerity measures such as cutting public programs, raising taxes and so on, we could push the labour workforce to increase production by working harder and longer, all while reducing consumption, given their reduction in expendable income.

The challenge is that not only are these measures politically unfavourable and usually avoided by politicians, but the general populace also doesn't tend to favour such measures, considering that austerity predominantly impacts the lower and middle classes and has an immediate negative impact on our quality of life. We also often overlook the demographic hurdles we currently face. Here are a few glaring facts that may give us some clues as to what to expect moving forward:

The Past

- The US population grew by 40% between 1950 and 1960.[15]
- The global population doubled between 1950 and 1987.[16]
- During the 1970s, the Baby Boomers began supporting themselves and entering the workforce, creating greater demand for goods, services and assets due to their high numbers.

The Future

- The percentage of senior citizen-aged Canadians (aged 65 and over) will increase by around 60% between 2019 and 2036, compared to an increase of under 10% for the younger population.[17]
- A study by the People's Bank of China revealed that *"China's population could halve in the next 45 years."* [18]
- At 0.35% in 2020, the US experienced their lowest annual population growth rate since at least 1900.[19]

As demonstrated above, we are currently undergoing a significant shift in demographics, transitioning from a period of rapid population growth to a complete reversal. With the aging of the population, the labour force is set to decline, posing significant challenges to the economy. This demographic shift places immense pressure on the economy and severely hampers the productivity of the workforce.

One long-term option for adjusting the "labour" lever could be incentivizing couples to have more children to increase the workforce. But, once again, the challenge is that we won't see much benefit from such a shift until long into the future. Moreover, numerous countries are attempting to directly incentivize child rearing but to no avail.[20] Within my personal friend group, many are still swayed by the pervasive messaging over the last two decades that warned of an impending global food crisis due to overpopulation.

Alternatively, we could pull the "enterprise" lever by promoting start-ups, new businesses, and innovation via tax incentives, government grants and reduced regulatory pressures. By doing so, we attempt to boost technological advancements to increase economic productivity and efficiency.

However, similar to the land factor, investing in technology and entrepreneurship requires adequate capital. Furthermore, it is also a time-consuming process with no guarantee of success. There is no clear timeline for when technological advancements will occur or at what point they will positively impact our productivity.

And that brings us to the more popular "capital" lever, which I will refer to throughout this book as monetary intervention or the monetary lever.

By stimulating the economy through monetary and fiscal policy, the government and central bankers can take measures which can:

- Lower interest rates, making debt consumption more favourable.
- Devalue the currency to promote spending and ease the burden of debt.
- Enable the government to obtain capital which they can direct to where they see fit, such as propping up failing companies that pose a structural risk to the economy or using this lever to adjust the others, by stimulating land, labour, or enterprise through financial incentives.

As you can probably guess, this is the quickest and most accessible lever, as its impact is immediate. However, as we will explore, there is no free lunch. Quick solutions come at a cost. In this case, such solutions reshape how people express themselves monetarily, thereby diminishing money's capacity to accurately reflect societal values.

So, in summary, of the four factors of production, the quickest and easiest solution to fix short-term economic pain is through the use of the monetary lever. Consequently, our economic system incentivizes monetary intervention to create change. And we are not the first ones to pick up on this! Governments have long recognized that the monetary lever is not only the quickest solution to enact change but also the only lever that has an immediate and direct impact on the economy. Other levers, such as land, labour, and enterprise, are often indirect or require a much longer time horizon for change to take effect. As a result, our monetary system has trended towards increased centralization over time, providing governments with greater oversight and the ability to intervene.

In light of this, it is worth taking a step back and exploring the history of the monetary system we interact with today. Understanding the origins of our current system can provide valuable insights into how it functions, its strengths, weaknesses, and potential for improvement.

HOW DID WE GET HERE?

Throughout history, the capital lever has been significantly more restricted than it is today, as money was often made of or backed by something of value, such as gold, i.e., up until January 30th, 1934, dollar bills were redeemable for gold.[21] Suppose a nation wished to expand the money supply. In that case, it must increase its gold reserves by:

- offering value via the trading of goods and services with trade partners
- extracting gold from the land
- pillaging gold from other nations

Given that gold is a challenge to source, this had two main results:

1. It limited the government's ability to intervene fiscally when the country fell on hard times.
2. The government would have to direct its energy toward the other levers—land, labour and enterprise—providing real economic value.

To those with an interventionist mindset, gold's backing to money was seen as a hindrance, so countries looked to ease the burden of sourcing gold by slowly adapting the currency and monetary system to suit their needs.

Although the centralization of money has happened many times throughout history, for the sake of brevity, we will focus on the US and its transition away from the gold standard. The US also serves as a compelling case study, as the US Dollar has evolved into the global reserve currency we use today.

In 1793 the US minted its first circulating coins: 11,178 copper cents.[22] This started the bimetallic standard whereby money had value because it was backed by metals such as gold or silver.

However, following the discovery of abundant gold deposits in Western North America, the United States transitioned to the gold standard in 1834.[23] Under this new system, the value of money became exclusively tied to gold, with all paper currency being redeemable for gold. The use of paper currency alleviated the burden of carrying around this weighty metal while still providing individuals with the opportunity to own gold.

Until the early twentieth century, money issuance was primarily in the hands of private commercial banks, with governmental authorities rarely issuing currency.[24] As fund manager and financial author Jesse Myers explains, with the US economy growing faster than the supply of money and above-ground gold, "prices shrank over time—we got more for less—we had deflation."[25] This stems from the nature of a gold standard, where the scarcity of gold can lead to a gradual appreciation in the currency's purchasing power— the same dollar affords more as time progresses. This trend is evident in the Consumer Price Index (CPI) data for the mentioned period, as depicted in Figure 1.1. While temporary inflationary spikes occurred during periods of war when the government temporarily abandoned the gold standard, issuing unbacked currency, it is noteworthy that prices resumed their deflationary trajectory when the peg was re-established after each conflict.[26]

....

SIDE NOTE: *The CPI serves as a measure of the general fluctuation in consumer prices over time, based on a representative assortment of goods and services. It provides valuable insights into the direction of price movements, indicating whether they are ascending or descending.*

....

Figure 1.1

The Consumer Price Index Before & After Central Banking

US Consumer Price Index, 1775 - 2012 (level, 1775=1)

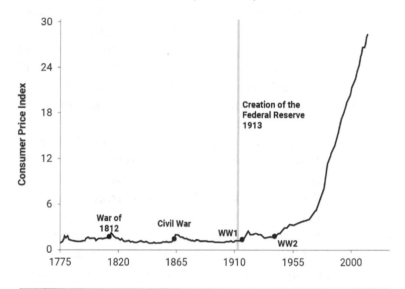

Source: Bureau of Labor Statistics. Historical Statistics of the US, & Reinhart & Rogoff (2009)

Whether by coincidence or design, the 19th century, while the US adhered to the gold standard, marked an era of immense growth, prosperity, and change. We witnessed the rise of:

- Human and civil rights
- American democracy
- The Industrial Revolution
- Free market systems with the emergence of the stock market
- Both the combustion and steam locomotive engines, which led to the extensive rail network, automobiles and airplanes
- Mainstream electrification

...and the list goes on.

However, as paper bills were significantly easier to trade over physical gold, it became rare for the holders of these bills to return to redeem the gold by which they laid claim. The commercial banks which issued paper currency noticed this and began issuing bills with no gold backing. Eventually, the bills in circulation laid claim to more gold than was warehoused. With no precedent in law, this was technically legal, so no charges were laid. From this proliferation of unbacked bills came the unintentional creation of the first fractional reserve currency system, in which only a *portion* of a bank's deposits are stored in reserve and available for withdrawal.

Fractional reserve banking presents a significant risk to the stability of any banking system. When a large number of depositors request their gold, and the bank has issued more money than it holds in reserves, it faces a challenge in meeting all the withdrawal demands. The news that the bank may run out of gold to back people's deposits can trigger a sense of urgency, prompting even more individuals to withdraw their funds before potential losses occur. This situation leads to what is known as a bank run, wherein the bank becomes incapable of fulfilling its financial obligations and ultimately becomes insolvent.

These risky banking practices spurred just such a series of financial panics at the turn of the century. Of particular note was the panic of 1907, which prompted the signing of the Federal Reserve Act in December 1913. This act was what gave rise to the Federal Reserve, a central bank designed to enhance the "stability" of the American financial system.[27] And this so-called *stability* would come through greater monetary control, as it was believed that, through monetary intervention, a central bank could alleviate financial stressors during periods of crisis.

It is important to note that this is the point at which money noticeably departed from a naturally emergent medium of exchange and toward something structured by those in positions of power.

....

FUN FACT: In Eustace Mullins' book The Secrets of the Federal Reserve, the origins of the Federal Reserve are revealed as a product of a covert conference held on Jekyll Island where the wealthiest individuals, accounting for a sixth of the world's wealth, gathered and conceived the idea of a central bank.[28] The result of this meeting was the Aldrich plan, which essentially laid the framework for the foundation of the Federal Reserve.

However, what makes central banking—our current monetary paradigm—questionable is the fact that not only was it conceived in secrecy by a select few private bankers, but it gives monetary oversight to these very same individuals, their compadres, and successors. Moreover, it was promoted through a nationwide propaganda campaign funded by commercial banks. This propaganda campaign was led by prestigious universities such as Princeton, Harvard, and the University of Chicago. Its objective was to persuade the American public to rally behind the Aldrich plan and advocate for its passage into law by Congress.

....

When the Federal Reserve Act of 1913 was signed, it introduced a requirement stating that newly issued dollar bills needed to be backed by a minimum of 40% gold reserves. Once again, money printing was limited due to the scarcity of gold.

But that was soon to change...

Over the coming years, whenever the US or another country on the gold standard needed capital, they would temporarily abandon their pegging to gold in order to expand their monetary supply. This influx of new currency was backed by nothing other than the government's promise that someone would accept it in exchange for their goods and services because it was legal tender. Not only that, but the additional currency also devalued the remaining currency in circulation by inflating the supply of money, and with more dollars chasing the same amount of goods, prices rose (Figure 1.1).

The first instance of this depegging from gold occurred during World War I (WWI). The US, struggling to fund the high expense of the war, temporarily left the gold standard. However, although this put the US in a better position to finance the war effort, the currency devaluation resulting from their monetary expansion led to rampant inflation, with inflation rates topping a staggering 18% before the US rejoined the gold standard in 1922.[29]

Although the roaring '20s led to significant social, economic, and political change, it wasn't long before the debts incurred during WWI, in conjunction with the Federal Reserve's decision to suppress interest rates so as not to impede Europe's ability to pay back their dollar war debts, laid the foundation for the Great Depression and, as I am sure you can guess, the next decoupling from gold, in 1934.[30]

At the height of the Great Depression, the government was feeling trapped. They wanted to increase the money supply to stimulate the suffering economy, but they did not have enough gold on hand to do so. They, therefore, had to think fast.

On the 5th of April 1933, President Franklin D. Roosevelt issued Executive Order 6102, "forbidding the hoarding of gold coin, gold bullion, and gold certificates within the continental United States."[31] US citizens with an excess of $100 worth of gold currency were required to exchange their gold for $20.67 an ounce (equivalent to $433 in 2021), far below the market rate. Immediately after receiving these large sums of gold from the public, the Treasury then raised the price of gold to $35 an ounce (equivalent to $733 in 2021).

Executive Order 6102 not only addressed the difficulty of obtaining gold, crucial for expanding the money supply, but it also yielded substantial profits for the government, which were then used to stimulate the economy. Furthermore, it incentivized holders of gold to convert their holdings into US dollars, bolstering the value of the dollar amidst a period of monetary expansion and central bank intervention. The strength of the US dollar stemmed from the government's deliberate manipulation of capital flow into dollars from gold, effectively shoring up the currency that would have otherwise experienced a decline.

Although this temporarily alleviated the issues the US was facing, it didn't last long. The US was, once again, restricted by the gold standard. The US had to figure out a way to obtain more gold if it wanted to expand the money supply further. The path to increasing their access to gold and stabilizing the dollar became apparent as the end of World War II neared.

With global tensions high, the US had become an ally to many nations when it entered the Allied Forces, and the US felt it was in a prime position to take advantage of this bolstered global positioning. In July 1944, high-ranking US economic officials met with many of the world's global leaders in Bretton Woods, New

Hampshire.[32] During this meeting, these leaders determined that the US would peg the dollar to gold while the rest of the world would peg their currencies to the dollar. This meant that most of the world's gold would pour into the US for safekeeping, depleting many countries of their domestic gold reserves.

Although this arrangement worked for all parties initially, as Mark Twain once said, *"History doesn't repeat itself, but it often rhymes."*

Fast forward to the late '60s and early '70s, when the US was at war in Vietnam. Once again, feeling confined by the dollar's backing to gold, the US decided to expand the money supply to continue funding the Vietnam War effort. This time, however, it wasn't just the dollar it was devaluing, but *every other nation's currency that had been pegged to the dollar.*

Understandably, many countries were unhappy about this situation. France took the initiative to send its Navy across the Atlantic to demand its gold back. This triggered a bank run on the central bank, with other nations quickly following suit.

As the US gold reserves were being depleted, they had to act quickly. If they continued on this path of giving each country their gold back, they'd eventually run out and have nothing left to give. And so, the gold standard had to be sacrificed for the continued functioning of the fractional reserve system. President Nixon formally ended dollar convertibility for gold, and the US dollar became the fiat currency we still use today.

....

FUN FACT: Since March 2020, the Federal Reserve has reduced reserve requirements to zero, eliminating reserve requirements for all US depository institutions.[33] This is still in effect as of writing in early 2023. Maybe "fraction-less" reserve banking is a little more accurate at this point?

....

The end of the gold standard became known as the Nixon Shock and is one of the key events in US monetary history.[34] From this day on, we saw the proliferation of so-called "fiat" currencies– a currency backed by nothing but debt and our faith in the government. The word fiat is Latin for "let it be done" and has traditionally been used in the sense of an order, decree, or resolution. Originally this order would have been given by an emperor or king, but today it is given by the state. The money we use today is no longer selected by the community or backed by something physical of value, such as gold. Instead, it is by decree. Money has value because the state says it does.

When you hear a government official say the US has never defaulted on its debt obligations, they're brushing over the fact that this transition off the gold standard was effectively a default on behalf of the US government. They did not follow through with their obligation to allow individuals and countries the ability to redeem their dollars for gold because they would have been unable to.

While we are at it, they have also defaulted on four other notable occasions throughout history[35]:

1. In early 1862, the US defaulted on its demand notes due to difficulties paying for the Civil War. These difficulties meant that the government took to printing paper money, or "greenbacks."
2. In 1933, the US defaulted again on its gold bonds. The US had promised its bondholders they could withdraw for gold coins and then refused to do so and offered them depreciating paper currency.
3. In 1968, the US defaulted once more by refusing to allow silver certificate holders the ability to exchange for silver dollars.
4. And the most recent default was in the spring of 1979 when the US could not make payments on maturing

Treasury bonds.[36] They later made these payments, but if we classify default as "the failure to meet an obligation," then that would mean the US as a nation has defaulted five times to date, including the Nixon Shock.

After the Nixon Shock of 1971, the world became a very different place. With US dollars no longer tied to gold, an era of significant monetary intervention began.

As can be seen in Figure 1.2, for the period when the dollar was at least partially pegged to gold, its purchasing power stayed relatively intact. Unfortunately, since 1971, although the minimum wage has risen in numerical dollar terms, its actual purchasing power adjusted for inflation has dropped to that of around the 1950s.

Figure 1.2

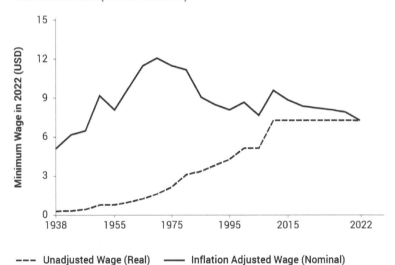

The Real Story Behind Minimum Wage
Real and nominal value of the federal minimum wage in the United States from 1938 to 2022 (in 2022 US dollars)

--- Unadjusted Wage (Real)   —— Inflation Adjusted Wage (Nominal)

Source: Bureau of Labor Statistics; US Department of Labor & Statista

Moreover, following the departure from the gold standard, US federal tax revenues have been consistently overshadowed by federal spending, as evident in Figure 1.3. A deficit occurs when expenditure surpasses revenue. On a personal level, we can all relate to the consequences when our spending significantly outweighs our income.

Figure 1.3

What Happened in 1971?
US federal surplus or deficit

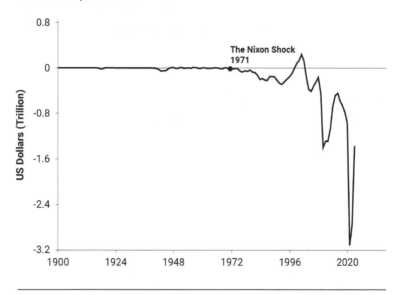

Source: US Office of Management & Budget

Since the proliferation of fiat currencies, not only have we seen far greater monetary expansion, as governments are no longer bound to gold, but also interest rates have become a more frequently used lever to incentivize debt consumption.

Over the last forty years, central bank intervention has meant that interest rates have declined from around 20% to the recent lows of roughly zero and, in some countries, negative. Meanwhile, the money supply has continued to rise unwaveringly to new heights (Figure 1.4).

Figure 1.4

Interest Rates vs Money Supply
Federal funds effective rate vs M2 money supply

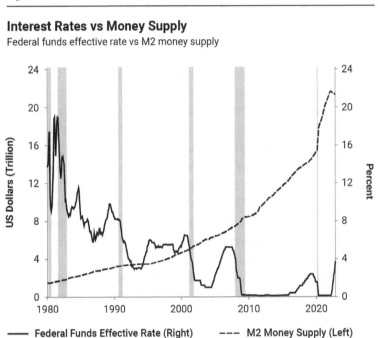

Source: Board of Governors of the Federal Reserve System (US)

I should also mention that the grey vertical bands in Figure 1.4 are economic recessions, such as the Great Recession of 2008. Looking carefully, you will see that interest rates are cut each time the economy experiences a recession. This is the monetary lever in action.

By lowering interest rates (solid black line), a central bank can ease access to capital. As a result, people borrow and spend more, stimulating the economy and expanding the money supply.

Looking at the graph once more, you may also notice that each time interest rates are cut, they never quite recover to their previous highs. As a result, we see an overall declining trend in rates over time. This is not by chance but a consequence of the interplay between interest rate adjustments and vulnerabilities within the economy. Each time interest rates rise, something in the economy breaks, such as:

1. **Increased interest payments triggering corporate defaults:** As interest rates rise, the cost of borrowing increases for businesses. This can strain their finances, leading to a higher risk of default on existing debts, particularly for companies with significant debt burdens.
2. **Devaluation of assets impacting bank balance sheets:** Rising interest rates can devalue the value of many assets banks hold. This devaluation can weaken the banks' balance sheets, potentially leading to insolvency if the losses are substantial or the banks are heavily exposed to such investments.
3. **Deterioration of the housing market:** When interest rates rise, it becomes more expensive for households to borrow money, especially for mortgages. This can make it harder for homeowners to meet their debt obligations, increasing mortgage defaults and placing downward pressure on the housing market.

These events put pressure on central banks to intervene in an attempt to minimize the negative consequences. However, the subsequent lowering of interest rates through such interventions perpetuates a problematic cycle. The cycle operates as follows: as the accumulation of debt increases, it necessitates lower interest rates, yet lower rates lead to further debt accumulation. Consequently, we are trapped in a continuous loop of escalating debt and heightened instability. Therefore, with each subsequent rise in interest rates, these economic disruptions tend to manifest earlier and with increased severity.

....

SIDE NOTE: Some readers may push back against this viewpoint by pointing out that in the first half of 2023, interest rates rose to levels not witnessed in nearly two decades. Central banks have been raising interest rates as a response to escalating inflation, aiming to curb consumer demand by increasing debt service payments and reducing disposable income. While these measures seem to be yielding results, with the CPI declining from its peak of nearly 10% in June 2022 to 4% as of May 2023, the banking system is currently grappling with over $700 billion in unrealized losses.[37,38] Unrealized losses refer to the decline in the value of an asset that has not yet been sold. By comparison, during the height of the 2008 great financial crisis (GFC), unrealized losses never exceeded $100 billion. The banking sector is on the brink of collapse, as evidenced by the bankruptcies of Signature Bank, Silicon Valley Bank, and First Republic Bank, which are larger in scale than the 25 bank failures experienced in 2008.[39]

....

Considering this scenario, I anticipate that either the Fed will, once again, cut interest rates to alleviate the burgeoning stress on the banking sector, or we may face systemic fragility issues that could rapidly escalate into more profound problems.

Furthermore, when central banks artificially suppress interest rates, it becomes exponentially harder to grow wealth through saving, so we are more likely to take on debt or take bigger risks to get ahead. When interest on savings was at 6%, our savings doubled every twelve years. At 1%, however, that same doubling would take seventy years. So much for saving! This may explain why we have seen a definitive downward trend in savings over the last five decades (Figure 1.5) yet an upward trend in debt (Figure 1.6).

Figure 1.5

To Save or Not to Save

US net saving as a percentage of gross national income

Source: US Bureau of Economic Analysis

As of March 2022, the US total debt (including household, government, and corporate debt) is more than twice the country's Gross Domestic Product (GDP)— the total value of goods and services produced within a country's borders each year. Overall, total debt has risen to 244% relative to GDP, up from 111% in March of 1980.[40] Moreover, since 1800, 51 out of 52 nations with government debt to GDP exceeding 130% defaulted.[41] As of now, the US is at 129% debt-to-GDP.[42]

Figure 1.6

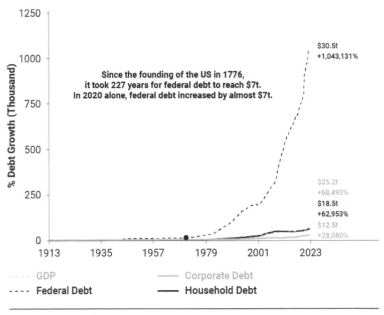

The Burgeoning US Debt to GDP
US federal vs corporate vs household debt vs GDP (1913 to 2022)

Source: Longtermtrends.net

Since the enactment of the Federal Reserve Act in 1913, Federal Debt has skyrocketed by a whopping 1,048,131%, reaching an astounding $30.5 trillion. Even more concerning is the omission of $173 trillion in unfunded liabilities as of December 2022, which includes future obligations like social security and Medicare payments.[43]

FUN FACT: There are two primary types of accounting:
1. ***Accrual Accounting:*** *Records revenues and expenses when they occur, providing an accurate financial picture.*
2. ***Cash accounting:*** *Only records current cash flows, neglecting long-term obligations.*

While the US government uses cash accounting, businesses must use accrual accounting. This allows the government to hide future liabilities, such as unfunded liabilities, since they aren't evident in immediate cash flows. This lack of transparency not only undermines accountability but also impairs informed decision-making regarding the government's financial health and long-term commitments.

Another perspective on the fiscal predicament of the United States can be seen through the analysis of renowned investor Stanley Druckenmiller, who emphasizes the following points[44]:

- The current US government debt stands at $32.1 trillion.[45]
- The Federal Reserve's balance sheet amounts to $8.36 trillion.[46]
- Tax receipts collected by the US government in 2022 amounted to $4.9 trillion.[47]
- Total spending in 2022 reached $6.5 trillion.[48]

When you remove spending from tax revenue, the deficit in 2022 was $1.6 trillion! Druckenmiller suggests that the country has reached a point of no return, trapped in a self-reinforcing cycle of debt. He further asserts that neither political party is willing to address entitlements, defence spending, or other sensitive issues. And as soon as one does, each party is quick to rally its affected voter or lobbying base by appealing to their interests and portraying the other party as the "bad guys."

With this looming debt burden, the Federal Reserve is stuck between a rock and a hard place. They either:

a) Intervene, further perpetuating the issue by bailing out fiscal irresponsibility with lower interest rates and capital injections through increased debt.

or

b) Allow the fiscally irresponsible and those laden with debt (which includes the government) to suffer the consequences of spending beyond their means. This would undoubtedly result in a significant depression where everyone will feel the effects, i.e., poverty, unemployment, financial hardship, social unrest etc. Such a scenario is likely to erode trust in both government and central banks.

You can probably guess which path they take... the path of intervention.

Why do they have to intervene?

Interest rates are essentially a measure of risk in the economy. If risk in the economy is low, people will typically lend money at a lower interest rate because they can be confident of having the money repaid. However, if economic stressors arise, such as increased job loss, debtors are more likely to fail to meet their debt obligations, so the risk of lending money is higher. Therefore, creditors require higher interest rates to adequately compensate them for the risk they are taking by lending their money.

In a free market where interest rates are free-floating—*interest rates that are determined by market forces of supply and demand*—as an economy heads into periods of uncertainty, rates tend to rise to account for the increased risk. As rates increase, capital naturally gravitates toward endeavours that offer reduced risk and greater value to society, leading to a realignment of economic priorities.

However, this poses a problem in a heavily indebted centrally controlled economy, such as the one we are in today. When interest rates rise, households, corporations, and governments must reduce spending to ensure they can pay their debt obligations. But if people aren't spending, money stops circulating. If money stops circulating, people will struggle to obtain capital, and if people lack capital, they'll fail to service debt payments, resulting in insolvency. These defaults can quickly lead to a systemic economic collapse in a system heavily encumbered by debt.

With this in mind, rising rates can quickly become a deadly blow to an over-indebted economy, with the working class bearing the brunt of the repercussions. Therefore, there is a strong motivation for the government and central banks to intervene in order to alleviate the burden of debt. Failure to do so may lead the general public, lacking sufficient context, to perceive them as the catalyst for the impending collapse.

So, to avoid the looming devastation of economic collapse, they intervene by lowering interest rates and expanding the monetary supply. This does a few things:

1. It devalues the currency, reducing the burden of debt. If the currency is worth less, so is the burden of debt.
2. With lower rates, debt consumption becomes favourable again, causing capital to flood into assets, elevating prices.
3. With rising prices, bystanders get a case of FOMO (fear of missing out) and take out even more debt to pile into assets, further driving up prices.

...which in turn leads to greater systemic fragility giving central banks all the more reason to intervene again, and again, and... again.

This brings us to where we are today. After decades of overusing the monetary lever to artificially stimulate the economy and avoid economic stress, we are in a vicious debt cycle. But it doesn't end there.

We now face a new challenge. We cannot continue along the path we are on due to the "law of diminishing returns," which states that the benefits derived from a certain endeavour will progressively decline as we allocate more attention and resources toward it. On the economic front, the more we rely on the monetary lever to stimulate the economy and prevent economic hardship, the less effective such intervention becomes.

Between 2008 and 2018, $1 in debt went from generating $0.48 to $0.42 of GDP across all major world economies (Figure 1.7). That's a 17.4% decline in ten years.

Figure 1.7

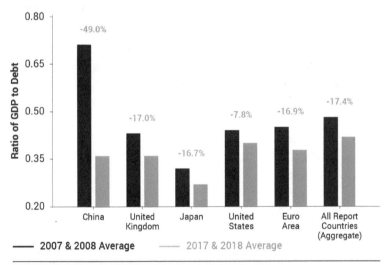

Debts Declining Ability To Positively Impact GDP
GDP Generating Capacity of Global Debt (All major economies)

Source: Bank of International Settlements

With the law of diminishing returns in full effect, maintaining our current growth trajectory requires escalating interventions involving exponentially more debt. Not only that but if we fail to continue to grow, our economy will collapse, given the size of the debt burden. We have a system that must grow indefinitely to outpace the impending burden of debt. Otherwise, it'll face collapse.

And this is not only true in the United States. In December 2022, Canada's total debt to GDP sat at an astronomical 398%.[49] This means for every \$1 of GDP, there was \$3.98 of debt. With a conservative average interest rate on this debt of 3%, Canada's GDP would have to grow by 11.94% (3% x 3.98) just to pay down the interest on its debt...let alone any principal.

Is this level of growth achievable?

Well, considering that between 1961 and 2022, Canada's GDP grew by an average of 0.76%[50] per year, we're a far cry from the desired objective. Even if Canada ceased debt accumulation and GDP were to sustain its historical average growth rate of 0.76%, total debt would still grow by 11.18% of GDP annually.

In the world of finance, this is called a debt spiral. Debt will inescapably continue to increase year after year, unless we see a dramatic, revolutionary shift in GDP growth.

Other prominent countries have similarly high debt to GDP ratios, putting them in a similar situation[51]:

- Japan: 505%
- Italy: 336%
- Spain: 332%
- UK: 308%
- US: 244%
- Global: 356%[52]

All these countries find themselves in a state of debt-dependence that creates a strong incentive for intervention, leading to a cycle of postponing the inevitable. This is evident from the fact that since the departure from the gold standard up until 2021, global debt has grown from less than $2 trillion to over $300 trillion. In contrast, GDP growth during the same period amounted to just $93.5 trillion. Notably, between 2009 and 2021, global debt soared by a staggering $185 trillion, while the corresponding GDP growth stood at a relatively modest $36 trillion.[53,54,55,56]

This raises the question: Have central banks, such as the US Federal Reserve, succeeded in alleviating economic stress and fostering price stability?

The Federal Reserve has a dual mandate to strive for *"maximum employment and price stability,"* which they believe can be achieved by targeting an inflation rate of 2%.[57] However, setting a specific target raises a concern known as Goodhart's Law, which states that when a measure becomes a target, it loses its effectiveness as a measure. In this case, the focus on achieving the inflation target can incentivize manipulation to achieve such a target, neglecting the original intention of promoting the well-being of the people and the overall health of the economy. As a result, the Federal Reserve may prioritize short-term goals at the expense of long-term financial stability and the overall welfare of the economy.

Case in point, in recent years, some banks have attempted to implement measures to enhance the stability of the financial system. However, these efforts were ultimately met with resistance and were unsuccessful as they posed a threat in the short term.

In 2018, Narrow Bank sought to obtain a US banking licence to create a risk-free banking service.[58] Unlike traditional fractional reserve banking, the Narrow Bank would deposit 100% of customer funds at the Federal Reserve for safekeeping and pass on any interest earned to the customer, making bank runs a relic of the past. Despite the seemingly straightforward nature of this model, the Federal Reserve rejected the bank's application.

Similarly, in 2021, Custodia Bank applied for a master account at the Federal Reserve with a similar premise to the Narrow Bank, but with a key difference[59]: the bank planned to over-collateralize customer deposits, holding 108% of deposited funds at the Federal Reserve.[60] They hoped this would increase its chances of approval, but the application was once again rejected.

In both situations, these banks were essentially declined because they were deemed "too safe," and as such, they posed a threat to the overall banking system... *which operates under a policy of zero reserve requirements.* The logic was if one bank were considered significantly safer than another, it could lead to nationwide bank runs at any and all fractional reserve banks as consumers opted to swap to the safer option, destabilizing the financial system. So rather than implementing measures to improve long-term customer security and safety, the Federal Reserve chose to reject these applications.

Even beyond the more specific target of 2% inflation, the mandate of "price stability" may not be in the best interest of what should be the Federal Reserve's true purpose, maintaining economic health.

Prices should naturally fluctuate as supply and demand find equilibrium. If prices are falling, this indicates demand is low or excess supply is entering the market, disincentivizing further production and vice versa. Through this ebb and flow, we would be better able to determine what the members of an economy value.

When we try to stabilize prices, we unknowingly decimate money as an accurate medium of expression, leading to a host of other issues.

However, pushing aside this understanding of price fluctuations being natural and healthy, let's see whether the Federal Reserve is meeting its mandate for price stability.

Looking back to Figure 1.1, which displays historical consumer prices and considering Figure 1.8 of the Dow Jones Industrial Average (an index which tracks 30 of the most prominent industrial companies in the US) priced in gold*, since the creation of the Fed, we have witnessed significantly greater volatility than before its inception.

Gold has been used as the denominator in Figure 1.8 due to its finite supply and enhanced price stability, making it a valuable reference point for this analysis.

Figure 1.8

---

200 Years - Dow/Gold Ratio

How many ounces of gold to buy the DJI Index (Log chart & before 1896, a surrogate index is used for the DJI Index)

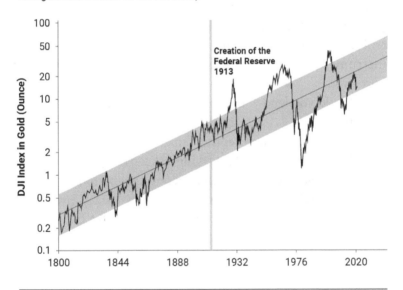

Source: World Gold Charts, http://www.goldchartsrus.com/

Furthermore, as of late 2022[61]:

- More than half of all countries are experiencing close to double-digit inflation, with the average inflation rate sitting at 9.8%. *If inflation remains at these levels, our savings will lose 60% of their value over the next ten years.*
- Energy prices have doubled globally in the last two years.
- Natural gas prices, in particular, have risen 600%.

If their mission is to create economic stability, one would have hoped the unparalleled monetary and fiscal intervention during the Great Financial Crisis would have led to lower economic fragility. Instead, Central banks globally cut interest rates an estimated 637 times in the six years following the GFC and purchased more than $14 trillion worth of securities and $8 trillion of negative-yielding government bonds— financial instruments representing a loan made by an investor to a borrower.[62]

Would you lend your money to be paid back less than you lent out?

It sure seems these central banks are throwing everything, including the kitchen sink, at trying to keep our global economy afloat. Yet each year we continue along this path of economic resuscitation through monetary intervention, the positive effects of stimulation diminish. That might not be such a big problem if debt came with no strings attached. But the more our debt grows, the greater the toll it takes on society. We're now in a world where the majority are simply trying to survive while living costs continue to climb. Presently, a majority of individuals struggle to make ends meet as living expenses steadily rise. Many people find themselves accumulating debt merely to meet basic family needs, leading to stress and guilt over living beyond their means, even in the absence of extravagance.

"Well... at least my money is safe now that the federal government fully insures my 'bank deposits up to $250,000 *through the FDIC*,' offering *protection* in case of a bank run."

Ahh, not so fast.

Just as our banking institutions run on a fractional reserve system, the Federal Deposit Insurance Corporation (FDIC) is no different.

As of 2022, the FDIC had just $125 billion in reserves to cover $9 trillion in customer deposits nationwide.[63] That's a reserve ratio of a meager 1.3%. While this may be plenty if one or two relatively small banks became insolvent, if a nationwide bank run ensued (like the type the Federal Reserve feared could be inspired by Narrow or Custodia Bank), there is a risk that the population would receive only 1.3 cents for every dollar in deposits lost... at best.

And as if this wasn't scary enough! Under bank "bail-in laws," banks have been granted the authority to employ the capital of creditors, including depositors, to address financial challenges. In other words, if a bank faces financial difficulties, they may be able to retain (bail-in) our savings deposits in return for a share in this otherwise failing institution.

CONCLUSION

As the monetary lever is the easiest to pull, it becomes the first course of action when times get tough. However, due to the limitations of gold and previous iterations of money, rather than addressing root issues as economic stressors arise, those in positions of power have looked to adapt the monetary system to alleviate short-term pain. As we will continue to explore, such actions have changed how individuals monetarily express themselves, eroding money's capacity to accurately reflect societal values.

This prompts us to ask: Are we considering the wide-reaching and long-term effects of pulling the monetary lever? Central planners would say, *"of course."* However, since the birth of central banking, there has been a strong case building that the world isn't necessarily better off for their interventions.

As John Haar explains, "Even if the new money and circulation credit does lead to real economic growth, it's a morally unjust arrangement because 1) it is involuntarily funded by real savers, 2) the risk of loss is involuntarily placed on real savers, and 3) it often relies on government intervention to prevent fractional reserve entities from collapsing."[64]

But maybe we are missing something. Perhaps we should give the interventionist approach the benefit of the doubt for the moment and, over the next two chapters, attempt to answer two questions:

"How does a system built around intervention impact us, the populace?"

"Is a system supported by intervention sustainable?"

....

SIDE NOTE: Figure 1.9 is the history of the US dollar summed up in a single picture.

....

Figure 1.9

The Evolution of the US Dollar Bill

1928 - Gold Standard

1934 - Gold Standard
Post Executive Order 6102

1974 - Fiat Standard

CHAPTER 2

THE HIDDEN COSTS
OF INTERVENTION

Why Meddling Has Led to a
Decrease in Purchasing Power

*"Inflation is when you pay fifteen dollars for the ten-
dollar haircut you used to get for five dollars when
you had hair." —Sam Ewing*

....

In the span of a single century, our purchasing power has
dwindled by a staggering 96% (see Figure 2.1). The stark reality
is that $100 today buys what $3.34 would have purchased a century
ago.[65] However, it's important to note that this loss in purchasing
power didn't simply disappear. Instead, it shifted into the hands
of the government and the banks—*those with the means to create
money*—granting them unrestricted control over its use. This
loss of purchasing power has created a formidable obstacle,
making it increasingly harder for individuals to meet their basic
needs, especially those shouldering the responsibility of caring
for their children.

- Are you feeling mounting pressure as gasoline and grocery prices soar unabated?
- Is the possibility of owning a home becoming an unattainable dream unless it is bestowed upon you through inheritance or unwavering familial support?
- And if homeownership isn't even on your radar, have you felt the weight of exorbitant rent relentlessly squeezing your wallet?
- Or perhaps you or your friends have been forced to uproot your lives due to rent hikes, leaving you scrambling to find an affordable place to live?

These examples epitomize the insidious impact of inflation, a force that continually chips away at our ability to secure a sustainable income without sacrificing precious time and compromising our overall well-being.

Figure 2.1

A Dollar's Worth
Purchasing power of the US dollar over the last century

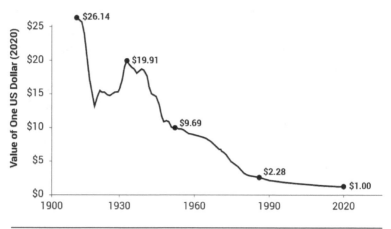

Source: Bureau of Labor Statistics - Consumer Price Index, Morris County Library of Historic Prices

Upon examining Figure 2.1, one might be inclined to think, "I earn far more than anyone did in 1913. Surely rising wages compensate for the decline in purchasing power." Unfortunately, the reality is not as straightforward. As we will delve into, wages have failed to keep pace with the soaring prices. And every year that our wage growth falls behind inflation, we're essentially experiencing a pay cut. If our employers were to openly declare a wage reduction each year, we would likely strike, revolt, or protest. Yet, the subtle erosion caused by inflation goes largely unnoticed.

This raises the question: What is it about our present-day monetary system that impairs our purchasing power?

Before diving into the nitty-gritty, let's first connect the dots between rising prices (inflation) and central banking.

As we have all experienced, inflation is a general price increase resulting in a currency's purchasing power falling. But let us dispel the notion that this deterioration is a mere coincidence or an inevitable force of nature. The truth is that the rise in prices is not arbitrary. It is a direct consequence of deliberate actions. When the money supply expands, when more currency enters the market, excess dollars compete for the finite quantity of goods available, and prices inevitably trend upwards. The mechanism behind inflation is rooted in the very fabric of our monetary system.

Consider for a moment that we have a pizza cut evenly into four slices. In this metaphor, the money supply is the number of slices: 4. If we double the money supply, it is not equivalent to doubling the amount of pizza. Instead, it would be equivalent to cutting each slice in half to create eight slices. We have not gained any additional pizza. We just have more slices, each smaller in size.

Put differently, owning one slice of pizza pre-monetary expansion equated to one-quarter of the pizza. However, post-expansion, your one-slice ownership has dwindled to one-eighth. Like the pizza's finite size, the value of goods and services underpinning our currency is limited at any given point. When we increase the money supply, which represents economic value, it follows that existing holders possess a smaller share of real-world value, given that no additional goods or services have been created, just monetary units.

This brings us to the next pertinent question: What causes an expansion of the money supply?

At the core of any monetary expansion lies a country's central bank, as it possesses three primary tools that affect the ease or difficulty of borrowing money, thereby influencing the supply.

Reserve Ratio: The reserve ratio refers to the percentage (traditionally around 10%) of deposits a bank must hold in reserves. When a central bank lowers the reserve requirements, banks can lend out more money, expanding the money supply. As an illustration, with a 10% reserve ratio, when a customer deposits $1000, the bank must hold $100 of this deposit in reserves. However, if the reserve ratio is lowered to 0% (as it was in March 2020)[66], that same bank can lend out the entire $1000 deposited by the customer.

Discount Rate: A central bank can also manipulate the money supply through adjustments to the discount rate. This is the interest rate on short-term loans by the central bank. By reducing (or increasing) the discount rate that banks are required to pay on short-term loans, the central bank can effectively raise (or lower) the availability of money. For example, if the central bank raises the discount rate, it becomes more expensive for commercial banks to borrow money from the central bank. Higher borrowing costs can discourage banks from borrowing funds. As a result, banks might lend less to individuals and businesses due to the increased cost of borrowing. Reduced lending by banks means that individuals and businesses have less access to credit, leading to a decrease in spending and investment. With lower spending and investment, the overall money supply in the economy contracts.

Monetary Policy: Through monetary policy, such as quantitative easing and tightening, a central bank can influence the money supply and direction of interest rates via purchasing or selling financial assets. When interest rates fall, it becomes cheaper for everyone to borrow, and with greater borrowing, the money supply expands.

With this in mind:

Central Bank Intervention → Money Supply Expansion → Inflation → More Income is Needed to Maintain Standard of Living

For the sake of brevity, let's look at the primary method impacting our money supply, quantitative easing.

MONETARY POLICY - QUANTITATIVE EASING

In May 2020, Jerome Powell, head of the Federal Reserve, was asked[67]:

"Where does it [money] come from? Do you just print it?"

His response:

"We print it digitally. So as a central bank, we have the ability to create money digitally."

While accurate, this is not necessarily the whole picture.

What would stop them from financially supporting everyone if they could simply print money without consequence?

Simply put, when new money enters an economy, it is not distributed evenly amongst its population. Instead, something known as the Cantillon Effect comes into play, whereby inflation resulting from monetary expansion is not uniform across goods, services, and assets. But rather, it primarily benefits asset holders and investors over wage earners, as asset prices tend to increase disproportionately. This Cantillon Effect is a result of how money enters our economy. Let me explain.

Within our current monetary system, there are two types of money.

- **Real Money:** This is the money we, the populous, interact with. We hold this money in our wallets and bank accounts and use it to purchase goods, services, and assets.
- **Financial-Sector Money (a.k.a federal funds):** You can think of this money as "behind-the-scenes" money circulating within the financial sector. Only entities with a direct account with the central bank can access this money, namely the big commercial banks, such as JP Morgan, Bank of America, Wells Fargo, etc. These banks cannot lend out this money, so we, the populous, never interact with it.

When a central bank senses economic pressure on the horizon and feels it is necessary to intervene, it does so through printing financial-sector money, *not* real money. This is called quantitative easing, or QE for short.

But the central bank can't just give banks a bunch of money to stimulate the economy, so what does it do...

These financial institutions with central bank accounts are private capitalistic entities. As such, they strive to maximize returns for their shareholders. They achieve these returns in various ways, one of which is investing in assets which generate a return, such as treasury bonds (government loans), mortgage-backed securities (bundled mortgages), corporate bonds (company debt), etc. When the central bank performs QE, it forces these financial institutions to sell them assets they request (within reason; there are certain assets central banks are currently unable to purchase).

Let's say Bank of America (BoA) holds $1 billion of government bonds, yielding 3% yearly. This means BoA generates $30 million in revenue annually from these bonds.

Now let's assume recent market data indicates that the US may experience economic stress on the horizon, so the Federal Reserve decides to implement QE.

To do so, they request that Bank of America sell them the $1 billion of government bonds, and in return, they are given $1 billion in financial-sector money, creating an exchange of assets rather than a direct giveaway of funds.

Now if you recall, this financial-sector money is not real money. It cannot be lent out to customers. That means that not only are these funds of limited benefit to Bank of America, but they had to sell their bonds, which were generating a nice little 3% yield per year.

So why would the Federal Reserve implement QE?

Given that Bank of America is a capitalistic enterprise that wants to generate returns for its shareholders, by changing the composition of its assets from government bonds to financial-sector money, the bank is compelled to go back out into the market and purchase more bonds or other interest-generating assets to generate the same returns it was before QE.

Because of this, two things happen:

1. **Asset Prices Rise:** With the commercial banks looking to purchase assets to generate returns, there is increased demand for assets. As a result, asset prices rise in response to this increased demand.
2. **Interest Rates Fall:** Bonds, whether government or corporate, provide a yield to the holder. When there is increased demand for bonds, yields fall, or in other words, interest rates decline to accommodate this increased capital looking to generate a return.

In summary, as the Federal Reserve, through QE, purchases assets from the financial sector, these banks then go out into the market and purchase more assets to rebalance their portfolios. In doing so, asset prices rise, and interest rates fall (reducing the burden of debt given reduced interest payments).

By now, you may notice how monetary policy, such as QE, impacts everyday folk. As asset prices continue to rise, the accessibility of acquiring assets becomes more laborious for individuals, while those who already possess assets can leverage their appreciation by utilizing debt, leading to higher levels of spending. Furthermore, the upward trajectory of house prices also translates into elevated rental rates. Ultimately, the effects of QE trickle-down, impacting the cost of living for everyone.

With the surge in asset prices placing a growing burden on people's income, an increasing portion must be allocated toward food and living expenses. This leaves individuals caught between a rock and a hard place: work more to make up for the difference or reduce spending in other areas.

Moreover, as asset prices increase and interest rates decline, this gives rise to several other byproducts that affect all of us.

Let's explore two of the primary byproducts of QE, financial repression and wealth inequality.

Financial Repression

As I'm sure most would agree, lending out hard-earned money to be repaid less is nonsensical. In a free market, interest rates invariably remain higher than inflation as individuals seek to factor in lending risks and guard against potential currency devaluation resulting from inflation. However, this is no longer applicable when monetary policy suppresses interest rates below inflation.

A concept introduced in 1973 by Stanford economists Edward S. Shaw and Ronald I. McKinnon, financial repression refers to the deliberate suppression of interest rates below the level of inflation, allowing debtors (borrowers), such as the government, to borrow money at artificially low rates to fund operations.[68] This greatly benefits debtors and is disadvantageous to creditors (lenders) who are no longer adequately compensated for the risks associated with lending. This financial repression has enabled the US to become the largest debtor nation with a total government debt of $32.1 trillion.[69]

In a free-floating interest rate environment, savers would typically enjoy favourable interest rates that provide a return on their capital, enabling their money to grow faster than inflation. However, the deliberate suppression of interest rates disrupts this natural balance. By artificially keeping interest rates low, the government indirectly shifts the cost of borrowing onto creditors, particularly pensioners and savers who rely on investment yield for financial security. These individuals, who diligently save for a better future, bear the brunt of suppressed interest rates, hindering their ability to build future security.

In essence, when the Fed artificially keeps interest rates low, it is a stealth tax on its currency holders. For instance, let's say you've diligently saved $10,000 and decided to invest in 1-year government bonds. In a free market interest rate environment, where market forces determine rates, you could expect a yield of 5% on your investment. With inflation around 3%, your real return (after accounting for inflation) would be 2%, providing a fair reward for lending your money to the government.

However, under financial repression, where the central bank artificially suppresses interest rates, the situation changes. In January 2023, 1-year government bonds were yielding only 5.7%, while inflation stood at 6.4%.[70,71] Despite the seemingly higher nominal yield of 5.7%, after subtracting inflation, you would actually be losing 0.7% of your invested capital each year. In this scenario, you find yourself essentially *paying* the government to borrow money from you, eroding the value of your savings.

In the book *The Great Rebalancing*, Michael Pettis, professor of finance at Peking University, demonstrates how China's policy of financial repression has resulted in a substantial transfer of wealth away from citizens.[72] Pettis estimates these suppressed interest rates result in an annual transfer of 3 to 8 percent of the country's Gross Domestic Product (GDP)— from savers to debtors like the government.

Assuming Michael Pettis's estimates of 3 to 8 percent are accurate, this would amount to a loss of between $532 billion to $1.42 trillion per year for households in China, based on the country's 2021 GDP of $17.73 trillion.[73]

Edward Chancellor's book *The Price of Time* further corroborates this by highlighting that China's interest rate suppression in 2001 and 2002 was *"partly intended to help banks handle their debt problems"* by giving these banks access to cheap capital.[74] However, as rates were held far below natural levels, *"Chinese depositors indirectly bailed out the banking system."*

Under normal circumstances, you'd never lend money and expect to be paid back less than what you lent out. But, in an environment where the government shapes the monetary system in their favour, you have no choice.

The UK also employed similar measures to liquidate its war debts after World War I and II. Between 1945 and 1980, the UK, as well as the US, experienced negative real interest rates, averaging –3.5%.[75]

During this period of artificially suppressed interest rates, the US government effectively received an annual subsidy equivalent to approximately 20% of its tax revenues through reduced interest expense. This substantial subsidy played a crucial role in alleviating the burden of the government's debt.

Moreover, financial repression has become even more pronounced in recent years. In June 2022, inflation-adjusted interest rates plummeted to a staggering -6.16%.[76,77] If these rates were to remain constant, it would lead to a devastating 45% loss of purchasing power over ten years.

So, when interest rates fall, people are no longer sufficiently rewarded when storing money in a savings account, a pension, or fixed-income products— all of which rely on interest rates to generate income. Without stable, safe vehicles to store our money that will keep up with inflation, our purchasing power is guaranteed to decline over time unless we take greater investment risk, which increases the potential loss of some or all of your investment.

To illustrate this, pension funds (i.e., managed 401k's or RRSPs) have return obligations they have to meet to ensure they can support their customers for retirement. To meet these obligations, they must invest their customer's hard-earned savings.

When interest rates are higher, say, 8%, a pension fund might be able to meet all of its payment obligations by simply investing in "safe" Treasury bonds offering low-risk regular interest payments.

However, when rates decline, this same pension fund may no longer be able to meet its obligations with conservative investments. Therefore, it must search for yield in riskier investments. This adversely impacts customers as greater risk means greater potential for default; in this instance, a default would mean the loss of people's life savings.

The more central banks engage in QE, the more savers, pensions, and investment funds will be pressured to engage in riskier activities, chasing riskier assets in an attempt to generate the same returns they once did. When these funds lose money or cannot meet their obligations, that loss falls back on the pensioners, parents, and anyone else saving for retirement.

The effects of this shift are already noticeable. The average American will retire with only 10 to 11 years of savings.[78] Given a retirement age of 63 years and an average life expectancy of 79 years, many retirees will run out of money with years still to live.[79] The situation is even more dire in countries like Japan, where the retirement gap is between fifteen and twenty years for males and females, respectively.

With no way of knowing how long you will live, people are stuck between working harder to earn more income to bridge the financial gap, extending their working years beyond the standard retirement age, or even finding themselves wishing for a shorter life to avoid running out of money. This dilemma becomes even more complex for parents who hope to leave a legacy for their children as the challenges of long-term saving are further compounded.

Wealth Inequality

Let's say you own a house worth $300,000 and have a mortgage of $200,000. Initially, you have a debt-to-asset ratio of 66%. However, if the government were to double the monetary supply and distribute these newly created dollars to the currency holders, then in theory, the value of your house would double. Given that your $200,000 mortgage stays the same, yet your house increases in value to $600,000, your debt-to-asset ratio will decline to 33%. Monetary expansion has eased your burden of debt. This sounds great for the asset holders, but what about all the currency holders with no assets? Unfortunately, they don't experience the same benefits.

Before the monetary expansion, someone with $300,000 in savings could buy your house outright with no mortgage. But, after, they would only have 50% of the purchase price.

That's a 50% loss of purchasing power.

In light of this, the other notable byproduct of QE is an increase in wealth inequality. As asset prices continue to rise, those who primarily hold assets, namely the upper class, benefit the most, while the working class, who tend to hold more currency, experience a decrease in their purchasing power as the value of their money declines. This results in increased wealth inequality as assets become ever-more unattainable for the working class, further exacerbating the cycle of this financial inequality.

When central banks, such as the Federal Reserve, target inflation and/or perform monetary policy such as QE, they effectively devalue the currency to artificially boost economic activity and ease the burden of debt.[80]

Therefore, it makes you wonder, if the currency is losing purchasing power, and the central banks openly tell you it will continue to do so, why would you hold your savings in the currency? You don't! Instead, you purchase assets that offset (if not benefit from) inflation, whose value rises in tandem with currency devaluation.

Figure 2.2

Historical Growth of Assets vs Wages

The annualized growth of the US average hourly wage is increasingly lagging behind US real estate & the stock market (S&P500 Index)

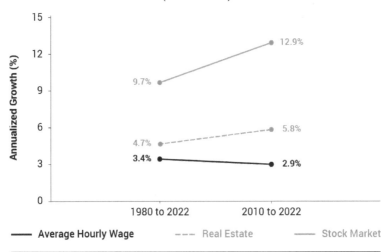

Source: Google Finance, DQJDY - Historical US Home Prices & Trading Economics

These QE byproducts (inflation and lower interest rates) have created a considerable divergence in the growth rate of assets to wages. And this divergence is only increasing (see Figure 2.2). The 2010-2022 annualized growth rate for the stock market and real estate is higher than the 1980-2022 annualized rate, showing a marked acceleration. Meanwhile, the average hourly wage growth is falling: a 2.9% increase in that 12-year period, down from 3.4% over the past 40 years.

As a result of our lagging of wages to asset prices, we have seen one of the greatest transfers of wealth from the working class to the upper class in recent history (Figure 2.3).

Figure 2.3

The Widening Jaws of Wealth Inequality
Share of total net worth held by the top 1% vs the 50th to 90th wealth percentiles

Source: Board of Governors of the Federal Reserve System (US)

SIDE NOTE: This inequality doesn't just happen on a societal level either. It also impacts nation-states. When a nation mismanages its money and inflation runs rampant, other countries, whose purchasing power has not declined at the same rate, are now in a position to purchase the country's goods and services at a discount, pillaging the nation's resources.

The suppression of interest rates creates a strong incentive for individuals to embrace debt as it becomes more affordable and appealing. In such an environment, people are more likely to borrow money even if their income and assets do not align with their desired spending and lifestyle. This leads to a situation where individuals end up living beyond their means, relying heavily on borrowed funds to sustain a lifestyle that exceeds their actual financial capacity. This excessive borrowing, in turn, contributes to the escalation of asset prices. Individuals may utilize debt to acquire assets like real estate or stocks, driving up demand and causing prices to soar. This pattern often paves the way for major asset bubbles and the distortion of market values.

During the Great Financial Crisis, the prevalence of NINJA loans (loans for individuals with "no income, no job, and no assets") exemplified the reckless lending practices fueled by low interest rates. These loans were given without proper assessment of the borrower's ability to repay, leading to a surge in mortgage defaults and contributing to the housing market's collapse.

Moreover, inflation distorts productive assets— an asset that offers productive use outside the financial realm, i.e., residential real estate for shelter, commercial real estate for storefronts, farmland for agriculture etc. As the currency's purchasing power declines, these assets become attractive as a means to protect wealth from inflation. This leads to a surge in demand for such assets, often driven by investors who have no intention of utilizing them for their intended purposes. They are primarily seeking a safe haven rather than contributing to their productive and functional use. Consequently, formerly productive assets in our economy have transformed into financial instruments, where the focus is solely on allocating money into assets to mitigate the impact of inflation. This trend exacerbates price escalation, making it increasingly harder for individuals with genuine needs, such as parents seeking a home for their children or small businesses in search of storefronts, to acquire these assets for their intended purposes.

Figure 2.4

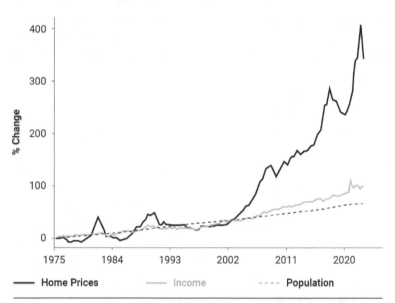

Growth in Home Prices vs Disposable Income vs Population
Percent change in Canada from Q1 1975 to Q3 2022

Sources: Data adapted from Mack, A., and E. Martínez-García. 2011. "A Cross-Country Quarterly Database of Real House Prices: A Methodological Note." Globalization and Monetary Policy Institute Working Paper No. 99, Federal Reserve Bank of Dallas, World Bank, Corplay

The Canadian Real Estate market offers a stark example of such behaviour (Figure 2.4). In my hometown of Whistler, BC, 61% of homes sit empty as wealthy investors primarily utilize these properties as a hedge against inflation without any intention of renting or residing in them.[81] And this issue isn't a localized problem. It's widespread, with many communities nationwide without the housing or businesses they need to thrive.

Lastly, as asset prices continue to climb and our purchasing power diminishes, we find ourselves compelled to invest significant time, energy, and intellectual resources in deciphering the intricate workings of financial markets, all in a bid to outpace inflation. And those too exhausted to dedicate time to grasping the financial markets, whether burdened by family matters, extended work hours, second jobs, or lengthy commutes, find themselves increasingly disadvantaged. Without such intervention, our money would naturally serve as a more reliable store of value, alleviating the necessity for extensive investing efforts.

CONCLUSION

So, what does all this mean...

First, monetary intervention exacts a toll on our most precious resource: time. As our purchasing power diminishes, we're forced to work longer (whether in hours in the week or years of our life) and pinch pennies that might have otherwise gone towards time-saving purchases. This means that we are essentially robbed of our time, leaving us less freedom to pursue the things that truly matter to us, whether it be raising our children, entrepreneurial activities, volunteering in our community, creative pursuits, or socializing with loved ones.

And second, when central banks step in to stimulate the economy, adding new money to the system or suppressing interest rates, such intervention does not evenly benefit the populace.

Instead, due to the Cantillon Effect, those holding assets benefit significantly more than wage-earners who swap their time for money.

We are now in a position where asset prices have reached unprecedented levels, making it exceedingly difficult for anyone looking to acquire certain investments, such as property. Wage growth has not kept pace with rising prices, preventing many individuals and families alike from achieving traditional financial and life milestones, such as buying a house, saving for retirement, or covering their children's educational expenses. Even basic necessities, such as feeding your family or filling up the car with gas, are becoming a challenge. To make ends meet and achieve a modicum of financial security, many are forced to work longer hours, leaving little time and energy for their personal lives. This is not just a minor inconvenience but a serious problem with long-term consequences across all of society. When our monetary system pressures us to prioritize financial security, we risk losing sight of what truly matters— our health, our relationships, and the well-being of our children.

How are we supposed to support ourselves and our families, let alone find meaning, when we're constantly trying to survive against a system that demands more and more of our time?

But... what if we could create a monetary system that empowers us to prioritize what truly matters? Maybe, we do stand a chance to resolve some of our challenges.

In the upcoming chapters, we'll continue to delve into our complex relationship with money, exploring how it impacts us in profound ways, and in nearly every sphere of life. By unpacking the hidden cost of money on society, we can then begin to envision a new monetary system that realigns incentives, promotes prosperity, and paves the way for a brighter future.

First, however, let's try to answer the question:

"Is a system supported by intervention sustainable?"

CHAPTER 3

THE FOUR STAGES OF ECONOMIC RUIN

Why Central Planning Often Leads Us Astray

"If you do not change direction, you may end up where you are heading." —Lao Tzu

....

M *any people* hold the belief that if we can only create more money, ensure we elect good people with good intentions, and spend this money on good things, then everything will be hunky dory.

But what if three goods don't make a right? What if this belief is a fallacy? And what if we are actually setting ourselves up for failure?

With this in mind, let's explore the path to economic ruin.

As emphasized in the preceding chapter, our societal framework operates on the foundation of trust. To participate in our existing economic structures, we rely on the assurance that central bankers not only prioritize the welfare of the people but also possess the expertise and insight to make well-informed choices that yield the desired outcomes. Yet, by placing unwavering trust in these public officials, we inadvertently disregard a fundamental principle of capitalism: *its inherent reliance on decentralized decision-making, where economic choices are made by a multitude of individuals and businesses based on their own knowledge and preferences.*

In capitalism, prices emerge, and decisions are made from a competitive free market environment encompassing the population's vast and diverse tastes and preferences. This decentralized approach allows for a dynamic and adaptive economic system that responds to the ever-changing needs of society.

....

DISCLAIMER: *Capitalism can often evoke strong reactions. If you are uncertain whether Capitalism deserves a seat at the table that is our global economy, feel free to read over Chapter Fourteen for a more in-depth exploration of the topic.*

....

Central planners, therefore, have the impossible task of gathering all the information needed to make accurate and informed decisions about our ever-changing, complex, and chaotic economy in an attempt to provide value that purportedly exceeds what the free market can deliver. Combining poorly informed decisions and a manipulable monetary system exposes us to the temptation of easy money and debt arising from short-term reactionary measures to alleviate immediate challenges.

The downfall of interventionist central planning becomes apparent in, what I call, the four stages of economic ruin:

1. Misalignment to Reality
2. The Death of Creative Destruction
3. Capital Flow Distortion
4. Decision-Making Impairment

Let's explore each one of these separately:

Stage One - Misalignment to Reality

Have you ever tried to help a co-worker with a complex task only to offer solutions that are irrelevant to the challenges they face? In doing so, you inadvertently add to their confusion and hinder their progress despite your good intentions. *I know I have!* This is a misalignment to reality on a personal level, where we misinterpret what our co-worker truly needs and unintentionally worsen the situation.

From an evolutionary perspective, it is crucial for a species to perceive reality accurately. We need to understand the threats to our safety, what is needed from us to obtain the necessities of life (i.e., food, water, shelter), and what opportunities are around us for enrichment. Failure to do so could lead to catastrophe. As M. Scott Peck aptly puts it in his book *The Road Less Traveled*[82]:

> The more clearly we see the reality of the world, the better equipped we are to deal with the world. The less clearly we see the reality of the world—the more our minds are befuddled by falsehood, misperceptions and illusions—the less able we will be to determine correct courses of action and make wise decisions.

The first stage of economic ruin occurs when there is a societal misalignment to reality.

In misalignment, we have a fundamental misunderstanding of the circumstances around us. We may perceive threats where there are none and ignore legitimate dangers. Given the consequences of this misalignment, it is worth asking ourselves, "Do we see reality as it is?"

We live in a world where human ingenuity constantly strives to get more for less through technological innovation and advancements in efficiency and productivity. One such advancement in technological efficiency is described by Moore's Law, which states that the "speed and capability of computers can be expected to double every two years, as a result of increases in the number of transistors a microchip can contain."[83] Said differently, the rate at which we can process information, and therefore the rate of technological growth, is exponentially increasing.

In the grand scheme of things, only in recent history have we seen the invention of:

- Cars and airplanes - reducing our time spent travelling
- Mass production - decreasing the cost of manufacturing goods
- The internet - aiding long-distance communication and increasing information-sharing
- Media digitization - making music, tv, film, literature, and more, available on demand and without the need for expensive and sophisticated equipment

We have also witnessed:

- More efficient machinery for easier raw material extraction, driving down the cost of natural resources.
- The development of computer applications and automated robotics that perform human tasks more efficiently, often reducing human error and dropping corporate operating expenses.
- Increased software and hardware efficiency in almost all digital disciplines

These lists go on and on...

As Jeff Booth masterfully explains in his book, *The Price of Tomorrow*, as technology advances and production costs fall, the marginal cost of production decreases. This gradual decrease in production costs should result in a natural tendency for prices to decrease over time, leading to ever-lower prices of goods and services for the end user.[84]

But if our technology is always making us more efficient, requiring less labour and time to perform the same processes, why, in most cases, do we face rising prices day-in-day-out?

At no other point has human ingenuity been used to receive less in exchange for more. Yet, for all our technology innovation, our current monetary system devalues the currency such that many goods continue to become more expensive and harder to obtain rather than cheaper and more accessible.

If saving time through increased efficiency is a measure of progress, then devaluing the currency, leading to more work and greater time commitment, must mean we are regressing, not progressing.

As highlighted in Chapter One, the Federal Reserve, through intervention, actively targets inflation of 2%. This may seem trivial, but as shown in Figure 3.1, over 30 years, that is a 45% loss of purchasing power. And if that inflation rises to 10%, such as in 2022, that 45% loss takes only six years.

Advancements in production efficiency should be inherently deflationary, meaning the prices of non-scarce goods, services, and most assets should fall in the long run. But because monetary expansion has outpaced the growth in productivity and technological advancement in our economy, we have instead witnessed a slow decay in our purchasing power and, in turn, an increase in the cost of goods, services and assets.

Figure 3.1

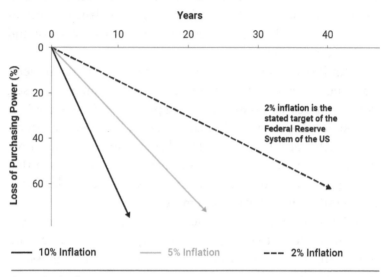

Impact of Inflation on Purchasing Power

2% inflation is the stated target of the Federal Reserve System of the US

Source: @anilsaidso

And here lies the critical flaw in our system: It relies on perpetual growth to meet the demands of mounting debt. Without sustained growth, the burden of debt becomes overwhelming, risking a catastrophic collapse of the economy. **The inherent problem is that our inflation-reliant system, which hinges on continuous expansion, clashes with the reality of our deflationary world, where prices persistently decline. This fundamental misalignment undermines the stability and sustainability of our economic framework.**

While central banks are targeting maximum employment, and we have a monetary system that requires more growth to service our ever-increasing debt service payments, technology is driving down prices, reducing profits, and eliminating jobs.

In the last 40 years alone, large companies, such as the ones listed in the S&P 500, have experienced a 70% increase in labour efficiency (Figure 3.2). A company that would have previously required ten employees now achieves the same output with three, i.e., in early 2023, Alphabet, the parent company of Google, announced it would cut 12,000 jobs and double down on its artificial intelligence (AI) efforts.[85] Of course, companies can keep employing ten people. But, at some point, competitors operating more efficiently will drive down prices, resulting in unsustainable overheads, pressuring such companies to adapt or close up shop.

Figure 3.2

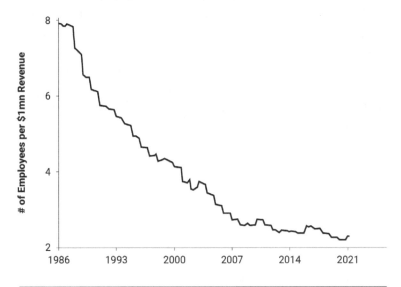

S&P 500 Is 70% Less Labor Intensive Than It Was in the 80s
S&P 500 total # of employees to total revenues ratio

Source: Bank of America Global Research

In today's landscape, corporations face unprecedented challenges in gaining a technological edge over their competitors due to the widespread availability and accessibility of technology. Gone are the days when exclusive access to costly technology provided a significant advantage to well-funded corporations. Now, many beneficial technological tools are affordable and accessible to all, levelling the playing field. As a result, companies are under immense pressure to stay relevant and deliver value to their customers. Failure to do so can hinder their ability to meet profit goals, ultimately leading to workforce reductions and layoffs. These intertwined factors illustrate why technological advancements often result in job elimination.

With this in mind, the relentless march of technological advancement, driving prices down and squeezing profits, forces companies to make difficult choices, often leading to worker layoffs. This downward spiral not only hampers governments in achieving their employment targets and reduces vital payroll and income tax revenues but also creates significant challenges for entities and individuals burdened with debt obligations.

The central banks' objectives of maximizing employment and stabilizing prices are misaligned to the reality of technological advancement. At some point, the system must collapse.

Intervention provides short-lived relief in the face of unceasing and exponential progress. After all, currency debasement and suppressed interest rates drive spending, which boosts economic growth. However, this effect is transient. If I lend you my money today in exchange for more tomorrow, you benefit by having more money today to meet your immediate needs, but you'll have even less tomorrow when you need to pay back the loan with interest.

On a small scale, this may be manageable. If tomorrow is Friday and you know you have a paycheque coming, but you need me to spot you $200 dollars so you can pay your rent on time, you may be confident that you can pay me back with interest. In this case, the primary concern is short-term access to capital. **But what happens when you borrow beyond your means? What happens when your future productive capacity is insufficient to pay your debt?**

Instead of receiving a regular paycheque for the work you have already completed, you rely on a one-time gig scheduled for tomorrow with an expected payment of $300. Fueled by optimism, you borrow money, confident that you will soon have the funds to repay it. However, when tomorrow arrives, your client unexpectedly cancels the gig. Now, not only do you find yourself unable to repay the borrowed amount, but you also face the pressing need to borrow more just to meet your basic expenses, such as buying groceries. As time passes, these expenses accumulate, and even if you eventually secure another gig that pays $300, it may not be sufficient to cover the accumulated debt. The cycle continues, leaving you trapped in a challenging financial predicament.

Given that traditional measures of economic growth, like GDP, are denominated in dollars, we're presented with a dilemma. As economic growth is becoming harder to achieve because technology is advancing and prices are naturally declining, we must use greater amounts of debt and inflation just to meet our growth targets, further destabilizing the system.

Nowhere is this more prominent than in Chapter One's Figure 1.6 (*The Burgeoning US Debt to GDP*), whereby since 1913, Federal Debt has increased by 1,048,131% to a whopping $30.5 trillion. To quote Jeff Booth:

If we are doubling our rate of progress on technology every eighteen months or so, and that technology is deflationary, then it is also logical to expect if it "only" took $185 trillion of debt over the last twenty years to fight the deflation and drive growth, then it might take that number again, but this time over the next thirty-six or so months. And eighteen months after that, a further $370 trillion. ... debt in itself is a massive drag on future growth because of interest payments on it. What about when we add another $555 trillion? ... Quite plausibly, to keep driving growth against an exponentially increasing technology deflation, global debt could become a number so high that the only way out is to hit the reset button.[86]

We should ask ourselves: Would asset prices be where they are today if our governments hadn't injected $185 trillion of new capital into the economy? Pricing across the board has been shaped by government intervention to meet particular economic metrics. As such, our economy is deliberately constructed and manipulated reality. This reality is misaligned with technology's inherent deflationary characteristics.

One notable byproduct of this misalignment to reality is the slow monetization of everything. As Charles Eisenstein lays out in his book *Sacred Economics*, GDP measures monetary exchange.[87] For an activity to contribute to GDP, it must involve a monetary transaction. Without such an exchange, the activity essentially goes unnoticed within the GDP framework, rendering it a narrow and inadequate measure of true growth. For instance, if I create a free educational course, it does not register in GDP, but the moment I start selling the course, even though it may impact GDP, its overall impact diminishes as people now have to pay for it.

In our ever-burgeoning world, the relentless pursuit of economic growth and the need to service mounting debt has led to the monetization of virtually everything around us, from tangible assets to intangible experiences. We must drive monetary growth in areas where monetary exchange previously did not exist. For example:

- **Entertainment and media:** Community events, local performances, and shared cultural activities used to provide free entertainment. However, the expansion of the entertainment industry, the development of media platforms, and the introduction of subscription-based models have led to the monetization of entertainment through ticket sales, subscriptions, and access fees.
- **Communication:** In earlier times, people relied on public spaces and community gatherings for communication. However, the advent of telecommunication networks, mobile phones, and internet services has led to the monetization of communication through phone bills, internet subscriptions, and various communication devices.
- **Water:** Historically, water was often obtained freely from local sources such as wells or rivers. However, with the rise of bottled water companies and the privatization of water resources, access to clean drinking water has been commercialized.

In the words of climate writer and entrepreneur Brianna Lee Welsh, "Community and social services are disqualified as irrelevant. Gifts of reciprocity deemed wasteful, if they cannot be converted for a fee. This logic motivates the conversion of forests into timber, water into bottles, ideas into intellectual property, social good-will into paid services."[88] But at what cost?

To fulfill mounting debt obligations, we find ourselves on a path where the monetization of previously free and accessible aspects of life becomes increasingly prevalent. Gradually, the very foundations of our existence become commodified as we are compelled to pay for what were once open and available basic necessities. This transformation is driven by the insatiable demands of our debt-based system, which perpetuates a cycle where growth becomes imperative to fend off collapse.

This brings us to our second stage:

Stage Two - The Death of Creative Destruction

Investopedia explains the concept of "creative destruction" as "the dismantling of long-standing practices in order to make way for innovation" and "a driving force of capitalism."[89] The process of creative destruction highlights two vital states in the business cycle that are necessary for effective decision-making: life and death. Without both of these states, we have no indicator of what works and doesn't work.

Creative destruction is essential for fostering new ideas, products, and businesses. Without it, our economy is at risk of perpetuating failure, stagnating, and eventually dragging down entire industries.

Netflix vs. Blockbuster is a prime example of natural creative destruction in business. During the early 2000s, Blockbuster dominated the video rental industry, boasting countless stores globally. In contrast, a small player at the time, Netflix offered DVD rentals through the mail with a subscription-based model.

However, as technology advanced, Netflix recognized the potential of streaming content over the Internet and shifted its focus to digital distribution, eliminating the need for physical rentals. In contrast, Blockbuster stuck to its traditional brick-and-mortar model.

The rise of online streaming and the convenience it offers transformed the industry. Netflix's innovative approach and willingness to adapt to changing consumer preferences gave them a significant competitive advantage. Blockbuster, on the other hand, failed to foresee the shift and underestimated the impact of digital streaming.

The outcome was striking: Blockbuster, once generating over $3 billion in revenue, spiralled into bankruptcy within a year.[90] Interestingly, Blockbuster had the chance to acquire Netflix for a mere $50 million back in 2000 but ultimately rejected the offer.

The Netflix vs. Blockbuster example illustrates how more agile and forward-thinking competitors can overtake businesses that fail to adapt to changing market dynamics and embrace innovation. When creative destruction can take hold, new ideas and technologies replace outdated ones, leading to the transformation and progress of industries.

You may be wondering, "What has creative destruction got to do with a misalignment to reality?"

Within a system which requires ever more growth and debt to continue functioning, corporations slowly emerge that are *"too big to fail."* Because of the systemic economic fragility in society, if these businesses were to collapse, we would experience a wave of defaults leading to widespread insolvency and whole sectors of the economy would cease functioning.

To prevent this from occurring, central banks step in as lenders of last resort, providing capital to these "too big to fail" institutions or any failing corporation that threatens the stability of our unsustainable economy. In doing so, they inhibit creative destruction. Companies that should have failed based on their conduct are able to continue their capitally destructive behaviour and consumption of ever-more resources. And because these established goliaths never die, there is little to no room for smaller competitors to take up the mantle and have their own shot at success.

In the fifteen years between 2007 and 2022, the Federal Reserve's balance sheet has increased from $874 billion to just shy of $9 trillion.[91] A tenfold increase from monetary intervention is propping up failing sectors of the economy.

We can see this balance sheet expansion in action when the Federal Reserve:

- Alongside the Treasury, authorized the purchase of $700 billion of toxic or underperforming assets through the troubled asset relief program (TARP) during the Great Financial Crisis,
- Gave banks access to funds at 0% interest rates to rebuild their damaged balance sheets,
- Purchased close to $6 trillion of financial assets, such as corporate bonds, during the pandemic as an emergency maneuver to prop up fiscally impaired companies.[92]

In the situations above, the government removed any financial risks from these now subsidized companies, saving them from business failure but consequently allowing them to continue with the negligent behaviour which got them into that mess in the first place.

Many of the banks we know and use today wouldn't exist without this. They would have had to collapse or either merge with or be bought for pennies on the dollar by more fiscally responsible banks. In an insightful talk[93] between risk analyst and mathematician Nassim Taleb and former UK prime minister David Cameron, Taleb reports that banks lost more money in 1982 and 1991 than they have made in the entire history of banking. And the scary part is that most of those banks still exist today.

Repeated bailouts teach the banking sector that if their insolvency is not an option allowed by the government, it is also not a risk they need to worry about. Their losses can be socialized (shared by taxpayers), while gains are privatized (reserved solely for their company and investors). As a result, there is little incentive to curtail excessive risk-taking. Not only does this further incentivize fiscal irresponsibility, but banks that would otherwise act with integrity can no longer compete in the market against the returns of those taking undue risk, pushing them to move up the risk curve to remain competitive. When there is no consequence for fiscal irresponsibility, greed is allowed to take the wheel, while value creation gets pushed to the wayside.

Central planning and intervention will inevitably expand in a system that allows for repeated failure and ongoing unproductive behaviour without natural consequences.

When short-term pain alleviation is paramount, second and third-order effects get disregarded in place of servicing immediate needs. In turn, the system uses increasing amounts of otherwise productive capital to mitigate this ever-growing list of emerging challenges. Central planners are stuck in a never-ending game of whack-a-mole with an ever-increasing number of economic issues.

As the famous British economist Friedrich Hayek expressed, "once the free working of the market is impeded beyond a certain degree, the planner will be forced to extend his controls until they become all-comprehensive."[94]

This leads us to the next stage.

Stage Three - Capital Flow Distortion

As explored in the Introduction, money is a powerful medium of expression. The more accurately our spending reflects our genuine beliefs, desires, and priorities, the more insightful and meaningful the information we can garner from our money becomes.

To reiterate some of the key points made in the examination of money as medium of expression, I highlighted that since we only have a finite amount of time, we cannot spend time on everything and everyone to the extent we might want to. We must make choices about how we express our finite, albeit unknown, quantity of time. From this, we can garner two interesting points:

1. As we interact with the world, we are constantly, and often subconsciously, prioritizing our wants and needs— deciding what is most important at this moment.
2. Given that when we work, we are renumerated for our time spent in the form of money, money can be seen as a way of storing time that we can spend in the future on whatever it is that we value.

For the most part, these interactions with the world are voluntary. We choose where to direct our time, energy, and money. But this may not always be the case. Just as language can be tainted through censorship, any mode of expression is susceptible to corruption, and money is no exception.

When the government robs us of our purchasing power through monetary expansion, this does two things:

First, they now choose where to spend this newly acquired purchasing power that was once ours by directing capital toward the industry or effort of their choosing. For example, suppose monetary expansion is undertaken in an effort to fund a war. In that case, citizens who are dissenters of that war will lose purchasing power, while the government uses their increased access to capital to continue that endeavour.

And second, this reduction in purchasing power limits our ability to express ourselves monetarily, as we now have less to direct toward what we do value. So not only are the hypothetical dissenters of the previous paragraph effectively forced into supporting a war that contradicts their personal values, but they also have less ability to spend towards what they do want, whether that's a comfortable home, nutritious food, a new video game, travel to loved ones, or anything else they might desire.

In this way, the action of money supply expansion alters how money is spent, distorting the natural flow of capital in the economy. *This also applies to other forms of intervention, such as regulation, capital controls, and spending restrictions or limitations, all of which alter capital flows and hinder our ability to express ourselves monetarily.*

Although these interventions are often done in the name of ameliorating short-term pain, by redirecting capital flows to failing areas of the economy, they are diverting capital away from viable and valuable areas— those that the populace would rather spend their money in. This perpetuates fiscal irresponsibility and threatens vital value-creating businesses.

In a world where the government didn't step in, would you have spent your hard-earned money supporting those failing businesses?

One such example is in our financial markets. Because we have become so accustomed to monetary intervention, asset prices—*such as equities*—no longer fluctuate based on corporate value creation but instead on central bank intervention. Today, most investors and funds allocate their capital based on the information one man, the central bank chairman, has to say.[95] If monetary tightening (reducing capital flows) is seen to be in the cards, assets pre-emptively decline in value, while if monetary easing (increasing capital flows) is on the horizon, prices start to soar.

Furthermore, because our government's monetary intervention supports failing areas of the economy, we can no longer recognize what is not working. A company may have longevity because it is successful or because it has been saved. As a result, we cannot learn from our mistakes. People will continue to repeat behaviours which do not add value to society.

To summarise the first three stages...

A misalignment to reality leads us down a rabbit hole of ever-increasing debt. Central banks then intervene to reduce short-term economic instability, but in doing so, they hamper the natural process of creative destruction. This, in turn, amplifies long-term economic fragility and distorts the flow of capital.

These three processes make way for our final stage.

Stage Four - Decision-Making Impairment

One way to look at stage four is through the lens of the relationship example from the first chapter. When the lines of communication in a relationship breakdown, so too does the relationship. We misinterpret what our partner needs, and they misinterpret what we need. It doesn't matter how much time and energy we invest if that effort doesn't include rebuilding the lines of communication. Without honest, clear communication, the relationship is doomed since we lack the capacity to understand what is needed to move forward. For a relationship to last, we must be able to communicate effectively, which better positions us to make more informed decisions, minimizing our exposure to unforeseen risks.

You can think of effective communication in our economy as unimpeded free market money. Such money allows for freedom of monetary expression, which—*through the principles of supply and demand*—provides insight into society's priorities. When we distort the channel of communication that is our money, we lose the ability to gauge what is valuable and what's not.

How can we expect to make informed decisions if we have a misaligned monetary system that incentivizes intervention, inhibits creative destruction, and distorts the natural flow of capital in the economy? If we are unable to see where value is truly being created?

Without freedom of monetary expression, the truth is obscured. We cannot know what society truly values, let alone what our economy needs. We are therefore making decisions constructed from partial or inaccurate information.

If we want humanity to flourish, we must ensure truth and integrity sit at the heart of our monetary system.

But this is currently not the case. In our current system, because our money supply is in a constant state of flux, governments, businesses, and individuals have no idea:

- what the free, unimpeded market deems valuable
- which companies should or should not exist
- what the actual risks in our economy are

Ultimately, these factors impact economic decision-making, eventually leading to failure.

Interest rates are a perfect example. Rates are traditionally a measure of risk in the economy. If rates are rising, it is because people are hesitant to lend as a result of elevated perceived risk. Therefore, we can gather that this may be a time to be cautious.

However, if the central bank suppresses interest rates, this gives us a false impression that everything is fine. With the illusion of security, people and businesses take on greater risk, leading to greater economic fragility. They are making financial decisions based on false information.

Moreover, this suppression of rates also pushes savers, such as pensioners in traditional yield-bearing assets, into riskier assets in search of greater yield and incentivizes debt consumption due to favourable rates— an environment ripe for mal-investment.

In 2022, this mal-investment reared its ugly head in the UK pension system. Suppressed interest rates meant that UK pension funds were severely underfunded, forcing them to resort to leveraging their assets to meet their obligations. The repercussions were devastating. By October 2022, approximately 90% of the UK's pension funds, representing a massive £1.5 trillion in assets, were on the verge of collapse.[96] Imagine yourself on the cusp of retirement after diligently saving throughout your career, only to face the possibility of your pension being wiped out in one fell swoop.

Fortunately for these individuals, the story took a different turn. The Bank of England, the country's central bank, intervened to avert disaster, but at a cost. The burden was shifted onto the taxpayers.

To recap, the four stages of economic ruin that can lead to collapse are as follows:

- **Stage One:** Misalignment to reality, where decisions perpetuate issues instead of resolving them.
- **Stage Two:** The misalignment sets the stage for the death of creative destruction. Central bank intervention props up failing businesses, inhibiting the natural process of creative destruction, which is necessary for fostering new ideas, products, and businesses.
- **Stage Three:** A lack of creative destruction leads to the distortion of capital flows due to intervention redirecting capital away from viable and valuable areas of the economy towards unsustainable, failing areas.
- **Stage Four:** This stage marks the critical point where the misallocation of capital, resulting from the first three stages, leads to inaccurate information, impairing vital economic decisions. At this point, the economy becomes increasingly fragile and vulnerable, and unless corrective measures are taken, this impairment will ultimately lead to economic collapse.

So, do you think a system built on intervention can stand the test of time? Can the current strategy of continually postponing catastrophe work indefinitely?

CONCLUSION

We live under a monetary system that uses our productive capacity to prop up failure and repay insolvent debt. This system will seem to function... until it doesn't. When we reach a point where the central bank cannot successfully control inflation, leading to hyperinflation, or those on the bottom rung of society can no longer afford to service debt payments, triggering a wave of defaults working its way up through society, devastating everything in its wake.

When I think of this, a quote by Seth Godin on juggling comes to mind: "Throwing is more important than catching. If you're good at throwing, the catching takes care of itself. Emergency response is overrated compared to emergency avoidance."[97] Our governments and central bankers are in the emergency response business. They're anchoring on outcomes, such as inflation and price stability, attempting to control results through intervention.

However, to build resilience in this ever-changing world, we must improve our emergency avoidance, such as building effective communication through freedom of monetary expression. Only then can we respond more appropriately, given that we'll be better positioned to decipher the world around us.

While our system hasn't yet collapsed due to its misalignment with reality, inhibiting creative destruction, or distortion of the natural flow of capital, it's just a matter of time before uninformed decision-making becomes the nail in the coffin. The need for unceasing growth is simply unsustainable.

What's more, we have a name for a system that requires growth to stay alive. When it comes to our economy we call it the fiat monetary system, but if we want to be accurate, the correct terminology is a Ponzi or pyramid scheme.

The US Government defines a Ponzi scheme as: "An investment fraud that pays existing investors with funds collected from new investors."[98] Our monetary system requires continual inflation to ease the burden of debt, all while enriching those at the top, and if they are unable to keep borrowing from the future, from the masses, the music stops playing, and the system collapses.

CHAPTER 4

THE LINK BETWEEN MONEY & BEHAVIOUR

How Our Money Shapes How We Act

"Whenever we seek to avoid the responsibility for our own behaviour, we do so by attempting to give that responsibility to some other individual or organization or entity. But this means we then give away our power to that entity, be it 'fate' or 'society' or the government or the corporation or our boss."
—M. Scott Peck, The Road Less Traveled

....

Financiers would benefit at the expense of 'widows and orphans'. Wealth would be redistributed from savers to borrowers. Creditors would be inadequately compensated for risk. Too much borrowing would take place. Money would flow abroad in search of higher returns. Asset price inflation would make the rich richer. The reduction of interest rates wouldn't revive a moribund [approaching death] economy. In short...forced reduction in interest rates imparts no benefit to a society.[99]

These are the words of John Locke, a leading 16th-century philosopher and political theorist from the book *The Price of*

Time by Edward Chancellor, and this quote perfectly underscores that the idea of monetary manipulation leading to a whole host of issues is not a new concept. Many people throughout the ages have warned of the effects of monetary intervention. That said, given the complexity of the financial system and (until recently) the limited literature surrounding the subject, this knowledge has only just started to trickle down into mainstream resources accessible to the general public.

....

SIDE NOTE: I find it fascinating that Locke's understanding of how a system that inhibits monetary expression ripples throughout society is as accurate today as it was in his day, over 400 years ago.

....

With the notion of financial intervention bringing about change being front of mind, let's take a look at how our monetary environment affects our behaviour, as this will assist us in building a solid foundation for understanding how money in its current form weaves its influence into areas such as government and politics, parenting, business, and our natural environment.

MONEY'S EFFECT ON BEHAVIOUR

In the old nature versus nurture debate, some argue that conditions such as ADHD, depression, anxiety, and obesity, among others, are a product of nature— they are simply a result of our genetics. However, work by doctors such as Gabor Mate or trauma specialists like John Bradshaw increasingly suggest that these conditions are, instead, a byproduct of our environment— when people are exposed to certain environments, they have a higher propensity for certain outcomes.[100,101] Said differently, these conditions are largely, in part, coping mechanisms developed during childhood.

Imagine a situation where your parents could not provide a nurturing space for your upbringing, where your environment lacked safety and security. In such a circumstance, as a child, you may have frequently found yourself in uneasy situations, triggering your natural fight, flight and freeze instincts. However, as much as you might have wished to defend yourself (fight) or flee (flight), you may have been unable to confront your parents directly due to your vulnerability and lack of autonomy. Consequently, you may have leaned towards "freeze," adopting emotional disconnection as a coping mechanism— whenever discomfort arose, you emotionally distanced yourself. Over time, this neural pattern became deeply embedded in your developing brain. As a result, when faced with discomfort in adulthood, your automatic response tends to be emotional detachment.

This theory offers insight into the evolving understanding of ADHD, characterized by ongoing patterns of inattention, and its potential root cause. It suggests that individuals may not be born with ADHD but could have developed it as a response to their early environment.

SIDE NOTE: It's important to acknowledge that it's not that genetics can't elevate the likelihood of these conditions. However, it's the environment that ultimately dictates whether such predisposition materializes.

With this in mind, we may believe that we are born with innate behaviours, but this is not quite accurate. Just as certain conditions are a product of our environment, so too is our behaviour.

If, as a child, our parents emotionally supported us, allowing us to experience a full range of emotions, we would be in excellent standing to explore the world from a state of growth (as we'll discuss in Chapter Five). While in this state, we are more able to push ourselves outside of our comfort zone, and we are far more emotionally capable of processing any challenges or failures effectively. As a result, a growth state enables us to be more adaptable to our ever-changing world and, more importantly, gives us the tools to recognize that failure is not only normal but also necessary. Recognizing mistakes is how we learn.

On the flip side, if our parents cannot meet our emotional needs, our ability to process failure, take risks, and push ourselves may be severely impacted.

I'm sure everybody has that one friend who micromanages their children and panders to their child's every need. Although it may seem like their children's emotional needs are being met through the parents' efforts, this is not actually the case. These well-intentioned, attentive parents tend to step in to solve their child's problems whenever their kid is in a position that elicits discomfort. Since these children are not allowed to sit with their discomfort and become comfortable with failure, these children also never have the opportunity to experience a full range of emotions, and often end up no better off than those whose parents are absent.

In such situations, the parent unwittingly inhibits emotional maturation and the child's ability to assimilate with their peers and society. Rather than trying to hand the world to our children on a silver platter, we should strive to support our children while at the same time assisting them in developing the emotional tools to be self-reliant and independent. The goal is to comfort and reassure kids in their moments of failure, not prevent them from ever experiencing it. As the famous parenting author Gary Ezzo would say, "prepare your child for the road, not the road for your child."

Who we are, our behaviour and our values are inextricably linked to our environment. Central planners trying to control the flow of money are no different from that micromanager parent attempting to control their children. They believe they know what's best, so they act on behalf of the individual. But in doing so, they're removing power from those they're trying to safeguard and support.

Just as our childhood environment influences who we become as an adult, our monetary environment plays a significant role in our behaviour.

Let's go over three such examples of how money in its current form impacts how we show up in this world.

Time Preference

The first and arguably the most important behaviour our money impacts is our time preference.

Don't worry. You're not alone if you don't recognize this term.

From inflation eroding our purchasing power, limiting our ability to acquire what we truly desire, to capital controls, restrictions, and regulations altering where we can allocate our funds, our monetary system not only dictates the boundaries of our spending but also shapes our inclination toward immediate consumption or saving for the future. And where we fall on this spectrum of spending or saving is determined by our time preference. You can think of the two ends of the time preference spectrum as:

1. **High Time Preference**, whereby our thinking is more focused on meeting our immediate needs.
2. **Low Time Preference**, in which our thinking places greater emphasis on future needs, delaying immediate gratification.

Instinctually, we are inclined towards immediate over delayed satisfaction, all else being equal. For instance, if given a choice between receiving $100 today or $100 a month from now, most rational individuals would opt for the immediate sum due to uncertainties associated with the future, i.e., what is the purchasing power of $100 in the future? Or will the items I desire be available? As a result, unless sufficient compensation for delaying gratification is available, we will most likely prioritize servicing our immediate needs.

Considering this, our inclination towards low or high time preference is heavily contingent upon the structure of our monetary system. To illustrate this, let's consider two monetary scenarios:

Scenario One

Our monetary system is structured so that interest rates adequately reward savers, and the currency functions as a reliable store of value, maintaining its purchasing power over time. This environment fosters low-time preference thinking, given that it incentivizes individuals to save. These savings can subsequently be used to acquire additional goods, resulting in enhanced utility and satisfaction.

Scenario Two

Our monetary system is structured so that we face financial repression (interest rates held below the inflation rate), and our purchasing power deteriorates over time, leading to inflationary pressures. As a result, the motivation to save diminishes, encouraging low time preference. Consequently, there is a heightened incentive to engage in consumption, accumulate debt, or invest in high-risk investments to generate returns that surpass inflation.

In light of these scenarios, the structure of our money dramatically impacts how we interact with the world.

Furthermore, the advantages of time preference extend beyond spending and saving. The well-known Stanford Marshmallow experiment conducted by Walter Mischel and Ebbe B. Ebbesen in 1960 shed light on this concept.[102] Kids were given a choice: have one marshmallow now or wait for a while and get two. This study revealed that those with a stronger ability to delay gratification (low time preference) tended to enjoy more favourable life outcomes in the ensuing decades. Subsequent studies in 1988 further supported these findings, revealing that individuals with low time preferences exhibited superior academic performance and were less prone to developing addictions or weight problems.[103]

In lower time preference societies where individuals possess the capacity to:
1. postpone the acquisition and enjoyment of goods, thereby saving and generating additional capital,
2. face problems head-on rather than pushing them off into the future, long-term technological advancement tends to thrive. Moreover, such societies experience enhanced peace and prosperity, as participants recognize that conflicts impede the seamless production of capital goods and the smooth functioning of economic activities.

However, the converse holds true for societies with high time preference. In such contexts, there is a tendency for debt to escalate, given that borrowing becomes more advantageous than lending. Rational individuals are inclined to spend as their currency loses its reliability as a store of value. Consequently, the pursuit of instant gratification by postponing challenges, along with dwindling savings and escalating debt that obstruct capital accumulation, leads to a subsequent reduction in productivity levels.

As should be evident, our current monetary system predominantly aligns with the latter scenario. We have a system that promotes high time preference thinking, as there is little incentive to save when the value of our money diminishes over time.

The challenge with a system geared towards immediate gratification, debt consumption, and spending is that rising prices begets rising prices. When we bring forward future spending (consciously or not) in an attempt to outpace rising prices, increased demand further elevates prices, feeding the beast that is inflation. And as inflation takes its toll, it becomes increasingly harder for individuals to sustain their livelihoods. Basic resources, such as housing, food, and electricity, become more expensive, leaving less room (if any) for the creature comforts previously within reach and enjoyed.

Maslow's Hierarchy of Needs provides valuable insights into our behaviour when we face such constraints. This foundational theory, often represented as a five-tier pyramid, offers a framework to comprehend our priorities and the factors that drive us the most. It helps us understand the fundamental needs that motivate human behaviour.

The five levels of the pyramid are:

1. **Physiological Needs** - food, clothes, and shelter
2. **Safety Needs** - health, resources, and job security
3. **Love and Belonging Needs** - friendship, intimacy, family, and belonging
4. **Esteem Needs** - respect, self-esteem, status and recognition, and freedom
5. **Self-Actualization Needs** - the desire to be the best we can be

Maslow states that before we can address our needs higher up the pyramid (such as tiers 3-5), we must meet the needs of those lower down, with our physiological foundation needing to be met first and foremost. If we are unable to meet our physiological needs, we cannot function optimally. Maslow considered physiological needs to be "the most important as all the other needs become secondary until these needs are met."[104]

As our focus shifts increasingly towards meeting basic survival needs, we risk losing our sense of self. When we lose touch with our true selves, we also lose our sense of purpose and become more susceptible to external influences. This process is referred to as dehumanization, where we start to lose sight of the essence of being human. Instead of living fulfilling lives, we find ourselves merely working to survive, missing out on the richness and depth of our human experience.

In summary, when our money no longer acts as a store of value, and we lack adequate compensation from saving, we are pressured into either spending as our purchasing power declines from one day to the next or taking on risk by investing our money to minimize the effects of inflation. Unknowingly, we have elevated our time preference from building future security to servicing immediate needs. This behaviour not only hinders sustainable economic growth and prosperity but also exacerbates inflation, making it increasingly more difficult to meet our basic physiological needs.

I would argue that many of the challenges we discuss in the coming chapters arise because our monetary system shifts our time preference, incentivizing people to spend and prioritize the short-term over building security for the future.

This leads us to our next behavioural change.

Compassion & Altruism

Compassion is the feeling of sympathy and sadness for those suffering and a desire to extend understanding to others and **altruism** is the practice of care for the welfare and happiness of others, even above or at the expense of our own.

These behaviours materialized out of a lust for the survival of both our genes and ourselves. They are evolutionarily advantageous and can be seen in other animals as well.[105] By being compassionate for those around us and other prosocial behaviours, we boost the chance of our small clan, including our relatives, surviving.

As Frans De Waal, in his article on empathy, puts it, having empathy and compassion serves two purposes[106]:

1. "Like every mammal, we need to be sensitive to the needs of our offspring."
2. "Our species depends on cooperation, which means that we do better if we are surrounded by healthy, capable group mates."

Money in its current form, however, has the potential to upend our inherent desire for compassionate and altruistic behaviour that has developed over millions of years of evolution.

When living under an inflationary system whereby our purchasing power is slowly declining, our attention turns inward, placing basic safety and survival needs ahead of external, altruistic, and compassionate endeavours— giving back is, understandably, not front of mind. This shift results in the individual prioritizing themselves above that of the collective. Not only do fear and anxiety now dominate, given our now uncertain future, but generosity also becomes costly as it can hinder future security.

As Morrie Schwartz, the iconic sociology professor, puts it, "When you get threatened, you start looking out only for yourself," which comes at the cost of our compassion and altruism towards others, as we prioritize our own personal security above all else.[107] This distortion only increases as our currency's purchasing power further weakens. Rather than looking to collaborate and support our community, we are incentivized to extract what we can from society to meet our basic security needs.

Although many individuals, such as the Dalai Lama, preach that we should practice altruism and compassion regardless of our situation, I would push back by saying that if the basic needs of the majority were met, it would be far easier for compassion and altruism to flourish. Therefore, a favourable environment goes a long way to assisting humanity on its road to compassion and altruism.

Meaninglessness & Apathy

Here are two facts about our monetary system that are often brushed over:

1. Monetary expansion is the unstoppable unilateral dilution of currency, which causes prices to rise.
2. When those in positions of power monetarily intervene, purchasing power isn't simply created out of thin air. Instead, it results from a movement of purchasing power from one area of the economy to another. Typically, this is from the currency holders to the government and the banks or from wage-earners to asset holders.

Another way to think about these two facts is that we have a reverse robin hood effect, shifting money from those with the least wealth to those with the most. For instance, between 1975 and 2018, approximately $50 trillion has shifted from the bottom

90% of the US population to the top 1%[108] To help understand the magnitude of this transfer, let's compare it to Africa. Africa is comprised of 54 countries with a combined GDP in 2018 amounting to $2.48 trillion.[109] In other words, the top 1% in the US has received more than 20 times the GDP of Africa's 54 countries over the past 43 years.

This loss of purchasing power has impaired our ability to express ourselves monetarily. At any moment, the government can extract value from the currency holders and spend it elsewhere. As we saw in Chapter Two, one significant repercussion of this dilution of purchasing power is that wages cannot keep up with asset prices.

- Purchasing a house becomes ever more unobtainable.
- Saving for your child's education is further out of reach.
- And buying groceries consumes a larger portion of your paycheque.

Furthermore, in a manipulated market, the middle and lower class, who central planners supposedly prioritize, suffer the most both on the way up and down. When times are good, prices rise faster than wages. This places greater financial strain on those at the bottom. As a result, they may need to take out loans to meet their basic needs.

While one might hope for some level of equalization during a market correction, it is once again the individual's living paycheque to paycheque who get hit hardest. As many of these individuals have limited cash flow, they are restricted in their ability to adjust their spending. If interest rates rise or banks start calling loans (the bank exercises its right to demand full repayment before the originally agreed-upon loan term expires) as risk starts to emerge in the economy, these individuals are the first to feel the effects.

The 2008 financial crisis provides a clear example of this. One in five Americans lost their jobs, and ten million people lost their homes, with the majority of those losses falling on the lower and middle classes.[110,111] Even after a decade, 65% of homeowners who went through a short sale or foreclosure and lost their homes have not yet purchased another home.[112] Meanwhile, those sitting comfortably were able to purchase foreclosed homes at fire-sale prices, and subsequently experienced massive wealth gain as the housing market recovered and soared to new heights.

While the intention of intervention is typically publicized to support those at the bottom of society, unfortunately, it often has the opposite effect. This crushes motivation and gives currency holders a sense of meaninglessness.

Although it is hard to measure meaninglessness, it is clear that we are witnessing a tremendous rise in mental health issues. US suicide rates are at the highest levels since World War 2, and in the Gen Z and Millennial generations, nihilism, defined as "the rejection of all religious and moral principles, in the belief that life is meaningless," is growing by the day.[113,114] In one article on nihilism, a fifteen-year-old named Luke said that it's not hard to be nihilistic "when you see how morally corrupt we all are."[115] He goes on to say, "I don't have much hope for the [human] race's future ... I think the state of the world will drastically affect the way young people perceive human existence."

It's not surprising that many members of younger generations feel a sense of helplessness in today's economic climate. Imagine graduating from college only to find yourself burdened with $37,787 of student debt (average in the US), struggling to make ends meet, and contemplating living out of your car just to survive.[116] Or questioning whether you'll ever own a home, as skyrocketing real estate prices make it nearly impossible to obtain mortgage approval on an average wage in most areas.

When it becomes harder to get by and future security and stability slowly evaporate, apathy and meaninglessness often set in, and productivity suffers. Why strive to be the best we can be when our future is so uncertain, money purchases less from one day to the next, and ever-growing debt payments consume more and more of our productive capacity?

Hopefully, the idea that our environment shapes our identity is becoming more evident. Another illustrative example lies in how our environment shapes our locus of control, which refers to an individual's belief about the extent to which they have control over the events and outcomes in their life, whether they perceive it as being primarily influenced by external factors or their own actions and decisions.[117]

While a significant portion of our locus of control develops during childhood, influenced by whether our parents supported our emotional needs, it continues to evolve throughout our lives based on our experiences, including the impact of our money on our perception of control over our lives.

Individuals with a strong internal locus of control believe they have the power to influence outcomes, take responsibility for their actions, and are less influenced by others' opinions. They often achieve high levels of success and attribute negative outcomes to their own shortcomings. On the other hand, those with a strong external locus of control perceive life as being controlled by external forces such as others, fate, or luck. They tend to blame others for their circumstances and may rely on others to determine outcomes. Other traits associated with internal and external locus of control include:

Internal Locus of Control
- Demonstrates a belief in their own capabilities and resilience
- Exhibits confidence and determination when faced with challenges or confrontation
- Tends to have better physical health

- Displays a strong sense of self-efficacy, sets goals, and works hard to achieve them[118]
- Reports higher levels of happiness and values independence
- Works effectively at their own pace

External Locus of Control
- Shows higher levels of stress and susceptibility to clinical depression[119]
- Often attributes circumstances to others rather than taking personal responsibility
- Quickly credits luck, others, or external factors for outcomes
- Feels a sense of powerlessness and believes they lack the ability to change their circumstances
- Responds to challenges with feelings of hopelessness or powerlessness, possibly developing learned helplessness

I have witnessed firsthand our monetary system's impact on the lives of people close to me. One conversation with an old friend stands out in my memory. A few years back, we were working together, discussing our plans for the future, when I asked about his thoughts on staying in Whistler, where we both lived. His response was filled with a sense of resignation and frustration. He sighed and said, "I don't know. The cost of living these days, the soaring real estate prices, and rental rates... It feels impossible to ever own a house or gain security. So, I've decided to stop caring about progression and live in the moment, to spend my money on enjoying myself and having fun."

Over time, I couldn't help but notice a deterioration in his mental well-being. One day, he opened up to me, revealing the inner struggles he had been facing bouts of depression, overwhelming feelings of meaninglessness, and an overpowering sense of helplessness. It was a reflection of our world, where control over our lives can often feel like an unattainable goal.

And his story is not unique. Many others face the weight of a system that appears to deny them the basic pursuit of stability and security. Dreams of a modicum of financial security slip further away, replaced by a sense of hopelessness and a loss of control over their own lives.

Through my friend's struggles, I came to understand the toll that a lack of control takes on a person's emotional well-being. It chips away at our spirit, casting a shadow even over our happier moments. It leaves us feeling like passive observers rather than active participants in our own lives. With this in mind, the structure of our monetary system holds significant influence over the productivity, motivation, and overall mental well-being of the population.

CONCLUSION

To summarise this chapter in a single sentence: **We are a product of our environment!**

Our money isn't simply something we use to transact. It impacts everything about how we interact with the world around us. In its current form, monetary incentives have created an environment wherein:

1. People focus primarily on spending and alleviating short-term pain
2. Compassion and altruism are pushed to the wayside as the majority simply try to meet personal security needs
3. We're experiencing a pervasive growth in meaninglessness and a lack of motivation

When our focus becomes consumed by external circumstances, such as the devaluation of our money leading to stress, we lose a sense of self as we have less attention available to devote to the things that truly matter in life.

Now that we have an awareness of how money impacts our behaviour, we are better prepared to look at how these behaviours carry through into the various facets of society, including many areas typically not associated with money.

CHAPTER 5

MONEY, PARENTHOOD, & SELF-IDENTITY

How Money Influences the Family Unit

"Don't limit your challenges; challenge your limits."
—Jerry Dunn

....

The parent-child bond is one of the fundamental necessities of human life. It is natural and intrinsic, and because of that, we might want to believe that it is immune to the potent effects of money.

But not only is this bond far from exempt from the far reaches of our monetary system, but it is also arguably one of the most critical areas impacted. Understanding how the foundational relationship between parent and child is shaped by money will also help illuminate how other areas of life are similarly transformed.

As we will discuss, our identity, social aptitude, emotional strength, and physical well-being are largely shaped by our experiences from conception through birth and during our formative years. If our parents faced substantial stress—*financial or otherwise*—during pregnancy, or if they were unable to provide the necessary emotional support during these crucial stages of development due to work demands or other factors, it can have lasting effects. This can manifest as impaired social skills, weakened immune system, hindered growth, and a range of other related byproducts.

With this in mind, before we can fully understand the critical connection between money, parenthood, and our sense of self, we must wrap our heads around the effects of parental stress during pregnancy and the significance of attachment. These two factors greatly shape our personal development and contribute to our overall identity.

---

*For those unfamiliar with the term parent-child bond, beyond the immediate bond between mother and child during pregnancy, the parent-child relationship extends to encompass the interaction between a child and their caregivers. These caregivers play a vital role in supporting and nurturing the child's physical, emotional, and social development, which form the bedrock of their personality, life decisions, and overall behaviour.

How Prenatal Experiences Shape Development

In situations of heightened stress, our bodies release hormones like cortisol, adrenaline, and noradrenaline, triggering a physiological response to potential threats. These stress hormones are also shared with the developing fetus during pregnancy. In her insightful book, *Nurturing Resilience*, Kathy Kain elucidates the potential repercussions of continuous maternal stress during gestation, saying, "If the mother experiences constant stress...these usually helpful hormones can instead have a negative impact on the development of the fetus."[120]

Extensive research has linked maternal stress to long-term effects on a child's development, including brain development, allergies, asthma, and restricted fetal blood flow. Moreover, maternal stress increases the secretion of corticotropin-releasing hormone (CRH), which can lead to a heightened threat response system in the developing fetus.

Our innate threat response systems, fight, flight, and freeze, evolved to enhance survival. However, an overly sensitive or constantly engaged threat response system can harm our overall well-being. In times of perceived threat, the freeze response slows down our breathing and blood flow to minimize potential bleeding from injuries and reduce movement, thereby lowering the chances of being detected.[121] Similarly, fight and flight responses engage or disengage bodily systems to maximize survival.

While these responses are beneficial in dangerous situations, repeated activation in the absence of threat poses significant risks to our health— suppression of essential physiological functions, like immune response, nutrient absorption, and restorative rest, while activating survival mechanisms, strains our physiological system. This chronic wear and tear contributes to increased health risks over time, impairing a child's access to vital physiological support systems.

The critical development period is between conception and three years when rapid neurophysiological growth occurs. Spending excessive time in survival physiology hinders the neurophysiological architecture needed for emotional regulation and immune system functionality.[122]

Understanding the profound influence of our early experiences on our neurological development makes it clear that disruptions, such as significant financial stress, during this time can significantly impact our perception of the world, ourselves, and others, even if those disruptions are often forgotten or overlooked. For example, children exposed to prenatal stress have:

- Higher risk for developmental delays, behavioural problems (such as ADHD, anxiety, and conduct disorders), and altered brain development.[123]

- MRI studies have revealed differences in brain structure and connectivity in children exposed to prenatal stress, particularly in regions related to emotional regulation and stress response.[124] These children also face an increased likelihood of developing mental health disorders like depression, anxiety, and PTSD later in life.
- Prenatal stress has also been shown to result in cognitive development impairment leading to lower cognitive abilities, lower IQ scores, and academic difficulties.[125]

As Kain lays out, adverse childhood experiences can lead to disrupted neurodevelopment, resulting in social, emotional, and cognitive impairments. These impairments can increase the likelihood of adopting health-risk behaviours, ultimately contributing to the development of diseases, disabilities, social problems, and even premature death.

But our development is not solely attributed to prenatal stress; the quality of our attachment to parents and caregivers also plays a crucial role.

The Importance of Attachment

Many mammals need minimal nurturing after birth since a large portion of their development happens in the womb. This can be observed in animals such as calves who can walk within 12 hours of being born. This is obviously not the case for humans.

Due to the limited size of the birth canal, only one-quarter of a child's brain growth and 10% of their neural wiring occurs inside the womb. The remaining three-quarters develop after birth, with 90% of neurological growth occurring by the age of three.[126]

Moreover, children's brains have billions more neurons than they need in their early years. Therefore, this convoluted synaptic mess needs to be pruned to create a brain that can effectively manage its varied list of responsibilities. This pruning is known as neural Darwinism and is the brain's way of adapting to its environment.[127] Circuits and connections that are regularly utilized are strengthened, while inactive ones are discarded.

With most of the brain's growth occurring in childhood, a child's early relational attachments and experiences are crucial as they determine how well their brain's architecture and neural networks will mature and govern such things as behaviour, relationships, beliefs, and learning. As Daniel Siegel writes in his book, *The Developing Mind*:

> For the infant and young child, attachment relationships are the major environmental factors that shape the development of the brain during its period of maximal growth...Attachment establishes an interpersonal relationship that helps the immature brain use the mature functions of the parent's brain to organize its own processes.[128]

Attachment can be seen as an evolutionary survival mechanism. As children cannot survive independently, they must attach themselves, through relationship building, to their primary caregivers.

In light of this, when a child's attachment needs are met, they are far better equipped to explore the world with a growth mindset rather than a protective one. These mindsets are defined as:

- **Growth:** We are present and comfortable in the moment. We can, therefore, better regulate our emotions. But more importantly, we learn to respond to stimuli rationally, impersonally and based on the present moment rather than our past being over-represented in our response to the present.

- **Protective:** We are not mindfully present in our surroundings but instead governed by past traumatic experiences imprinting apprehension about what may happen in the future. When we attempt to quell internal discomfort, we are held hostage by stress and anxiety. We respond in any way that we have learned reduces the uncomfortableness of the present, whether beneficial or not.

It is important to note that children and adults alike can only be in one of these two possible states at any one time.

Suppose you are scuba diving in the Great Barrier Reef and suddenly realize you are running out of oxygen. You will naturally transition into a state of protection, focused on removing yourself from the present situation and towards safety. All your attention and efforts will be directed away from the natural beauty of the world around you and toward survival. It doesn't matter how incredible the fish, coral, and surrounding scenery are. You will be focused on the imminent threat of suffocation, not whatever you originally hoped to gain from your scuba diving excursion.

Building on this idea, we usually require more than just oxygen and physical orienting when we become lost and out of touch with the world around us before we can return to a growth state. Psychological orientation is just as crucial to a child's development. Children increasingly need direction as they age to gain a sense of their values, morals, passions, reality, and an understanding of why things happen and what things mean.

While the life-or-death scenario of a scuba diving mishap is an extreme example, this protective state can be triggered anytime our well-being is threatened. Therefore, while our innate biological protection mechanisms, i.e., fight, flight, and freeze, serve a vital role in potentially dangerous situations, the ability to effectively self-regulate sets growth and protective individuals apart. While the self-protection response of a growth individual only engages when a threat is present, this is not the case for protective individuals— those governed by the past. Their nervous system may be overly sensitive or remain in a constant state of threat response even in the absence of real danger, which, as mentioned above, can lead to numerous health issues later in life.

With this in mind, attachment is vital not only for health but for children to establish their authentic selves, enabling them to avoid many conflicts that arise from trying to conform to external expectations. When we embrace our authenticity, we expand our capacity to listen to our inner voice and pursue endeavours that truly resonate with our true selves. Honouring our authentic desires can lead to a more meaningful and fulfilling life. Moreover, authenticity empowers us to act with greater integrity, as it grants us greater clarity about our values and morals. When we are true to ourselves, our actions, self-expression, and choices reflect our genuine beliefs, fostering trust and deeper connections with others. Ultimately, authenticity allows us to live a life that is genuine, purposeful, and in harmony with our deepest essence.

Moving forward, when we talk about authenticity, we are referring to our ability to locate our own personality, values, and spirit, regardless of the external pressures to act otherwise.

This raises the question: How can we maximize physical and psychological orientation in children to promote authenticity?

The Parent-Child Bond

As the world-renowned physician Gabor Mate puts it, "attachment enables children to hitch a ride with adults who are, at least in the mind of a child, assumed to be more capable of orienting themselves and finding their way."[129]

In a peer relationship, both the child and their friend explore the world simultaneously, with similarly limited experience and knowledge. On the other hand, parents and elders have decades of hard-earned life lessons and wisdom to pass down. With solid, secure parental attachment children are more open to accepting advice from their parents and elders, which assists them in learning necessary life lessons, values, and morals unattainable from typical peer relationships.

Furthermore, when a child develops a solid parental attachment, this acts as a foundation for them to confront the world from a state of growth, as parents promote:

1. **Unconditional Love**: Parents often strive to establish an unconditional love bond, making it clear that although they may disagree with certain behaviours, their love towards the child is not dependent on the child's behaviour. This assists the child in growing up knowing that love is not temporary and based on their actions. The child can then express themselves fully, taking greater risks without fear of judgment. This comfort with pushing boundaries and trying new things assists in maturation and psychological growth.

2. **Exploring One's Authentic Self**: Parents often enable a safe environment for children to feel comfortable expressing themselves both emotionally and physically. When a child is rejected by their peers as a result of their behaviour, it often leads to "I am not worthy, I am not good enough, I need to hide who I am because it is unacceptable." This doesn't support healthy emotional processing as it pressures conformity. Instead, parents often explore why their child is behaving the way they are and try to meet the child's needs.

This reduces the risk that the child feels lost, helpless, and lonely— pervasive in today's teens and young adults.[130] In search of connection, they have put others before themselves. In doing so, they have lost sight of who they are, their values, and what they need at any given moment.

Although a peer relationship or two may not go as expected, if the child's need for love and support is being met through their parental relationship, the child should be able to recognize their uniqueness and stay true to their own burgeoning values. A child with a strong sense of self is much less likely to cave to their peers' suggestions against their better judgment. This uncommonly self-assured child will feel free to be who they want to be around their friends with reduced fear of judgment— not necessarily because they believe everyone will automatically accept them as they are, but because they will not fear that their own worth lies in their peers' opinions, or that their authentic choices could make them any less deserving of love and respect.

Peer Attachment

When children lack a secure foundational parental attachment, their developmental journey relies heavily on their peers as companions and guides. However, being led by fellow inexperienced individuals without the maturity and wisdom of parental figures poses risks. Not only does it elevate the risk of these children being exposed to potentially unproductive or destructive behaviours, but it also restricts their perspective of the world, narrowing their understanding of its vast possibilities. Additionally, due to their limited life experience, the connection formed with peers tends to be superficial, lacking deeper emotional bonds. Seeking similarity becomes the least vulnerable form of attachment, leading children to strive to resemble each other in appearance, temperament, thoughts, preferences, and values.[131]

In these peer relationships, both the developmental psychologist Gordon Neufeld and world-renowned physician and author Gabor Maté posit that the primary goal of a child who lacks sound parental attachment is to keep their connection to their peers intact.[132] They do not prioritize the "growth" of their identity but rather the "protection" of their social safety in fear of rejection. This often results in the suppression of emotions, likes, beliefs, passions etc., all in an attempt to fit in. As Maté explains: "Maturation requires that the child first becomes unique and separate from other individuals. The better differentiated she becomes, the more she is able to mix with others without losing her sense of self."

In essence, a solid parental attachment will help children better learn how to locate their authenticity and regulate their emotions more effectively.

What is often misunderstood about trauma is that it is subjective. Many children aren't traumatized because they were physically hurt, but instead, they were alone with their hurt, or in other words, their internal pain. They had no one to speak to honestly and openly and had no outlet within which to express themselves.

Inside the shell of a traumatized person is a healthy individual who has never found true expression in their life.

And here is where the problem lies. The deterioration of our currencies, creating relentless upward pressure on prices, forces parents to work more just to make ends meet. As a result, not only does **financial stress during pregnancy increase**, but **parents have less time available for meaningful interactions with their children** after birth and during their crucial developmental years.

If successive generations increasingly depend on peer attachment, the detrimental effects on society may quickly become overwhelming. For example, suppose a child's emotional needs are neglected, and they grow up to become parents. In that case, their own children may be even more likely to suffer, being two generations removed from secure parental bonds. Could this be one of the reasons behind the despondency we observe in the current younger generation?

We need to look no further than our ancestral nomadic hunter-gather tribes or the local indigenous populations to realize that for millions of years, tight-knit community support, enduring parental, and elder attachments, and passing down knowledge have been the norm. These conditions have been essential for survival, ensuring the well-being of pregnant individuals and the upbringing of children. They have facilitated the reduction of prenatal stress and enabled the transmission of essential knowledge about the land, culture, heritage, and our environment's dangers and opportunities.

Now, as Sebastian Junger, in his book *Tribe*, highlights, "A person living in a modern city or a suburb can, for the first time in history, go through an entire day—*or an entire life*—mostly encountering complete strangers. They can be surrounded by others and yet feel deeply, dangerously alone." [133]

Just like a child needs a sense of self, how can humanity flourish if we don't have a clear sense of who we are or what we want?

Although there are many factors at play, Figure 5.1 depicts that since a transition away from the gold standard, we have seen a tremendous rise in depression, as well as ADHD, and obesity. Even more alarming, one in three youth aged 13 - 18 will face an anxiety disorder and every year [134,135]:

- One in five Americans receives a mental disease diagnosis.
- Suicide kills more than 48,300 individuals in the US and 800,000 people worldwide, making it the second most common cause of death in the US for teenagers aged 15 to 24.
- Drug overdoses claim 81,000 lives per year in the US alone.

Figure 5.1

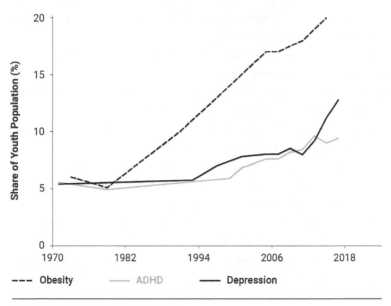

The Rise of Disorders & Illness in Youth

Prevalence rates for obesity, ADHD, & major depression in youth

Source: European Journal of Human Genetics

Given that money consistently ranks as the number one stressor in life—*affecting 73% of Americans*—and is the second leading cause of divorce, could it be contributing to the health challenges we face through its impact on prenatal mothers and parental attachment?[136,137,138]

Every parent I know shares a deep desire to reduce stress and forge a strong bond with their children, fulfilling their inherent need for attachment and unconditional love. However, growing financial pressures often demand increased work commitments in today's world. Many households rely on dual incomes to make ends meet, leaving self-care and domestic tasks to be tackled after work or on precious days off when parents are already exhausted and in need of rest. As a result, crucial aspects of parenting often get relegated to the backburner of an ever-growing to-do list. This unfortunate reality leaves parents with limited time and energy to support themselves or truly connect with their kids and cultivate this essential relationship. It's a frustrating situation that many parents face, as the one thing they yearn for the most is more **time.**

Figure 5.2

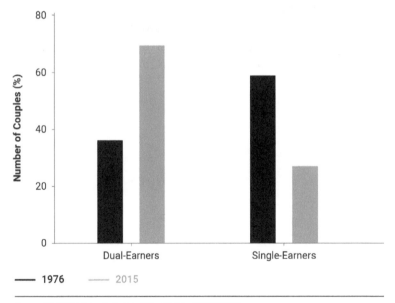

The Rise of Dual-Earner Couples
Comparing the number of dual-earner vs single-earner couples with at least one child under 16 in Canada from 1976 to 2015.

Source: Statistics Canada, Labour Force Survey, 1976 & 2015

Greater awareness of effective parenting strategies and the detrimental effects of prenatal stress and insecure parental attachment are helpful. But without spare time, many parents will simply be unable to commit the energy to self-care or to upgrade and enhance their special bond with their children. Case in point:

- Over the past 40 years, dual-earner families in Canada have doubled from around 35% of families to 70%, while the number of single-earner families has more than halved (Figure 5.2).
- In the US, dual-income households have grown by 40% between 1967 and 2010, and only 7% of all US households consist of married couples with children in which only the husband works.[139,140]
- And Japan is in a similar situation. Dual-income households now account for over two-thirds of all households, up from one-third in the 1980s (Figure 5.3).

Figure 5.3

The Changing Working Family Dynamic

Number of dual-earner couples vs households consisting of an employed husband & a non-working wife in Japan

Dual-Earner Couples ———— Employed Husband & Non-Working Wife

Source: Labour market reform in Japan to cope with a shrinking and ageing population,
ResearchGate

The maxim that "time is money" carries dire consequences in this context.

THE LINK BETWEEN PARENTING & MONEY

When we work, we are remunerated for our time spent in the form of money. Whether working as a tradesperson, teacher, or pilot, we must expend time to accumulate money.

Conversely, by investing money, we can reclaim precious time and gain greater freedom in how we utilize our non-working hours. For instance, purchasing a dishwasher eliminates the time spent on cleaning up. Acquiring a vehicle reduces time commuting. Enrolling in education enables us to save considerable time in trial and error. In each of these examples, we're bypassing the time-consuming tasks using money.

But, when the value of our time expended diminishes, meaning the money we receive for each hour of our time no longer has the same purchasing power, we are forced to work more, consuming more time, in order to maintain the same standard of living. An increased workload comes at the expense of our precious time for ourselves and our loved ones. For example, when parents and caregivers are compelled to work longer hours to offset the effects of inflation, it not only raises the risk of financial stress but also deprives their children of crucial parental bonding and learning opportunities. Consequently, there is a shift from parental guidance to reliance on peer influence. In 2020, statistics revealed that 84% of working mothers didn't take time off due to financial constraints, with 57% stating they had no alternative but to continue working.[141]

Moreover, data suggests that financial stress causes people to delay having children.[142] In the late '60s, the average age of Canadian mothers at first birth was 23.[143] The average age has currently risen to 29. As a result:

- Women are having children out of their reproductive prime, increasing the risk of complications and health issues, increasing the burden on the healthcare system.

- We experience a generational gap as population growth slows, leading to an aging population and potential strains on social welfare systems and healthcare services.

And to add fuel to the fire, as we work longer hours to make up for our loss of purchasing power, we have less time to spend with our children, socialize, pursue personal interests, and engage in critical thinking. This lack of free time can make us more susceptible to stress and anxiety as we struggle to balance our responsibilities with our personal needs and desires. Additionally, it can limit our ability to fully participate in and contribute to society in our desired manner, ultimately undermining our well-being and sense of fulfillment. Without time for rest and fulfillment, many parents struggle to be the type of parent they want to be, even when they do spend time with their children.

In short, a decrease in purchasing power directly impacts our quality of life by affecting not only the time we, as parents, can spend with our children but also the quality of that time. To illustrate just how impactful purchasing power is on our time, let's crunch some numbers in a few examples.

Let's say I earn a salary of $50,000 per year and plan to save for my child's college education. The average annual cost of an undergraduate degree at a state college is $26,290, and after pinching some pennies, I estimate that I can save $6,000 per year.[144] So in the absence of inflation, it would take 17 years to afford a four-year degree totalling $105,160. Not ideal if you have any unexpected expenses at any point during your child's childhood, but just about feasible. However, the story takes a different turn when we factor in inflation.

As a rule of thumb, American college tuition increases on average 8% per year.[145] Assuming a constant inflation rate, even in year one of my savings plan, the cost of tuition has increased by $8,412, more than the $6,000 I could save, making it impossible to achieve my goal.

All in all, in the absence of inflation, I could save for my child's college tuition just in time for them to head off to college. However, with an inflation rate of 8%, it's unlikely I'll ever be able to afford even the first year of their college unless I significantly increase my income.

Take a moment and let it sink in: think about all the extra time you'll have to spend at work in a futile attempt to try and support your child's education. It's a sobering thought, but the harsh reality, given our monetary climate.

Figure 5.4

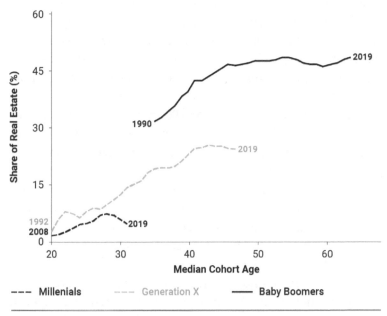

The Millennial Homeownership Slump

Share of American real estate owned by each generation, by median cohort age

Source: Federal Reserve Distributional Accounts & The Washington Post

And inflation doesn't just concern education. In recent years, food inflation has topped 14%, 11% and 8% in the Emerging Markets, US and Eurozone, respectively. And on the investment front, in 1970, an average person had to work 28 hours to buy a single share of the S&P 500 stock market index. [146,147] Fast forward to February 2023. [148] It now takes 125 hours to purchase that same share, reflecting the increased strain on those attempting to build security.

Or take, for example, housing. Compared to fifty years ago, purchasing a house has become far harder due to the significant rise in the house price-to-wage ratio. [149,150] In 1970, this ratio was around four. Today, it exceeds eight. This means the average home now costs eight times the average person's wage, compared to just four times in 1970. And this ballooning is much worse in desirable locations such as Whistler, BC, where the average house is a casual 106 times the average wage. [151,152]

This dramatic change in the affordability of housing has had a demonstrable impact on younger generations and families. As Figure 5.4 demonstrates, in 1990, when baby boomers reached a median age of 35, they owned almost one-third of American real estate by value. Fast forward to 2019, when the median age of millennials was 31, their ownership of American real estate value stood at only 4%.

The decline in real estate held by each generation starkly highlights how, more than ever before, prices are affecting a generation's ability to enter the property market. [153]

- Silent Generation (Born between 1928 - 1945): $7.2 trillion
- Baby Boomers (1946 - 1964): $15 trillion
- Gen X (1965 - 1980): $7.2 trillion
- Millennials (1981 - 1996): $1.1 trillion

And the situation doesn't look to be improving. Today, 81 countries are experiencing double-digit inflation. [154] That is almost half of all reporting countries. To put it into perspective, if inflation hovers around 10% for the next decade, without similar increases in wages, we can expect to lose 65% of our purchasing power. At this rate, we will need almost triple the amount of money to buy the same goods and services in ten years. This highlights the unfortunate reality that in the face of inflationary pressures, we are pressured to work harder and longer, sacrificing more of our valuable time in order to maintain our standard of living.

As noted in Chapter One, between the '50s to the '80s, we experienced a remarkable global population boom. When the baby boomer generation entered the workforce, this demand further elevated the prices of consumer goods.[155] Due to the rapid rise in the number of individuals earning a wage and looking to spend, demand outstripped supply. Alongside these rising prices, we experienced rising debt levels as individuals and families could no longer afford what they previously could without financing. This can be seen in the increasing levels of various debts in Figure 5.5.

With the burden of debt and purchasing power erosion greater than ever, dual-earner families, let alone single-earner families, struggle to cope. This puts a significant strain on the parent-child relationship as parents must either get by on less or increase their income to make ends meet. For many families, this means working longer hours, sometimes by getting an additional side gig or even a second full-time job. After preparing dinner, organizing the house, and finishing chores (if they are lucky enough to be able to be home for dinner), they have little energy left to direct toward quality time with their children.

From my experience as a child of divorced parents raised effectively by a single mother, I have seen firsthand how our parent-child relationship was impacted due to my mother's work requirements. With my mother having to work to support my two siblings and me, we looked to our peers for emotional support as our mum worked diligently to put a roof over our heads. And my situation is not unique. Almost one-quarter of households today are single-parent households.[156]

Figure 5.5

The Growing Debt Burden
Combined non-governmental/corporate debt

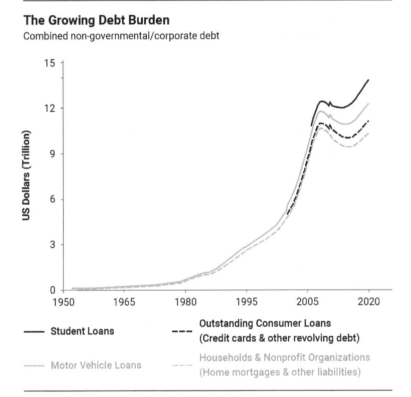

Source: *Board of Governors of the Federal Reserve System (US)*

However, what is truly alarming is the convergence of multiple challenges:

- Rising financial pressures due to the erosion of purchasing power
- The increasing prevalence of dual-earner families
- A looming population crisis

In countries such as Canada, the US, and several developing nations, we are witnessing the slowest population growth in the past century. This demographic shift is significant considering that countries like China, once concerned about rapid population growth, now face the prospect of a staggering 50% decline in population over the next 45 years. The magnitude of this decline is cause for serious concern and warrants our attention.

With an ever-growing debt burden, parents must work more to get ahead or meet their rising debt payments. Who will pick up the slack if our labour workforce is cut in half, or will we see a further decline in the work/family balance?

CONCLUSION

Reducing prenatal stress and fostering secure parental attachment is crucial for optimal childhood development. These factors play a significant role in shaping a child's brain architecture and neural networks, influencing their social, physical, and emotional well-being. Moreover, a strong parental figure serves as a guiding compass, allowing children to discover their authentic selves and express their needs verbally, physically, and emotionally. This freedom to explore and grow enables children to navigate the world with confidence, reducing the likelihood of feelings of being lost, helpless, or lonely.

However, while reduced stress and secure attachment can offer powerful benefits in child development, when this vital bond becomes impaired or disrupted, it can quickly spell trouble, negatively impacting the child's emotional, social, and cognitive development.

I would argue that one of the primary assailants in this impairment today is our money, which, as we have explored, is slowly and, at times, rapidly losing its purchasing power. With our savings losing value, are we incentivized to save? Of course not. We might as well buy the newest flat-screen TV or techno gizmo. And as we feel the effects of inflation, we won't have the option to look after ourselves during pregnancy or take time away from the workforce when our children are young. Instead, we may feel pressure to ramp up our personal working hours and maybe even take on a second job.

All of this results in a chain of negative consequences:

Financial pressures → Adverse childhood experiences → Disrupted neurodevelopment → Social, emotional, and cognitive impairments → Increased likelihood of adopting health-risk behaviours → Development of diseases, disabilities, and social problems

Money profoundly impacts our most fundamental pillars of life: health, connection, and authenticity. Therefore, how we choose to approach money will greatly impact our future and the world around us.

....

SIDE NOTE: *If you believe that only our children's health is affected by our financial surroundings, think again. Our immune system and nervous system are intimately linked. This is why, when we're emotionally stressed, we get sick, & where we're sick, we are more easily triggered emotionally.*

Considering that financial stress ranks as a top global stressor, it's no surprise that we are facing a health epidemic. Our nervous systems bear the relentless burden of monetary stress, significantly impairing our immune system in the process. Addressing these monetary stressors is crucial for our overall health and well-being.

....

CHAPTER 6

MISMANAGEMENT, IRRESPONSIBILITY, & RISK-TAKING

How Easy Money Disrupts Business

"The most important thing to remember is that inflation is not an act of God, that inflation is not a catastrophe of the elements or a disease that comes like the plague. Inflation is a policy." —Ludwig von Mises

....

W hen capital is abundant, such as when debt is cheap because interest rates are low, individuals, governments, and businesses become less conscientious about where they direct their funds. This is a problem! In a world of never-ending monetary expansion, the need to productively allocate capital declines, leading to a vicious cycle of misallocation. As a result, our productive capacity becomes consumed by ever-increasing debt service payments, with far-reaching consequences for our economy.

In this chapter, we will explore how our current monetary system disrupts the natural functioning of businesses, beginning with its impact on innovation.

Innovation Suppression

The term "zombie company" may sound like something from a horror movie, but it's a very real phenomenon in the business world. A zombie company is a business that cannot support itself financially but continues to operate through debt accumulation. These still-functioning but debt-dependent businesses play a critical role in disrupting the natural flow of capital. A lack of financial viability in a company often indicates that its product or service fails to generate sufficient revenue to cover operational expenses or that the company has been financially irresponsible, rendering it unable to meet its debt obligations. In a free market, such a business must either restructure or close up shop.

However, when the government intervenes to make it cheaper and more accessible for companies to borrow capital, the number of these zombie companies in our economy increases. This propping up of unsustainable companies prevents or postpones the natural life cycle of a business from playing out.

New businesses must now compete with an ever-increasing number of zombie companies, making it ever more challenging for these up-and-coming businesses to succeed and prosper. Instead of focusing on innovation, these businesses must use a portion of their resources to compete with companies that should not exist.

What's more, in the US, the prevalence of zombie companies is only increasing, with their presence in almost every sector. In July 2020, a staggering 19% of all publicly listed US companies were considered zombie companies, indicating a significant disruption in the natural flow of capital.[157] The trend is even more pronounced when we examine the Russell 2000, a US exchange-traded fund that tracks 2000 small-cap companies (a company valued between $300 million and $2 billion). Over the past decade, the number of unprofitable companies in the Russell 2000 has swelled eightfold.

Figure 6.1

The Rising Trend of Unprofitable Companies
Number of Unprofitable Companies in Russell 2000

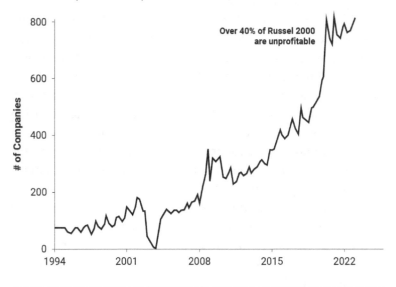

Source: Bloomberg, Morgan Stanley Wealth Management GIC as of Sept. 30, 2022

We must ask ourselves, "when the government steps in by directly bailing out fiscal irresponsibility or suppresses interest rates, indirectly supporting such companies to continue functioning, what message does this send?"

The initial thought is, "Why shoulder responsibility when there is no risk of incurring losses?" By bailing out businesses, they become increasingly incentivized to act irresponsibly, as they can depend on government support in times of trouble. Moreover, fiscally responsible businesses witness failure being rewarded, which prompts them to adopt a more risk-taking approach, either by accumulating more debt or taking on additional risks to match the benefits enjoyed by their irresponsibly managed counterparts.

All in all, capital misallocation begets capital misallocation, as bailouts create a vicious cycle where everyone is incentivized to capitalize off future bailouts rather than creating value in a fiscally responsible manner.

The misallocation of capital is compounded when monetary intervention leads to the direct distribution of money to the general public. For instance, during the COVID-19 pandemic, the Federal Reserve lowered interest rates and injected trillions of dollars in an attempt to stabilize the economy. As a result, investors, fueled by cheap, if not free, capital, started pouring their money into speculative assets. Some aimed to front-run the inflationary consequences of expansive money printing, while others simply sought to benefit from fortuitous windfalls resulting from government stimulus.

And this was the culture when GameStop, an outdated and near-bankrupt company, became a national headline. A group of amateur investors on the Reddit forum "WallStreetBets" noticed that hedge funds had heavily shorted GameStop's stock; given GameStop's status as increasingly irrelevant in the gaming industry, these hedge funds were betting that the company stock price would fall.[158] Seeing an opportunity to "stick it to the man," the Redditors started buying GameStop's stock en masse, driving up the price and causing the hedge funds to lose billions of dollars.

At one point, the stock price touched $483.00, up from $2.57 nine months earlier. That's an 18,693% increase! Ultimately, the once-failing company gained a second wind. While several factors contribute to the dynamics of speculative fevers, including the power of social platforms that facilitate collective efforts and the gamified nature of financial exchanges that promote speculation, it is crucial to recognize that access to capital plays a pivotal role in driving and sustaining these trends. Without the availability of capital, such speculative frenzies would struggle to gain the momentum necessary for their proliferation.

And this wasn't the only company whose price soared as a result of easy money.

In a story that seems almost too wild to be true: a company in bankruptcy, over $18 billion in debt, saw its stock plummet over 95% in a matter of months.[159] But then, thanks to monetary intervention triggering a speculative fever, a bidding war on the trading platform Robinhood ensued, with over 170,000 users jumping on board, causing the stock price to skyrocket 400%.[160] This is the story of Hertz.

After this price appreciation, the company was able to raise $5.9 billion in new capital, reducing its debt by $5 billion.[161] But this close call didn't exactly teach Hertz a lesson. The company opened up nearly $10 billion in new loans and credit lines, allowing it to continue its fiscal irresponsibility with no consequences.[162]

The pandemic has seen a proliferation of companies decimated by the crisis and filing for bankruptcy. But this hasn't stopped investors from piling into these companies and causing their stock prices to surge, divorced from any semblance of fundamental value. For instance[163]:

- J.C. Penney surged 167% in the three weeks post-bankruptcy.
- Whiting Petroleum soared 835% in the two months following its bankruptcy.
- And Pier 1 Imports stock saw a 200% increase in two days at one point following the bankruptcy.

These capital flows are a testament to how distorted and irrational financial markets have become, with investors chasing speculative gains and ignoring the underlying realities of these companies' bankruptcies.

What does all of this tell us about intervention? For one thing, easy money and government intervention do not promote value creation or innovation. Instead, unnatural capital flows divorced from reality allow failing companies to continue their economically destructive behaviour. And while Hertz may have come out on top this time, it's hard not to wonder: what are the long-term consequences of this?

This leads us to our next byproduct.

Unproductive Capital

A "unicorn" is the term venture capitalist Aileen Lee coined to describe unlisted startup companies valued at $1 billion or more, typically having never turned a profit.[164] According to Lee, as most successful companies go public, "startups that reached this mark are so rare that finding one is as difficult as finding a mythical unicorn."

However, although unicorns may have once been a rarity, by 2022, they were practically a dime-a-dozen, with more than 1,191 of them operating, up from 43 in 2013.[165,166] The total value of these unicorns globally now totals some $3.85 trillion.

You wouldn't be alone if you were to attribute this rise in unicorns to the immense technological advancement in recent years. However, I would argue that the more pertinent cause is how our money functions.

Between 2008 and 2015, a period characterized by near-zero interest rates, there was a significant surge in the number of unicorns founded each year. During these seven years, figures skyrocketed by nearly 600%, rising from 29 unicorns established to 175.[167] But, as interest rates began to rise in 2016, this growth subsided, highlighting their susceptibility to interest rates.

As for why, since easy access to capital extends a company's runway before cash depletion, and this longer runway increases a business's chance of positive cash flow and success down the line, low-interest rates are used to justify the astronomical values of these unicorns.

While low-interest rates can extend a company's runway and increase its chances of success, it's important to note that this does not guarantee success. In fact, even with these favourable financial conditions, most startups fail— 90%, to be specific.[168]

By propping up failing companies with low-interest rates and cheap capital, we risk perpetuating financial irresponsibility and diverting valuable resources away from more promising opportunities. Instead of prolonging the agony, we should focus on encouraging the responsible allocation of capital, even if that means accepting some short-term losses.

It's also important to highlight that the trend of capital flowing into unicorns is further exacerbated when interest rates are suppressed below that of inflation. In such an environment, investors seeking yield flee traditional yield instruments and interest-bearing accounts into riskier assets to protect against inflation, which only adds to the already mounting flow of capital into unicorns.

One of the more infamous unicorns in recent years was Theranos.

At its height, the consumer healthcare technology startup which claimed to revolutionize blood testing was valued at a lofty $10 billion.[169] Their goal was to create a machine that could take a single blood sample and test it against hundreds of markers to give an accurate health profile.

However, this dream never quite turned into a reality.

Theranos, which promised to revolutionize the medical industry with its breakthrough blood testing technology, ultimately failed to deliver on its claims. It was later discovered that over 200 of the tests the company claimed to conduct were outsourced to external labs, and the tests it performed on its own equipment were unreliable and produced inaccurate results. Ultimately, patients ended up receiving false diagnoses for everything from cancer to diabetes.

In early 2022, Elizabeth Holmes was eventually found guilty of three counts of wire fraud and one count of conspiracy to conduct wire fraud, but not before she decimated more than $700 million of investors' money.[170] Once again, the availability of capital, whether sourced from inflation-hedging investors or direct government intervention, played a crucial role. Without access to such cheap capital, Theranos may have encountered significant challenges in securing the necessary funding to establish itself, thereby minimizing the risk of capital destruction.

Another example of a company that has significantly benefited from easy access to capital is Tesla, the electric car manufacturer that aims to revolutionize the industry. While not technically a unicorn, as it is now publicly traded, Tesla's growth has been fueled by the same monetary interventions that propped up Theranos.

Despite taking 18 years to become profitable, Tesla has seen its valuation skyrocket in recent years, where at its peak, it was the sixth most valuable company in the world.[171,172] But does its stock price represent the real value it creates?

It can be difficult to comprehend just how much money flowed into Tesla stock. In 2021, Tesla sold 301,998 cars globally while boasting a market capitalization of $1.2 trillion.[173,174] And $1.5 billion of Tesla's $5.2 billion in net income that year came from government subsidies.[175] That same year, Ford sold thirteen times more cars than Tesla, with 3.9 million vehicles sold and a net profit of $17.9 billion.[176,177] Yet, Ford's market capitalization was only 8.3% of Tesla's, at around $100 billion.[178]

What's even more concerning is that during this same period, Tesla's market capitalization was $500 billion larger than the combined market capitalization of Toyota, Volkswagen, Mercedes-Benz, BMW, GM, Ford, Stellantis (Fiat Chrysler and PSA), Honda, Hyundai, Kia, Nissan, and Renault.[179]

It begs the question: Is Tesla really worth more than the entire automobile sector combined? Or Is investor speculation artificially propping up capital flows?

Price-to-earnings (PE) ratios often serve as a crucial indicator for gauging an investment's payback period. For instance, if a company has a PE of 21 (The average of the 500 companies in the S&P), the investor should expect a payback time of 21 years based on earnings.

At its peak, Tesla's PE ratio was a lofty 1,386, meaning it would take an ungodly 1,386 years for an investor to expect a return given current earnings.[180] So investors in Tesla are doing so without any hope of a return in their lifetime based on the company's current profits. Their only hope for a return lies in faith that Tesla's value creation will somehow balloon and be reflected in its stock valuation. They are betting on astronomical growth for the company rather than the present reality.

When central banks suppress interest rates, they inadvertently postpone the need for businesses to create value in a timely manner, as fiscal failure is pushed into the future. Consequently, more capital flows into companies that have yet to prove their viability, diverting capital away from productive assets.

Figure 6.2 demonstrates losses in some of the more prominent companies of today. *This is capital destruction on a grand scale.* Uber's total losses have surpassed $23 billion, $8 billion for Snapchat, $7 billion for Airbnb and Lyft, $6 billion for Palantir, and $5 billion for Nutanix. Bloom is then close behind with $2.5 billion, and WeWork, before bankruptcy, had been estimated to have accumulated losses of roughly $10 billion by March 2021.[181]

Figure 6.2

Tech Company Losses vs Year of Existence
The cumulative losses of prominent tech companies vs year of existence

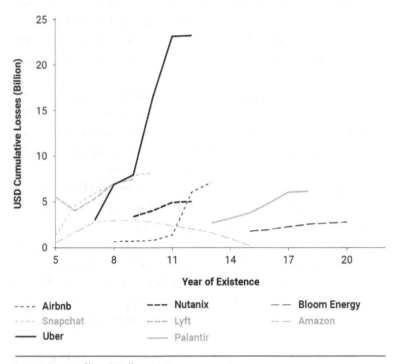

Source: Company filings & Wolfstreet.com

And the scary part is that these are just a select few of the businesses profiting from monetary manipulation, but that list is endless. This misallocation of resources is unsustainable and ultimately undermines the success of our economy.

Let's now take a look at how intervention triggers a rise in regulation.

Regulation

Regulation today permeates nearly every aspect of society:

- Government regulations have a significant impact on businesses.
- Environmental regulations impose compliance costs on industries with environmental impacts.
- Labour regulations protect workers but increase labour costs for businesses.
- Consumer protection laws require businesses to meet quality standards and provide accurate information.
- Health and safety regulations necessitate increased investment in administration and safety measures.
- Financial regulations create compliance challenges for financial institutions.

This rise in regulation has been fueled by malinvestment and inefficient capital allocation in an attempt to protect society. However, these problems haven't naturally emerged! Instead, they are byproducts of interventionist practices propping up fiscal irresponsibility.

As previously discussed, monetary intervention by the government often leads to the misallocation of capital, fostering unproductive behaviour. Such behaviour poses a significant threat to the stability of a functioning economy and jeopardizes the continued viability of an unsustainable economy. As a result, those in positions of power are incentivized to react with ever-greater regulation in an attempt to quell the resulting fiscal irresponsibility and unproductive behaviour. However, given that the regulatory policies are not addressing the underlying cause of these reckless business practices—*monetary intervention*—regulation only further perpetuates unproductive behaviour.

With this in mind, regulation in an unsustainable system slowly percolates throughout every area of society, impeding innovation and sucking up capital, further exacerbating any problems.

One such example of this is that of London's financial district.

In the late 1970s, there were fewer than 80 financial regulators in the City of London, which amounted to a ratio of one regulator for every 11,000 city workers. This changed in 2008. The global financial crisis led to a surge in regulatory oversight. As a result, "the ratio of UK financial regulators to finance employees fell to 1:300."[182]

This trend is not unique to the UK either, as it also shows itself in the US. Since 2008, US banks have spent billions hiring thousands of compliance and regulatory officers to keep up with the growing financial red tape. In 2013, JP Morgan Chase announced it would hire 13,000 compliance staff at a cost of $4 billion, and by the end of 2014, Citigroup had a total of 30,000 compliance officers.[183]

Furthermore, Figure 6.3 illustrates that this issue isn't specific to finance. Since 1970, there has been a significant surge in the number of administrators compared to physicians, mainly due to the rising regulatory burden and bureaucratic obstacles that healthcare professionals face in complying with the stringent requirements imposed by healthcare governing bodies.

Or take American education.[184] While student and teacher numbers have only increased by 7.6% and 8.7%, respectively, between 2000 and 2019, the number of district administrators has surged by a staggering 87.6%. As administrators take centre stage, I can't help but wonder about the potential long-term impact on learning. This shift of capital from teachers to administration may warrant reflection on how it could affect the quality of education and the overall learning experience.

Figure 6.3

Growth in Physicians vs Administrators

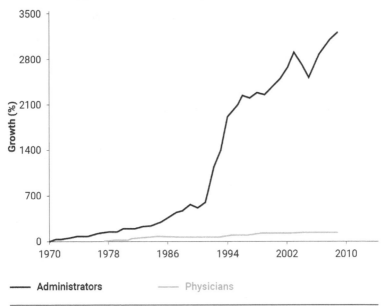

Source: Bureau of Labor Statistics: NCHS: Himmelstein/Woolhandler analvsis of CPS

In each of these examples, an unfathomable amount of capital is sucked up under the umbrella of regulation. The marked increase in compliance costs due to this rise of regulatory bodies has forced companies to divert resources from other areas to keep up with the regulatory burden and, in some sectors like healthcare, also increase the cost of their services.[185] According to one report, "hospitals spend $1200 on compliance every time a patient is admitted."[186]

With this in mind, we can see how increased regulation impacts capital allocation. With more and more capital directed toward maintaining administrative and regulatory staff, less capital is available for true value creation. This leads many corporations to focus on maximizing paper growth through financial engineering rather than driving real beneficial change. This is now a common strategy, as companies seek to create the appearance of growth without the risk and effort of developing real innovations or productive assets. As a result, our financial system has become increasingly oriented toward speculation and financialization rather than creating tangible benefits for society.

Therefore, we are at a point where:

1. The economy has become so heavily financialized that many companies can generate greater returns through investing and share buybacks (Figure 6.4) than when directed toward capital expenditure or research and development. This is when a company repurchases its own shares from the open market to potentially boost stock prices. As Edward Chancellor explains in his book *Price of Time,* "Over the previous decade, America's largest public companies spent more than half their total profits on buybacks."

2. Regulation in certain industries, such as traditional energy, is so cumbersome that it is almost impossible to reinvest capital into operations.

To illustrate such behaviour, as of the second quarter of 2022, Apple, sitting in the top spot, has spent a staggering $557.39 billion on buybacks over the past decade.[187] This figure is so large that it exceeds the total combined market capitalization of 494 of the 500 companies listed in the S&P 500.

Apple directs capital toward share buybacks, so they can artificially elevate their stock's price-to-earnings ratio. While the actual earnings remain unchanged, reducing the number of outstanding shares elevates the earnings per share. This tactic creates the illusion of growth for investors, but in reality, it's merely financial engineering.

Figure 6.4

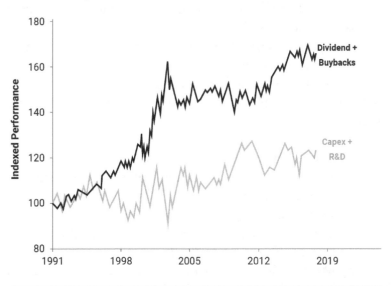

Equity Market Performance vs S&P 500 by Uses of Cash
as of October 26, 2017

Source: Goldman Sachs Global Investment Research

Instead of creating value in the real economy (the production and consumption of goods and services), these companies are simply trying to maximize returns in the financial economy (banking, investing, and the buying and selling of financial products). Rather than investing in capital expenditure or research and development (R&D), two areas essential for continual operation and value creation, corporations see greater benefit in directing their capital toward share buybacks. This creates a problem. When capital is no longer being put to productive use, productivity and value creation slowly break down, and economic fragility ensues.

Finally, when debt is cheap, mergers and acquisitions to buy out competitors become more favourable. This decreases competition in the market, ultimately leading to monopolies and other fateful side effects, further reducing the drive to create beneficial change. Thanks in no small part to this consolidation, the total number of listed US companies has almost halved over the past two decades.[188]

The pharmaceutical industry provides a glaring example of this trend, where companies are prioritizing the buyout of smaller pharmaceutical firms and their medical patents over investing in research and development. Two notorious instances highlight this issue:

1. **Valeant Pharmaceuticals:** Fueled by accessible financing, Valeant pursued a strategy of acquiring existing medications and drastically inflating their prices. One case involved Syprine, a drug used to treat a rare genetic disorder. After gaining control of Syprine, Valeant raised the price from $652 to $21,267 per bottle.[189]
2. **Martin Shkreli's Turing Pharmaceuticals:** In 2015, Turing Pharmaceuticals obtained the rights to Daraprim, a crucial drug used in the treatment of parasitic infections. Following the purchase, they increased the price from $13.50 to $750 per pill.[190]

All things considered, the rise of regulation and the associated increase in compliance costs have significantly burdened businesses. This, in conjunction with the manipulation of money, has led to a shift in capital allocation towards financial engineering and away from genuine value creation. As a result, value creation is a mere afterthought in the great financialization of everything, with stock-based compensation and other methods of financial engineering to drive up the stock price being the primary focus of corporate executives.

If we continue down this path, I can't say the future looks very rosy.

This leads us to one final byproduct that intervention has on businesses: a lowering in the quantity and/or quality of goods and services.

Quality Breakdown

Imagine for a moment that the government doubles the total supply of dollars in the system. In theory, prices would double, and the currency's purchasing power would be halved. This would leave producers of goods and services with three options:

1. They could double the price of their product or service to maintain their current margins. However, this would most likely drive away customers.
2. They could maintain the current price, but they would take a hit on their margins and, therefore, their bottom line.
3. They could maintain their margins and current price but reduce the quantity or quality of the inputs that make up their product or service, resulting in less value or a lower quality product or service.

Unfortunately, businesses, driven by their profit motive, often lean on option three, with option one a close second. In some instances, businesses may even employ a combination of both strategies, resorting to "shrinkflation," where prices increase while the size or quality of the product decreases.

As a result, we have this byproduct of inflation whereby the quality/value of our products or services declines over time. And this can be observed not only in grocery stores but also in major construction projects.

For instance, the 102-story-tall Empire State Building, completed in 1930, took only 410 days to build and cost $40 million ($560 million in 2022 dollars, adjusted for inflation).[191] In contrast, the 94-story-tall construction of The One in Toronto began in 2017, and its estimated completion date is 2024, a seven-year build with a total cost of $1.5 billion.[192]

Similarly, the world's first nuclear submarine, the USS Nautilus, cost $58.2 million ($680 million in 2022 dollars, adjusted for inflation) and took only 1,173 days to complete, starting in July 1951.[193] In comparison, the USS Gerald Ford, which began construction in August 2005, took 12 years to complete and cost $18 billion.[194]

Or consider the iconic Golden Gate Bridge.[195] In 1933, the project was completed in just four years and cost $23.8 million, equivalent to $540 million today. Now, fast forward to 2014, when a decision was made to add a suicide net to the bridge.[196] Construction began in 2018, but despite ongoing efforts, the project has yet to be completed and is now expected to cost a staggering $400 million. To put that into perspective, the cost of the suicide net alone is nearly the same as the total price to build the entire bridge back in 1933.

The convergence of inflation and rising regulation, which drives up prices due to unnecessary administrative costs, poses significant challenges to our cost of living and the quality of products and services. This phenomenon explains why product quality is declining over time, even after accounting for inflation.

CONCLUSION

Hopefully, the above information has stoked cause for concern regarding the negative consequences of monetary intervention and its impact on innovation and capital allocation within the business environment.

In short, as we have witnessed greater intervention, we've seen a rise in regulation, leading to a shift in capital allocation toward financial engineering and away from genuine value creation. These byproducts erode the foundations of a thriving economy and pose a threat to its longevity. However, although regulation may sound like a great option to fix such issues, in most situations, it only further incentivizes destructive business decisions and diverts resources away from more viable and sustainable ventures.

As we have seen, the impact of our monetary decisions on the economy and society at large is undeniable, as evidenced by these trends. But its impact doesn't stop there. Money's influence not only touches businesses but extends to the halls of government, shaping policies, elections, and power distribution.

CHAPTER 7

SHORT-TERM THINKING = LONG-TERM PROBLEMS

How Our Money Impacts Government & Politics

"As soon as you allow politicians to determine that which is bought or sold, the first thing bought and sold will always be politicians." —El Gato Malo, Gato's Law[197]

....

As the saying goes, "power corrupts, and absolute power corrupts absolutely."[198] Nowhere is this more evident than in the realm of government.

Elected officials often promise one thing on the campaign trail, only to do something entirely different once they are in office. This necessitates the question: How can we ensure that those in power remain accountable to the citizens they represent?

According to Jörg Guido Hülsmann, the German-born economist, the key is to make the government financially dependent on its citizens, which "addresses the fundamental political problem of controlling the people in office once they are there."[199]

However, with the government's ability to print unlimited amounts of money, our current monetary system has seemingly no government dependence on its citizens. As a result, the balance of power has shifted away from the people and towards those in positions of power. With a system that allows the government to go into debt and access capital without limit, we have created a system where the government's ability to spend is more dependent on imaginative financial intervention to avoid collapse than on the taxpayers themselves.

As the great economist Friedrich Hayek predicted, people would seek security instead of independence under a central-planning regime. This warning rings true in the current state of Western democracy. In theory, democracy is meant to represent the will of the people, with elected individuals making decisions as such. However, problems arise when money and politics become intertwined, causing values to become skewed and short-term thinking to prevail. In today's context, there appears to be a greater emphasis on virtue signalling rather than actual implementation of meaningful change.

While our currency has managed to maintain some degree of value, albeit deteriorating, since departing from the gold standard, the ongoing use of monetary intervention raises concerns about the long-term viability of our political system. Worldwide we have seen declines in essential democratic functions (Figure 7.1). With this in mind, let's investigate the relationship between money, government, and politics.

In our current state-controlled, growth-oriented economy, intervention is a necessity to keep the system alive. However, as we have discussed, over time, this approach leads to a devaluation of our currency, worsens wealth inequality, and puts the stability of our economy at risk through mounting debt.

Figure 7.1

Declines Across the Board

From 2005 to 2021, we experienced declines in all regions & subcategories highlighted in the 2022 Freedom in the World report.

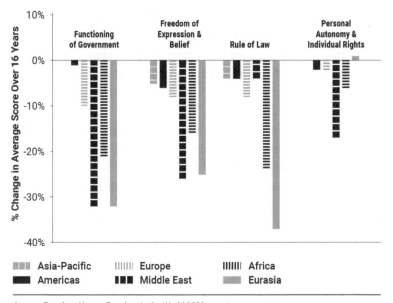

Source: Freedom House, Freedom in the World 2022 report

On the governmental and political side of things, these effects are noticeable in several ways:

First, the populace, feeling the heat of economic hardship, is incentivized to vote for immediate relief rather than considering the long-term effects of their decisions. This short-sightedness pushes politicians to act urgently without considering potential negative consequences.

Second, with the state controlling the money printer, the free market's need to provide value to obtain capital is eliminated. This has two major consequences: fiscal irresponsibility becomes even more pernicious, and the free market struggles to compete with the government, which can expand and encroach on private sector jobs.

Third, when the government controls the money supply, it has the power to control the narrative and silence opposition by controlling media corporations.

Fourth, intervention can distort economic signals, impacting our ability to make sound decisions.

Fifth, governments are incentivized to protect their currencies at all costs, even if this is at the expense of the populace. This can include waging war to maintain the fiat currency, especially in the case of the US.

Sixth, economic stress fractures can cause the lower and middle classes, those most affected by inflation, to revolt. This opens the door for extremist political parties or controlling structures to emerge, claiming to have the solution to people's pain.

These byproducts of monetary intervention form a feedback loop of increasing regulation and erosion of rights and freedoms. In Chapter Ten, we will explore the rise of extremist political parties and totalitarianism. But for now, let's delve into the other byproducts listed above.

Alleviate Immediate Pain

For a significant portion of the US population, approximately 64%, the reality of living paycheque to paycheque is an undeniable struggle, and their immediate priority is finding relief from their financial hardships.[200] In this context, the question arises: would you support a politician who promises to provide financial support through stimulus packages, assisted living programs, and tax cuts, or would you favour a politician who emphasizes fiscal responsibility and advocates for austerity measures? Most people tend to lean towards the former option.

When the government controls the money supply, politicians can make short-term promises that appeal to the majority of voters. Consequently, our political system becomes structured in a way that encourages momentary decision-making—*a.k.a high time preference thinking (as discussed in Chapter Four)*—often at the expense of long-term stability. In other words, our monetary system shapes the behaviour of politicians.

Unfortunately, however, the individuals who vote for such politicians will continue to struggle once that stimulus money has been spent, as the monetary expansion results in further devaluation in the dollar, exacerbating their financial situation and perpetuating the cycle of living paycheque to paycheque.

When we vote to alleviate interim pain, we unconsciously welcome greater economic intervention. That intervention leads to the financial consequences outlined in previous chapters, which then require further intervention. This leads to a cycle of ever-advancing government control, including increased capital controls, restricting our ability to spend freely in keeping with our genuine desires.

The sad truth is that this cycle is perpetuated regardless of political affiliation. Politicians will usually favour intervention to mitigate the immediate effects of fiscal irresponsibility in a system that rewards short-term thinking. There's no incentive for them to consider the long-term consequences of their actions. One reason for this is that if they don't act fast enough and meet the needs of their constituency, they risk losing power to someone more willing to intervene.

Case in point. During the late 1990s and early 2000s, there was a push by politicians to increase homeownership rates in an attempt to grow their voter base by showing support for the American Family. This led to policies and initiatives that encouraged mortgage lenders to offer loans to borrowers with lower creditworthiness. While this initially appeared beneficial by allowing more people to become homeowners, it eventually contributed to the subprime mortgage crisis and the subsequent global financial crisis of 2008. The focus on short-term goals of expanding homeownership without adequate consideration of long-term sustainability and risk management played a key role in the eventual collapse of the housing market.

The inevitable result of a state-controlled monetary system is that it trends toward intervention and away from the free market because the majority usually votes for momentary relief. As a result, there's usually no real incentive for deep reflection on the part of the government or the people.

Why are these issues emerging?
What may be the cause of the challenges we are facing?
How can we alter our own behaviour to resolve these issues?

Furthermore, when the government can print money to fund its operations, this often leads to reactiveness rather than proactiveness because there is less urgency to consciously save and plan for effective capital allocation.

Given that the government can rely on money creation to cover its immediate expenses, the absence of constraints on the availability of funds can create an environment where saving and careful capital allocation are undervalued. In such a scenario, there is little incentive for proactive measures that require disciplined saving, planning, and strategic investment. This can foster a culture of short-term thinking, where rather than engaging in long-term decision making to maximize value creation, there is a tendency to prioritize immediate needs and react to present challenges— often at the expense of long-term sustainability.

All in all, when those in positions of power have control over the monetary system, they can use it as a band-aid solution to temporarily mask economic issues rather than taking responsibility for their actions. This creates a system that prioritizes short-term gain over long-term interests and encourages reactivity instead of proactivity. Rather than addressing the root causes of the problems at hand, such behaviour leads to a cycle of constant intervention and a lack of accountability for those in power.

This brings us to our second byproduct.

Fiscal Irresponsibility

Capitalism, characterized by private ownership of resources and the means of production, and driven by competition and profit-seeking, is often lauded as a powerful engine of value creation. For a business to succeed under a capitalist system, it must offer products or services that are valuable enough to convince consumers to pay for them. If a business struggles to provide value, it will ultimately fail.

Ideally, the same standard would apply to the government. However, the pressure to offer value diminishes when the state controls the monetary system. If obtaining capital required providing value, politicians would be incentivized to think long-term, making choices that would benefit society in the long run. In contrast to that ideal, under the current system, if the government lacks the funds to operate, it can simply increase the monetary supply, extracting value from its citizens to finance its activities. This lack of incentive to offer value often leads to short-sighted decision-making, as politicians prioritize the most immediately visible solutions that can assist them in elections over true value creation.

While many individuals and businesses need evidence of value creation to obtain capital, the government and those in charge of the money printers are not beholden to the same standards. They can devalue the purchasing power of others, directing capital flows in ways that meet their immediate needs rather than the needs of society as a whole. This centralization of power ultimately undermines the fundamental principles of capitalism, where individuals have the right to engage in voluntary exchange and pursue their own self-interest in the marketplace. This leads to a less equitable society.

One such example of this fiscal irresponsibility and pain alleviation can be seen in our use of subsidies and bailouts, creating and perpetuating non-productive pursuits.

The Distortion & Destruction from Subsidies & Bailouts

During the era of British Rule in India, the capital city of Delhi grappled with a problem: a significant population of venomous cobras.[201] To address the problem, the British Government devised a plan that involved providing financial incentives in the form of a bounty for every dead cobra. However, this well-intentioned subsidy backfired, and the cobra population multiplied instead of decreasing.

The subsidy inadvertently created a lucrative opportunity for individuals to capture and breed cobras solely to claim the bounty. Consequently, resources and efforts that would have likely been channelled into more productive endeavours were diverted toward cobra breeding. So, what is it about subsidies that often leads to unproductive behaviour?

A government subsidy or handout is financial assistance the government provides to certain individuals, organizations, or industries. These subsidies can come in the form of cash payments, tax breaks, or other forms of support to help alleviate financial burdens or to encourage certain activities. Subsidies are often provided to promote economic growth, social welfare, or specific industries.

This raises an important question: If individuals or corporations are only motivated to perform specific actions due to subsidies, do these actions truly reflect the most efficient and effective utilization of these resources?

In a free market, an exchange only occurs when both parties' subjective and unique needs are met. In the case of subsidies and handouts, as money can be obtained through monetary expansion, the government often makes no direct financial gain and expects no reimbursement in the form of products or services, nor do they need to. If reimbursement is not needed, value creation and fiscal responsibility quickly fall by the wayside. Therefore, when an action takes place that otherwise wouldn't have without subsidies, we can conclude that it either does not provide satisfactory economic value or is an unprofitable venture altogether.

Take corporate subsidies, for example. They often have three negative impacts that ultimately result in value destruction:

1. They divert productive labour away from in-demand goods and services towards endeavours that provide less economic value than the resources consumed in production or the resources that would have otherwise been produced, i.e., in the renewable energy sector, government subsidies have, at times, resulted in the overproduction of solar panels and wind turbines, leading to a surplus of these goods that exceed market demand. This has diverted productive labour and resources away from other non-subsidized energy production methods, which may have greater demand and offer great value.

2. They incentivize companies to redirect labour and capital away from productive, in-demand goods and services and towards government grant and subsidy paperwork, ultimately creating a drag on economic growth.

3. Companies that would otherwise fail due to lack of demand or fiscal mismanagement are propped up via subsidies, further diverting otherwise productive capital and labour towards unsustainable ventures.

If the general populace wouldn't have directed their capital into these areas of the economy, what makes the government think that it is necessary?

When you step back and alter how you view subsidies, you quickly realize they are simply coercive payments from taxpayers to sectors of the economy that the government favours. These sectors are supported beyond their true value to society, hindering the pressure to innovate and achieve sustainable profits without government assistance.

That's not economic development. It is economic destruction.

With this in mind, subsidies often:

- Encourage moral hazard—*the risk or likelihood of reckless behaviour arising from being protected from the consequences of one's actions*—as they provide a safety net for companies engaging in fiscally irresponsible behaviour, leading to a cycle of poor financial decisions.
- Divert capital and labour away from productive sectors, hindering necessary restructuring for long-term growth.
- Create an uneven playing field, favouring certain businesses or industries at the expense of others, resulting in a misallocation of resources.

Although subsidies may promote growth or provide temporary relief in certain situations, they ultimately perpetuate fiscal irresponsibility, impede necessary restructuring, and distort capital flows.

Great Financial Crisis Bailouts
When there is no emotional or physical attachment to our money, much less care goes into capital efficiency. This lack of care was particularly evident during the 2008 Great Financial Crisis, whereby the US housing market went from boom to bust due

to lax monetary policy, triggering an explosion of speculative investment vehicles and derivatives.

Rather than going into the depths of why this speculation occurred, let's turn our attention to the intervention that ensued after the bubble had burst.

Under the guise of stabilizing the financial markets and putting in place *"consumer protections"* to support the people, the government intervened on a level never seen before.

As Dr. Nomi Prins recounts in her book, *It Takes a Pillage*, by the third quarter of 2009, the government bailout had totalled an astonishing $13.3 trillion[202]:

- $7.6 trillion from the Fed,
- $2.5 trillion from the Treasury (Including the $700 billion Troubled Asset Relief Program),
- $1.5 trillion from the Federal Deposit Insurance Corporation (FDIC),
- $1.4 trillion joint effort and a $300 billion housing bill.

Dr. Prins draws the shocking comparison that this total amount is "more money than the combined costs of every major US war (including the American Revolution, the War of 1812, the Civil War, the Spanish-American War, World War I, World War II, Korea, Vietnam, Iraq, and Afghanistan), whose total price tag, adjusted for inflation, is $7.2 trillion." And that was only the start.

Dr. Prins also remarks that:

- $50 trillion in global wealth evaporated in a two-year span,[203]
- $7.5 trillion in losses in the portfolios and pension plans of everyday folk,[204]

- $2.0 trillion in retirement plans and individual retirement accounts (IRAs) lost income,
- $1.9 trillion in traditional defined-benefit plan losses,
- And lastly, $3.6 trillion in non-pension asset losses.

Moreover, this was all while over 30 million Americans lost their jobs.[205]

All in all, subsidies and interventionist monetary policy played a large part in the loss of $65 trillion, not including the $13 trillion in taxpayer-funded bailouts.

Some may justify this by saying, "Yes, $13 trillion is expensive. But it was to save us, the consumer." Although this is one potential viewpoint, I'm inclined to agree with Dr. Prins when she remarked, "I don't think the financial sector bailout has ever been about fixing the problem; it's been about using the crisis as a pretext for the greatest transfer of public wealth into private hands in monetary history."

After years of lenient monetary policy, dead bodies started to emerge. But rather than allowing the natural process of creative destruction to occur, those in positions of authority opted to instill fear and utilize public funds to protect their positioning and provide bailouts to the parties responsible.

When a system enables the privatization of profits and the socialization of losses, malinvestment is an inevitable byproduct. Both Goldman Sachs and Morgan Stanley avoided collapse after receiving $10 billion of bailout money. Even more alarming. After losses of $27.6 billion, Merril Lynch received $10 billion and still paid out $3.6 billion in bonuses the same year.[206]

Imagine for a second that you were a big bank, and you knew that in a worst-case scenario, the government would intervene to bail you out, socializing your losses. Would you prioritize the safety and security of your customers' funds, or would you take speculative risks to increase your banks' returns and your own personal bonuses? By examining the banks' above actions, it's clear to see which path they chose to take.

However, it is fair to ask: Why did the government decide to bail out the banks in the first place? Simply put, for an economy that depends on perpetual growth and consumption, banks play a critical role in enabling corporations and consumers to access capital. Without them, our burgeoning, unsustainable system would have collapsed, exposing it for what it is.

But even if we accept that the bailouts were needed to avoid total system collapse, the recession bailouts could have been carried out at a considerably lower cost. Consider that approximately 5.1 million foreclosed properties underpin $1.4 trillion in subprime loans. If the government had simply bailed out the subprime loans, this costly problem could have been avoided at a fraction of the expense, equivalent to just 1.7% of the all-up losses of $78 trillion. Dr. Prins observes that it would even have been cheaper for the government to "[buy] up every residential mortgage in the country— there were about $11.9 trillion worth at the end of December 2008."[207] These types of inefficiencies arise when there is a disconnection between those who earn the money (the public) and those who spend it (the government).

Despite the various choices made, as we have extensively examined, attempting to mend a system that necessitates constant growth and increased intervention with more money is a futile endeavour. Ultimately, these subsidies fueled further fiscal irresponsibility and resulted in economic devastation of an unimaginable magnitude.

This brings us to the pandemic, another event that saw significant subsidies and bailouts.

Pandemic Subsidies

As the COVID-19 pandemic swept across the world, governments stepped in with subsidies to support individuals and struggling companies. While this support seems necessary at first, it raises an important question: Are these subsidies creating the right incentives?

As we examine the impact of these government interventions, we must consider whether they are ultimately helping or hindering the economy's future health.

Let's look at two types of pandemic subsidies, those supporting businesses and those assisting people.

As of late 2023, we are still navigating the ongoing pandemic. Therefore, we have limited insight into the long-term effects compared to the GFC above. Once the dust settles and we gain greater perspective, evaluating the impacts on our society and the world at large will be interesting.

Business Subsidies

During the pandemic, the US government injected nearly $5 trillion into the economy, with approximately $1.7 trillion allocated toward supporting businesses.[208] In addition, the federal reserve purchased $13.7 billion worth of corporate bonds, further supporting the private sector.[209]

These transfer payments were essentially handouts from taxpayers to government-favoured businesses, organizations, and industries. While this money may have assisted businesses, billions ended up propping up companies that would have otherwise failed or did not need the capital, diverting productive capital and labour away from more viable ventures.

These subsidies ultimately prevented a necessary restructuring required for long-term growth and prosperity.

Subsidies for the Individual

Between March and November, the Canadian government announced that it had spent $322 billion supporting the Canadian economy, with over $81.6 billion being sent to 8.9 million individuals through the Canada Emergency Response Benefit

(CERB), providing $2,000 per month to those whose income was impacted.[210]

For many, it can be hard to comprehend just how much money this is, so let's break it down. In 2020, 28.6 million Canadians filed taxes, and almost 30% of them, or 8.2 million individuals, reported an income of less than $25,000.[211] When the CERB was introduced and provided $2,000 per month, or $24,000 annually, many people in this income bracket faced a difficult question: Why work when I can earn the same amount without working?[212]

The Canadian government's subsidies have created a situation where approximately 30% of the population can afford to stop working without facing immediate financial consequences. I am surprised Canada didn't experience greater fallout in the business sector. That said, more than a quarter (26%)[213] of Canadian companies have faced labour shortages, high employee turnover or resorted to hiring individuals they would not have otherwise considered.

Moreover, if the UK is anything like Canada, this may explain why recent data from the UK's Office for National Statistics (ONS) indicated that in 2020 an unprecedented 54.2% of the population, or 36 million people, lived in households that received more in benefits than they paid in taxes.[214] How can an economy sustain itself in the long term if half of the population takes more than they contribute?

You may have heard the saying, "there's no such thing as a free lunch." In this situation, this couldn't be truer. Although workers receiving handouts may be benefiting, businesses are not.

In a free market economy, as wages are determined by supply and demand, wages typically increase when there is a worker shortage, attracting more workers into the labour force. However, when the government intervenes by providing a wage subsidy, this distorts the natural equilibrium of the labour market, placing immense pressure on businesses.

When governments hand money out to individuals, employees are no longer incentivized to seek employment, severely impacting businesses. Given that these businesses will now struggle to find workers, these subsidies impair business operations, potentially threatening their viability.

While pandemic subsidies have been a key topic of discussion in recent years, it's worth noting that government subsidies have long been a part of economic policy, especially farming-related ones.

Farming Subsidies

Government subsidies have had a significant impact on the food and farming industry. Although a detailed analysis of this topic could fill an entire chapter, I will keep this short and get straight to the point.

When governments step in with subsidies, they put themselves in a predicament that often ends in increasing subsidies over time. Take, for instance, a group of farmers who receive subsidies in the form of a fixed price higher than the market rate for their crops. With higher profits, these farmers are incentivized to produce more of these crops.

And this is where the problem arises. With the incentive to produce more crops, we experience a surplus of particular products, which the government must now pay to transport and store. Over time, not only does this surplus grow, but it also puts downward pressure on market prices and reduces farmers' profits. As a result, the government must subsidize farmers even more for their losses.

This increase in subsidies has to be funded from somewhere, so either taxes rise to meet the cost or there is increased monetary intervention to account for increased subsidies, which then has negative consequences for other farmers and corporations that do not receive subsidies. Higher taxes create a challenging environment for these businesses to thrive and grow, and they impede the development of non-subsidized sectors.

A well-known example of this process occurred in the Soviet Union during the 1970s and '80s when wheat production was heavily subsidized.[215] As farmers produced more, they earned more. Subsidies increased in each subsequent cycle. This led to a significant wheat surplus, causing bread prices to fall sharply. The government then had to subsidize the state trading network by reimbursing losses from selling cheap bread.

While the decrease in the price of bread for the average consumer may appear to be a positive outcome of the subsidies, it is important to note that that:

1. Nothing is free. There's always a cost, and someone ultimately bears the burden. In this case, these subsidies are funded either directly through taxation or indirectly through monetary debasement (inflation).
2. And, more importantly, these prices do not reflect the true cost of production, transportation, storage, and other associated expenses.

As a result, subsidization inherently poses various threats to the environment, as it often leads to the overuse of natural resources. This overuse can cause irreversible damage to the ecosystem, such as soil degradation, water depletion, and deforestation (but more on that in the next chapter). Ultimately, these effects harm not only the environment, but also compromise the sustainability and productivity of the industry itself, which can have severe long-term consequences.

Moreover, food subsidies have had negative consequences beyond the realm of economic productivity or our environment. In addition to promoting unproductive behaviour, they have also had a detrimental impact on public health domestically and globally.

Since the 1920s, grain farmers have received subsidies in the name of supporting farmers and regulating the supply.

> **FUN FACT:** *Did you know that almost 90% of US agricultural subsidies are given to just three types of grain— corn, wheat, and soy?*[216] *These crops form the foundation of processed foods, while less than half a percent of subsidies go toward fruits and vegetables. Even more alarming is that tobacco (cigarettes) receives four times more subsidies than fruit and vegetables.*[217]

Given the artificial supply of capital to grain farmers, this has led to an overproduction of grain. With "Big Food" taking advantage of this cheap grain, it is now almost impossible to escape it. Grain is in everything! As Kate Deering points out in her book, *How to Heal Your Metabolism*, "From gluten-enriched breads to wheat pasta, cookies to crackers, soy sauce to salad dressings, ice cream to candy, Americans are becoming grain addicts."[218] This overconsumption of grain-heavy foods is not only contributing to numerous health problems globally but decimating our soil quality.

And the issue of food subsidies extends beyond just grain. In the 1970s, government policies aimed at increasing corn production resulted in a surplus of corn crops. This surplus led to the widespread use of high fructose corn syrup (HFCS), a substance far more harmful than table sugar. HFCS is now commonly found in processed foods, soft drinks, and fast food and is a major contributor to the obesity epidemic society faces today.

This is the world we live in...

The regulatory board members who determine the inclusion and recommendations of foods in nutritional guidelines have significant financial ties to food or pharmaceutical companies (95% in the most recent proposed guidelines).[219] Additionally, the studies influencing the decision-making process are frequently funded by organizations that stand to gain from government food recommendations, i.e., During the 1960s, the Sugar Research Foundation (SRF) quietly provided financial compensation to Harvard researchers to discredit the connection between sugar and heart disease.[220,221,222] The researchers willingly generated findings that aligned with the SRF's agenda. Rather than attributing heart disease to sugar, Harvard and the SRF shifted the blame towards cholesterol and saturated fat. Unfortunately, the subsequent six decades of dietary policies emphasizing the negative effects of fat have coincided with deteriorating health among Americans. Numerous studies have since emerged, validating the role of fats, including saturated fat, in a balanced and comprehensive understanding of nutrition.

The situation becomes even more concerning in the realm of pharmaceuticals. The government channels billions of dollars into the pharmaceutical industry each year while simultaneously controlling the regulatory process. To make matters worse, government staff often receive royalties from successful drugs or vaccines.[223] Given the glaring conflict of interest, this raises significant doubts about the safety and effectiveness of pharmaceutical products.

As Calley Means, the former Coca-Cola consultant turned whistleblower, says: "Are we as a society — when close to 80 percent of Americans are overweight or obese ... going to ask why people are getting so fat, why people are getting so sick, why people are getting so depressed, all at the same time?"[224]

In summary, government subsidies have had far-reaching consequences on the food and farming industry. While initially designed to support farmers and regulate supply, subsidies often lead to overproduction, price reductions that increase government dependency, environmental damage, and negative health outcomes. Moreover, subsidies can create a cycle of increasing support over time, which eventually leads to the waste of taxpayer money.

And while the government may appear to be solely responsible for providing subsidies, in reality, taxpayers' money is being used to fund these programs. As a result, it is ultimately the responsibility of the citizens to bear the burden of not only supporting the industries deemed valuable by the government but the negative consequences and capital destruction resulting from misguided subsidies— According to the Organisation for Economic Cooperation and Development, for every $5 of support that is provided, only $1 of income is generated, meaning that $4 of resources are essentially wasted.

As we wrap up our discussion on subsidies and handouts, it's worth taking a closer look at another prominent area often subject to government intervention: housing.

Housing Subsidies

Housing subsidies have recently become a popular tool for governments to conjure up support from the public, who overwhelmingly struggle to afford a home. But just like the other subsidies we have explored, unfortunately, they come with their faults.

First, by subsidizing the purchasing of homes, the government artificially increases demand for real estate, further pushing up prices and making it harder for the average person to get ahead without assistance.

Second, when programs exist, such as the Australian shared equity home buyer program (through which the government contributes up to 40% of new homes and 30% of existing homes in exchange for a percentage ownership of your house), it creates a situation where homeowners may feel compelled to prioritize the government's interests to avoid the risk of losing their homes.[225] This level of control can be concerning as it places individuals relying on assistance in a vulnerable position under the government's authority.

Lastly, when affordable housing is prioritized as a government agenda, the focus on maximizing its access can often override viability, leading to shortcuts being made. As Minnesota's American Experiment describes, "affordable housing goals turned into mortgage quotas that continued to be raised over time, reaching by 2008 an almost impossible 56% of loans that had to be made to people that were at or below median income. To reach goals, underwriting standards had to be reduced. Three percent down payments became zero down payments."[226] In the end, the significant deterioration in underwriting standards in order to offer mortgage loans to lower income Americans became a major contributing factor to the fragility that resulted in the Global Financial Crisis.

And if the repercussions of 2008 weren't enough of a warning as to the dangers of housing subsidies and toying with underwriting standards, as of May 2023, Fannie Mae and Freddie Mac will introduce new fees called loan-level price adjustments (LLPAs), where customers with higher credit scores will subsidize those with lower credit scores.[227,228] Fannie Mae and Freddie Mac are the same government-sponsored mortgage giants which suffered massive losses totalling $47 billion in their single-family mortgage businesses during the financial crisis.[229] Because of their insolvency risk, the government had to intervene and take them over. Now, with these new fee adjustments, a homebuyer with a 740 credit score and a 15-20% down payment will face a 300% increase in their surcharge fee, from 0.25% to 1%, while someone with a score of 620 and a 5% down payment will enjoy a significant reduction from 3.5% to 1.75%. With such incentives favouring debt consumption, are we headed towards a recurrence of the events seen in 2008?

Just like the others listed, housing subsidies have only further distorted capital flows, resulting in economic stress and capital destruction.

Public Sector Expansion

When one entity has the potential to print money at no cost to itself while everyone else has to expend time and energy to earn money, this entity will grow disproportionately faster and larger.

In this case, that entity is the government, in conjunction with the banks.

As we've seen, under our current system, governments can enact monetary intervention and run endless deficits at the expense of currency holders. At the same time, banks can conjure up money out of thin air and then lend this money out, all while charging interest. Not only is this a surefire way for these entities to capitalize off average citizens, but it also makes it practically impossible for the private free market to compete.

What's more, **how can you compete against an entity that prevents competition?** Many organizations in the public sector are legal monopolies, as the private sector is not allowed to compete. For instance, BC Hydro is the only electricity supplier in British Columbia, Canada, and ICBC is the only car insurance provider. When there is no competition or motivation to generate a profit, productivity and efficiency suffer. For instance, British Columbians, on average, pay $1,832 per year for car insurance through the government-run company ICBC.[230] In contrast, Nova Scotia, New Brunswick, and Prince Edward Island residents pay $891, $867, and $819, respectively. The lack of competition in the government system leads to inefficiencies, resulting in higher consumer prices.

Building on this idea. Over the past two decades, the US government has consistently operated at a deficit, with that deficit growing larger and larger.[231] This kind of fiscal irresponsibility would quickly cripple most private businesses, as it impairs cash flows and leads to insolvency. But since the government can always create a new influx of money and there are often no repercussions to fiscal responsibility, they can pay above-market wages, slowly absorbing the labour force. In Canada, government (a.k.a public sector) jobs, on average, pay 9.4% more than private sector jobs, and in the US, you can see a clear divergence in public vs private sector jobs dating back to the '50s in Figure 7.2.[232]

Figure 7.2

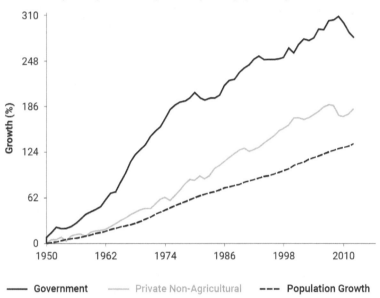

Unfettered Government Job Growth

Government jobs vs private non-agricultural jobs vs population growth

Source: *Global Economic Analysis & FinancialSense*

Even more alarming is that, according to the Fraser Institute, in Canada since the pandemic, the "public sector accounts for a large majority (86.7 percent) of all net new jobs created. Meanwhile, there has been almost no net job creation in the private sector (including self-employment)."[233]

The governmental power that serves effectively as a money printer doesn't just benefit the government in its job creation but also the lending market. With their money printer, the government can provide favourable terms (i.e., lower interest rates) to public entities as it never has to turn a profit.

Such was the case in 1979 when a two-tiered interest rate system emerged in China.[234] Under this two-tier system "cheap loans were originated by state banks for state-owned enterprises," while "more costly credit was provided by back-alley banks to private enterprises." This system gave state-owned enterprises a big leg up while the private sector struggled to compete. New private businesses had to quickly prove viability or interest payments would drain cash flow.

If we continue down the path of deprivatization, the public sector will gradually swallow the private sector as it simply cannot compete.

Propaganda and Silencing Opposition

In a paper[235] by Marius Dragimur, he reveals that in a study by the Open Society Foundations (OSF), 31 out of 55 countries surveyed use state funding to manipulate media.

Although there are various means to control the media, including regulation, legislation, physical attacks, and threats against journalists or media owners, financing has always been the most effective method. Therefore, given the financial struggles faced by the majority of independent journalism outfits, especially those outside the Western world.[236] This creates an opportunity for government funding to exert direct and indirect influence over the media.

With this in mind, when governments have access to easy money, they can suppress a significant portion of the media sector by providing financial support to media outlets and journalists aligned with their agenda while neglecting or even suppressing independent, critical voices. In some countries, this control is so pervasive that the government either directly or indirectly controls the entire media industry.

Dragimur also highlights that governments use various financial strategies to dominate the media sector. These tactics can be grouped into four primary categories:

- Public funding for state-administered media,
- State advertising,
- State subsidies,
- And market-disruption measures.

The first three categories involve direct funding, while the last one includes strategies that aim to distort market perception, impair the financial health of independent and critical media, or bolster the media outlets that support the government.

While we may be well aware of the intimidation of journalists in some countries with authoritarian governments, like Russia or North Korea, it may sound far-fetched, but this type of manipulation also happens closer to home. In my home country of Canada, the government announced in its 2019 budget that it would provide nearly $600 million in subsidies to specific media outlets of its choosing.[237] And that doesn't include the more than $1 billion the Canadian Broadcasting Corporation (CBC) receives annually from taxpayers. In addition, the Journalism Labour Credit allows "qualified" organizations to apply for a 25 percent refundable tax credit, with a cap of $13,750 per employee. While the government claims these subsidies are intended to support journalism broadly, government funding can also serve as a means of controlling and influencing the media, which can be a dangerous tool for any government to wield over its citizens. For example, Margaret Munro, a journalist at PostmediaNews, uncovered documents obtained through access to information that revealed the involvement of communications managers, policy advisers, political staff, and senior officials in drafting and vetting "media lines."[238] This discovery highlights how openness is being compromised and manipulated to serve the government's political agenda, as further confirmed by Kathryn O'Hara, President of the Canadian Science Writers' Association.

Imagine running a media outlet and being offered significant funding, but with the condition that you only display certain content or portray the government in a specific light. Would you compromise on journalistic integrity to secure free money? Now, add in the pressure from corporate board members and shareholders who prioritize profits above all else. This combination of factors creates a clear incentive for content censorship.

And while the American government may not have their own broadcasting company like CBC in Canada, ABC in Australia or BBC in the UK, they still very much subsidize the news industry. In David Westphals insightful article, "American Government: Its Always Subsidized Commercial Media," he notes that:

> There's never been a time in US history when government dollars weren't propping up the news business. This year [2009], federal, state and local governments will spend well over $1 billion to support commercial news publishers through tax breaks, postal subsidies and the printing of public notices. And the amount used to be much higher.[239]

Westphals goes on to recount that in the late 1960s the government forgave approximately 75% of print publications' periodical mailing expenses at the cost of around $400 million per year (which amounts to about $2 billion today, adjusted for inflation). Much of this subsidy disappeared after the Postal Reorganization Act of 1970 and subsequent cutbacks. However, the Post Office still provides a discount on postage costs, amounting to about $270 million annually.

Furthermore, this intervention in media doesn't just encompass traditional media but everything from search engines to social platforms. For example, in 2022, the New York Post reported that "the FBI had paid Twitter nearly $3.5 million of taxpayer cash to ban accounts largely linked to conservative voices and target so-called 'foreign influence' operations."[240] Additionally, a 2018 report showed that Google's parent company Alphabet had received $766 million in federal funding since 2000, all while, according to *The Guardian*, "Google's search algorithm appears to be systematically promoting information that is either false or slanted with an extreme rightwing bias."[241,242]

And while we're at it, in 2017, journalist Matthew Caruana Galizia was locked out of his Facebook account after sharing a post about the Panama Papers, which exposed a vast network of 214,000 tax havens that involved wealthy individuals, public officials, and entities from 200 nations.[243] These records reveal how these parties utilized shell corporations to engage in fraudulent activities, evade taxes, or circumvent international sanctions. And as you probably guessed, between 2010 and 2018, Facebook received $333 million in government funding.

All things considered, when a government controls the money supply, it has the power to control the narrative and silence the opposition by controlling media corporations. George Orwell once said: "All the papers that matter live off their advertisements, and the advertisers exercise an indirect censorship over news." When reliance on advertisers shifts to dependence on government financing, the same indirect—or *direct*—influence is not inconceivable.

Distorts economic signals

Arguably, the primary pitfall in a centrally planned economy is how it interrupts the natural flow of supply and demand. With an interventionist mindset driving decision-making, governments influence capital flows, undermining the natural forces of competition in the market and shifting the relative levels of supply and demand, as we saw in the case of farming subsidization.

Through regulation and monetary policy, governments direct money to sectors of the economy they deem valuable rather than requiring sectors to depend on what the free market considers valuable. This allows them to put out brush fires which could risk exposing the system for what it is: a time bomb of unserviceable levels of debt. At best, this approach to crisis management prolongs the inevitable collapse and leads to ill-informed choices along the way, and at worst, we experience economic stagnancy and a total breakdown in supply chains.

For example, rather than allowing the free market to drive supply and demand, Stalin—*operating under the economic theories of Karl Marx*—believed that to advance the Soviet Union, society needed to revolve around the heavy metal industry.[244] During 1949-1953, he envisioned 95,000 people working in the metal industry. He wanted metal production to increase by 49% and pig iron production to rise by 80%.

However, a problem arose. The centrally planned economy did not know how to handle the high energy demands of these sectors or the shortages in raw materials. This not only meant that ore was inefficiently processed, impacting human health and the environment, but metalworks also cropped up like weeds, depleting supplies of coking coal at an unsustainable rate. As a result, colossal limestone mining operations irreversibly impacted the local environment, and more progressive sectors of the economy were chronically underfunded as the lion's share of funds were directed in service of Stalin's goal.

When the Soviet Union's Communist party finally came to terms with the fact that they were economically and technologically almost a decade behind the rest of the world, they voted to shut down more than half of all plants. As a result, 853 of the 1,557 industrial plants operational in 1956 had been shut down by 1965. This forceful, misguided decision-making had catastrophic implications. In the town of Sered in Slovakia, a 30-hectare-sized hazardous slagheap containing toxic nickel waste poisoned the local people, with preschoolers in the area frequently experiencing conjunctivitis and inner ear infections. Even now, the Czech and Slovak Republics are still coming to terms with the ramifications of the Communist industrial experiment.

And this misguided, unilateral industry driving isn't unique to Stalin. Before and after the Great Financial Crisis, China prioritized the steel industry— regardless of market indicators. Today, they produce over half the world's steel.[245] Although the pre-2008 real estate boom and general infrastructure growth created a much-needed surge in steel demand, Chinese supply continued to outstrip demand due to excessive investment in steel plants.

After global steel prices fell a further 30.6% in 2015, "having already fallen four years in a row: 7.8% in 2011, 11.6% in 2012, 7.6% in 2013, and 16% in 2014," Chinese steelmakers continued to increase production, despite declining prices and profitability:

- 881 million tons in 2011,
- 951 million tons in 2012,
- 1.07 billion tons in 2013,
- and 1.13 billion tons in 2014.

The collapse of steel prices had far-reaching consequences on the global economy. From January to October 2015, a staggering 72 billion yuan ($11.2 billion) in combined losses were incurred by 101 medium-sized and large steel companies.[246] This not only strains the environment due to the unsustainable sourcing of resources but also depletes otherwise productive capital. Furthermore, Chinese manufacturers selling steel at a loss exert pressure on foreign steel manufacturers, who struggle to compete on price and may be forced to shut down their operations. The resulting overreliance on Chinese steel, as illustrated in Figure 7.3, only amplifies economic fragility.

Figure 7.3

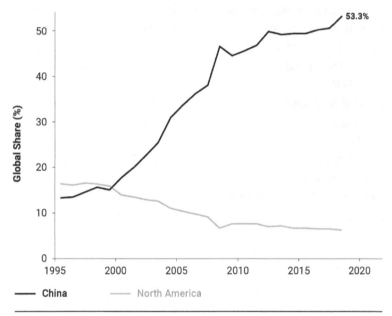

The Growing Chinese Steel Monopoly
Percentage share of world steel production - China vs North America

Source: Worldsteel & Wolfstreet.com

One final example of economic distortion is that in 2014, as Greece was in turmoil due to excessive government debt, financial mismanagement, and unsustainable fiscal policies, the European Central Bank (ECB) started offering banks targeted financing against the collateral of loans to companies and households.[247] Although this financing was supposed to create stability, it also gave the central bank the power to decide what debt was eligible for support. They could, therefore, direct capital to areas of the economy they deemed favourable in their mission of stability.

But it didn't stop there. Two years later, the ECB felt it was necessary to add investment-grade corporations to its list of eligible assets.[248] With this move, they openly favoured large companies over small ones.

And the ECB wasn't the only central bank to do so. The Bank of England followed suit and extended its bond purchases to foreign corporations as long as they were seen to be contributing to the UK economy.[249]

We are now in a position whereby, as of February 2020, the German government has guaranteed 40% of all new corporate loans.[250] Meanwhile, in France, that figure stands at 70%, and in Italy, it's over 100%, as old maturing credit is migrated to new, government-guaranteed schemes.

This is the new normal, and governments everywhere are following suit. By telling banks which sectors benefit from guaranteed loans, the governments can control capital flows to where they see fit.

Without subsidized credit, many state-owned and state-supported enterprises would collapse. These central banks obfuscate that reality by stepping in to "stabilize" failing companies. The challenge we now face is that as our system allows for intervention, in the eyes of the government, it has become not an option but an imperative to intervene.

We're so accustomed to intervention that we find ourselves in a situation where the absence of government intervention during a crisis is often perceived as the problem, while their involvement allows them to claim credit for averting a potentially worse outcome and portray themselves as saviours.

Understanding the ways in which intervention can distort free market economic decision-making is crucial to comprehending the broader implications of our monetary system.

War

As covered earlier, the US dollar holds the position of the global reserve currency. This is one of the principal ways that the US maintains its global power. However, in holding reserve currency status, the US government is in a bind:

Does it protect its position as the global reserve currency at the expense of its economy?

or

Does it focus on its economy at the expense of potentially losing reserve currency status?

This paradox is known as the Triffin dilemma, after renowned Belgian-American economist Robert Triffin. As the global reserve currency, the USD facilitates the majority of international trade. This creates a constant demand for dollars. Therefore, to maintain reserve currency status, the US must ensure global USD liquidity meets demand. In other words, they must keep USD easily accessible to people and nations.

To maintain high liquidity levels, the US must:

1. Outsource manufacturing and encourage a consumer culture to provide global USD liquidity. Doing so creates a movement of domestic dollars internationally through foreign goods consumption.
2. Lower interest rates and debase the currency to encourage a consumer culture.

Ironically, while the US is concurrently outsourcing manufacturing to secure global USD liquidity, they are also trying to achieve full employment. This further incentivizes the lowering of rates and the debasement of the currency to tempt businesses to grow and increase hiring.

The premise of the Triffin paradox is that as the global reserve currency, you cannot maintain reserve currency status, grow your manufacturing base, and preserve sovereignty simultaneously. And as shown in Figure 7.4, no nation in history has ever maintained its global hegemony indefinitely.

Figure 7.4

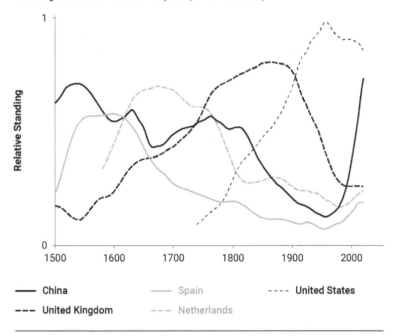

Relative Standing of Great Empires
Standing level relative to other empires (1 = all-time max)

Source: Ray Dalio, www.economicprinciples.org

With the US directing all its energy and resources into protecting the reserve currency status, we inevitably see healthcare, infrastructure, and domestic manufacturing sacrifices. Eventually, these sacrifices will hollow out the US and its global hegemony, but in the meantime, the US is incentivized to act in the interest of the USD rather than its populace. This can be seen in US military spending.

Before we experienced the prevalence of fiat currencies, those in power were limited in their ability to fund wars. First, they could only go to war if they had saved up the capital and resources to do so and had support from the populace. Second, if the war was not going as planned and resources were being depleted, it was in the best interest to call off the war effort or face harsh consequences. This minimized casualties and ensured wars didn't drag on through artificial funding, i.e., monetary expansion. In our current system, however, this is not the case.

Figure 7.5

The Reality of US Government Spending

Data from 2015 & all $ values in thousands

	Mental Health + Addiction	Counter Terrorism
Government Spending	$5,376,090	$146,000,000
Deaths	95,331	58
Dollars Spent Per Death	$56	$2,522,413

The US government allocates a staggering 44,731 times more resources to combatting terrorism-related deaths than mental health & drug addiction deaths.

Source: The National Council for Mental Wellbeing, National Intstitute of Mental Health & Stimson Study Group on Counterterrorism Spending

In times of perceived threat, governments have the ability to finance wars by tapping into the wallets of the people through methods such as taxation, debt issuance, or money printing, regardless of whether it aligns with the desires of the populace.

Let's look at war through the lens of US military spending. Figure 7.5 is a table that compares government spending on mental health and drug addiction to the military's counter-terrorism budget and then looks at total deaths and the dollars spent per death.

Beyond the egregious disparity in counterterrorism and mental health spending specifically, the US spends 450% more on the military than on healthcare overall.[251]

Figure 7.6

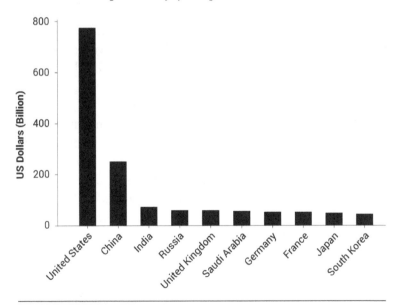

Top 10 Countries by Military Spending
Countries with the highest military spending worldwide in 2020

Source: Bank of America Global Research

Although initially jaw-dropping, this expenditure makes more sense when you realize that if the US lost its reserve currency status, we would see a significant drop in demand for the USD, threatening the US. If they were to lose that status, the US would no longer be able to capitalize off its global positioning, and it most definitely wouldn't be able to expand the money supply to the same extent without major repercussions and destruction of the USD's purchasing power. Given the situation, the US is highly incentivized to protect its global reserve status, which can be seen in the significant military spending in Figures 7.5 and 7.6.

In 2020, the US spent 308% more than China and more than the subsequent ten countries combined. As Loren Thompson puts it in her *Forbes* article, "Five percent of the world's population is trying to cover fifty percent of the world's military bills with only a quarter of the world's wealth."[252] What's more, the Pentagon awarded Lockheed Martin $75 billion in contracts, surpassing the total budget of the State Department and the United States Agency for International Development combined.[253] As a result, the average taxpayer's annual contribution towards weapons contractors amounts to $1,087, while only $270 is allocated for kindergarten to grade 12 education.

So where does this military spending go?

With the understanding that the US is incentivized to challenge anyone who attempts to interfere with its power, let's dig into some examples of how and where the US directs their immense global authority and military power.

While there have been numerous instances of US military overreach, two particularly relevant cases concern Muammar Gadhafi and Saddam Hussein.

In 2009 Gadhafi, the de facto leader of Libya, proposed the idea of the gold dinar to the states of the African continent.[254] His proposal was to implement a currency backed by gold and facilitated by the transition from selling oil in dollars to selling oil for gold. The gold dinar would be a way to divert oil revenues towards state-controlled funds and away from the US.

Given that Libya is home to Africa's largest oil reserves, with 2.9% of the total known global reserves, and considering most of the global oil trade is done in the dollar, which greatly strengthens the dollar, this posed a threat to the US's financial supremacy.[255,256]

So, unsurprisingly, the US responded.

First, the US supplied Libyan rebel opposition with millions of dollars of military equipment, "such as vehicles, radios and medicines," to prolong the conflict and weaken Gadhafi.[257] Then in October 2011, the US, in conjunction with NATO, called an airstrike on Gadhafi loyalists forcing Gadhafi and his inner circle to flee. While fleeing, he was captured by Misrata-based militias and ultimately executed.

As expected, with Gadhafi's death also came the death of the gold dinar. Libyan oil was never priced in the gold dinar, and the dollar remained the dominant currency in the oil trade.

These military operations in Libya cost US taxpayers $726 billion in 2011 alone.[258] That is roughly $2 billion per day.

The US claims the intervention was necessary under humanitarian interventionism grounds.[259] However, not only could human rights foundations not find any evidence to support this, but in 2015 Wikileaks released a US Department of State document emailed to Hillary Clinton in March 2011, which detailed that Gadhafi's government held 143 tonnes of gold intended for the establishment of the gold-dinar.[260,261]

This evidence exemplifies that the US knew about Gadhafi's plans for the gold dinar. Therefore, given the sequence of events, it seems far more likely that the US recognized that the dollar was under threat of attack and felt it needed to react rather than a humanitarian push was required.

Or consider the case of Saddam Hussein. Iraq ranks fifth in the world for its large oil reserves, accounting for 8.7% of the global total.[262] In October 2000, Hussein announced that Iraq would switch to selling oil in euros— a move that similarly could have significant implications for the US economy and its global financial dominance.

By February 2003, Iraq had sold 3.3 billion barrels of oil under the new currency, totalling 26 billion euros.[263] Soon after, in March 2003, the US military, partnering with British troops, invaded Iraq and overthrew Saddam. Just three months later, Iraq was back to selling its oil in dollars.

Similarly to Gadhafi, the US has claimed they invaded Iraq to promote human rights. They based this on the idea that Hussein had deep ties to terrorist organizations such as al-Qaeda and secretly held weapons of mass destruction (WMD). However, as there have never been any verified links between Saddam and al-Qaeda, nor any evidence supporting WMDs in Iraq, it is entirely possible the intention was to protect the dollar, using the public fervour around terrorism following 9/11 as a cover.[264]

Even though empirical evidence indicates that military spending is detrimental to economic productivity and growth, the dollar's power nonetheless depends on a strong military, and the military depends on a strong dollar.[265,266] Without either, the US would be unable to continue its inflationary narrative.

....

FUN FACT: Inflation, originally defined as an increase in the quantity of money, has undergone a transformation since being co-opted by governments. It has been redefined as simply a "price increase," portraying it as an external threat beyond their control, necessitating their vigilant fight against it.[267] However, the inescapable truth remains that inflation is primarily a consequence of money supply expansion, which given that it is the governments that govern and control the money supply, they are the architects of inflation. Thus, if they truly desire to halt inflation, the power to do so lies within their hands.

....

Misleading humanitarian/terroristic war narratives and the military serving as a capital sponge will continue as long as misaligned monetary systems exist. Under such systems, what is right does not matter, but rather what allows these unsustainable systems to persist. To give one last example, in August 2022, the Senate passed the Inflation Reduction Act, granting an astounding $80 billion in extra funding to the Internal Revenue Service (IRS).[268] This allocation would enable the IRS to recruit 87,000 additional agents, enhancing their capacity to oversee the financial affairs of American citizens.

In a striking display of inconsistency, a mere few months later, the Senate resoundingly blocked a bill to ensure transparency and accountability of Ukraine war funding, currently sitting at over $75 billion of taxpayers' money.[269,270] Such contrasting decisions cannot be overlooked; they serve as a clear testament to the priorities held by the government.

United States congressman and former presidential candidate Ron Paul once remarked: "It is no coincidence that the century of total war coincided with the century of central banking." The findings of R.J. Rummel, in his book *Death by Government*, further confirm this, in which he estimates that governments killed a staggering 169 million people during the 20th century.[271] Even in specific cases, like Iraq, the consequences of maintaining dollar hegemony resulted in more civilian deaths than those attributed to Saddam Hussein's alleged inhumane acts.[272]

These shocking numbers underscore the devastating consequences of central banking and unchecked money printing. Many wars are fought under the pretense of democracy when in reality, they are simply a way to support failing fiat currencies, with military spending being used to ensure certain currencies maintain their global status. The consequences are deadly.

CONCLUSION

In light of everything discussed, our current monetary system has shifted the balance of power away from citizens, creating a situation where the government's ability to spend is more dependent on financial intervention than on the taxpayers themselves. This has created a system that incentivizes short-term political thinking, the silencing of truth, and conflict over cooperation, ultimately putting the stability of our global economy at risk.

Although the relationship between money, government, and politics is a complex one, we must carefully consider the long-term implications of intervention. Therefore, to conclude this chapter, I would like to leave you with the following thought: We fear death and change not only in life but also in business, money, and government. We cling to the familiar, resisting the unknown at all costs, yet this only prolongs failure, mismanagement, and ill health. Embracing change and letting go of outdated practices is essential for growth and vitality in all areas of life.

As should be evident by now, the impact of our monetary system goes far beyond pure economics. However, no monetary discussion is complete without addressing its implications on our environment and consumption habits. In the next chapter, we'll focus on how money plays a role in the health of our planet.

CHAPTER 8

MONEY'S TOLL ON OUR PLANET

How Monetary Policy is Amplifying Environmental Destruction

"If you think the economy is more important than the environment, try holding your breath while counting your money." —Guy McPherson

....

Humans, in our current form, have roamed this planet for around 300,000 years.[273] If we condense human history into a full-length two-hour movie, each minute will represent 2,500 years of history! Isn't it astounding to consider how far we've come?

Now, take a guess at when the introduction of modern-day central banking would appear in such a film.

Given that the Federal Reserve Act was signed in 1913, it would appear in the last three seconds of the movie. What's more, the transition off the gold standard would be a mere one second from the end. Yet, the implications of these events have already altered the course of humanity and have had a profound impact on the parent-child bond, our businesses, our governments, and our politics.

Therefore, in an era where fiat money reigns supreme, we must ask ourselves: What is the cost such money imposes on our planet? Our existing monetary system propels us toward a precarious future characterized by rapid resource extraction and consumption. As we tirelessly strive to outpace inflation and relentlessly pursue economic growth, we are unwittingly creating a wake of environmental devastation. This unrelenting exploitation depletes the very resources that form the bedrock of life itself, casting a shadow on the sustainability of our existence.

In this chapter, we'll explore the effects that our financial system has had on our planet.

In 2022, Earth.org, a global environmental movement championing sustainable economic policy, identified the following issues as among the most pressing and critical[274]:

- Some 1.3 billion tons of food meant for human consumption (a third of the total produced) is wasted.
- In 1950, the annual global production of plastic was around 2 million tons. By 2015 that number had increased to 419 million tons. Most of it is not recycled, and much of it cannot be sustainably repurposed.
- Every hour forests the size of 300 football fields are logged.
- Globally, more than 68 billion tonnes of topsoil are lost each year. That is 100 times more quickly than it is naturally replaced.
- According to the UN Environment Programme, textile dying in the fashion industry alone is responsible for over 20% of the world's wastewater, or around 93 billion cubic meters. This is on top of the 92 million tons of textile waste annually.[275]

The above-mentioned issues result from unbridled consumerism, devastating our planet and its natural resources.

But what do all these have to do with our monetary system?

Money, in the form of debt, currently drives our economy, and consumerism is the engine behind it. With 68% of the US GDP rooted in consumption, the Federal Reserve's goal of a 2-3% GDP growth rate is primarily a call for more consumerism.[276] Our system necessitates continuous growth in consumer spending to enable debt-laden companies to fulfill their financial obligations.

And herein lies the problem: When technology deflates the cost of goods and services, this spells disaster for a debt-based economy. Without sustained growth in consumerism, the system simply cannot function, as corporations that rely on consumer spending to stay afloat can no longer meet their growing debt obligations.

Therefore, as prices decline, central banks must increasingly intervene to stimulate consumption. This, combined with the fact that the correlation between energy usage and GDP over the last 60 years has been 99% (as GDP increases, so does energy consumption), begs the question[277]: Where will all the energy and resources come from to fuel this increasing consumerism?

Whether it's drilling for oil to create plastics or mining for minerals to produce microchips for our devices, there's no escaping the fact that our environment will suffer from increased exploitation due to the rising demands of consumerism. As consumer needs grow, so does the demand for natural resources.

One of the most remarkable aspects of the free market is its innate ability to balance prices in response to supply and demand dynamics. This organic ebb and flow of prices play a vital role in conserving natural resources. When there's a surge in demand for a commodity like gold, prices naturally rise to accommodate the heightened interest. Mining operations can now branch out and mine in more costly areas which would otherwise be unprofitable. In turn, the supply of gold entering the market increases. *And this is where the market self-regulates through price.* If demand stays the same while supply rises, prices will drop. Eventually, it'll no longer be economical for these operations to mine in these otherwise unprofitable areas, so mining stops again.

This natural feedback mechanism regulates supply, minimizing the possibility of overproduction and environmental impact. Rising prices signal to the free market that supply is limited, while falling prices signal an oversupply.

What's more, this impact extends beyond mining and encompasses consumption as well. When prices rise due to supply shortages, it serves the hidden advantage of incentivizing innovation and the exploration of alternative resources while also acting as a deterrent for those who cannot afford these scarce resources. This reduction in demand plays a crucial role in preventing further depletion of limited resources and promotes their responsible utilization.

However, when governments intervene this is when problems start to arise. This intervention shows itself in a myriad of ways:

- When artificially acquired capital, such as through subsidies, enters the economy, this leads to an uptick in consumption, disrupting the natural balance of supply and demand.
- When interest rates are artificially suppressed, debt consumption becomes more favourable, increasing consumption, often beyond people's means.
- When inflation devalues the currency, holders are incentivized to spend (or invest) today rather than save for tomorrow.
- If capital controls prevent money from flowing into certain areas of the economy, other areas unnaturally benefit by receiving a greater share of purchases.
- If price controls cap the cost of certain resources to ensure affordability and ease of access, we experience unnatural demand.

When any of these conditions are met, capital no longer exhibits its default, free market flow. Instead, it pools in subsidized or government-supported areas, increasing demand for specific resources. And the more we witness a distortion in the flow of capital, the greater our natural environment is impacted. For instance, when governments step in, such as by capping energy prices, it disrupts the economic signal indicating supplies are low. Consequently, individuals, corporations, and governments end up consuming beyond what they could otherwise afford. If the government refrained from intervening, these individuals might have been compelled to seek more affordable alternatives, such as using public transit instead of personal vehicles or implementing energy-saving measures in their homes. This shift would naturally reduce demand. In essence, price caps and subsidies, by suppressing prices and increasing demand, only worsen resource depletion.

On top of this amplified consumption contributing to environmental degradation, it also creates two additional negative effects:

- It exacerbates inequality as prices rise far more than normal for those who do not have access to the government subsidies that are forcibly lowering prices, such as the poor in developing countries.
- If resource depletion wasn't enough, rising prices incentivize short-term uneconomical and environmentally unfriendly solutions to fill the supply shortage exacerbated by intervention.

The Aral Sea in Central Asia is a haunting example of environmental destruction caused by such behaviour. In her UN Chronicle article "Dry Tears of the Aral," Beatrice Grabish exposes the catastrophic effects of the Soviet's aggressive policy of agricultural expansion.[278]

Thanks to the Soviet Union's relentless pursuit of cotton, just 65 years ago, Central Asia experienced rapid depletion of what was once the world's fourth largest lake, with a volume of 1,093 km3, to just a mere 100 km3 today.[279] The United Nations Development Programme (UNDP) called this tragedy "the most staggering disaster of the twentieth century."

Figure 8.1

The Shrinking Aral Sea

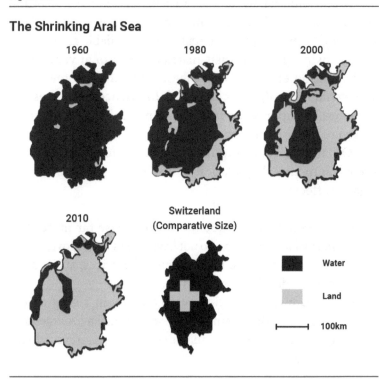

Source: Adapted from Philip Micklin, Western Michigan University

Although cotton had previously been cultivated in Central Asia, beginning in 1959, the Soviets' plans for cotton cultivation were a departure from previous practices. The Aral Sea region was selected for its ideal conditions: two large rivers, the Syr Darya and the Amu Darya, that could provide ample water to support the intensive farming of the crop.

A little over 20 years later, it seemed like the plan was successful. Cotton output reached 9 million tonnes, making Central Asia the fourth-largest cotton producer in the world. However, as subsidies suppressed prices and cotton demand continued to grow, the lake eventually couldn't handle the unnatural water demand from cotton cultivation, and cracks began to show.

As the Aral's water volume started to drop from overuse, fertilizers and pesticide concentrations meant the water became poisonous for fish and animal populations, not to mention people, and cotton harvests began to decline due to the increased soil salinity surrounding the sea. "The once thriving fishing and canning industry evaporated, replaced by anemia, high infant and maternal mortality, and debilitating respiratory and intestinal ailments," and illnesses, starvation, and poverty now plagued the region.

The 3.5 million people in and around the region witnessed "their health, jobs and living conditions literally go down the drain." And to top it all off, "without the moderating influence of a large body of water, the seasons [of Central Asia] have become more extreme." Summers, which were already scorching, became much hotter, drier, and longer, and winters, even colder, icier, and drier.

Artificial agricultural expansion through subsidies doesn't just impact the local communities and environment, but also the surrounding continental climate. Many of the environmental and economically challenging situations listed at the start of this chapter arise from intervention. By subsidizing sectors of the economy and suppressing interest rates, we not only incentivize borrowing but also allow individuals to live beyond their means and purchase and extract natural resources at prices below what the free market deems sustainable.

When intervention impairs the free market from self-regulating prices, the consequences impact everyone. The Aral Sea crisis serves as a stark reminder of the consequences of unchecked consumption and the dangers of disregarding the long-term impact of our actions.

But are we truly learning from history's mistakes?

Our monetary system, with its emphasis on consumption over savings, is a ticking time bomb. When central banks artificially suppress interest rates, the temptation to borrow and spend becomes irresistible. What would normally be unaffordable is now made possible through debt. Suddenly, we can bring forward future expenditure to the present, artificially increasing our consumption.

I vividly recall meeting some friends for a mountain bike ride a few years ago and being taken aback. To my surprise, three of the five friends had recently acquired brand new, high-priced trucks worth over \$50,000, despite their income levels not aligning with such substantial purchases. Instead, they were relying on zero-interest financing to sustain these acquisitions. This perfectly highlights the excess resource consumption as a result of easy money.

The findings of two studies conducted by Hurst and Stafford (2004) and Parker et al. (2013) provide further support to this behaviour as they investigated the impact of interest rate reductions on household spending and consumer spending resulting from economic stimulus payments.[280,281]

In the first study, Hurst and Stafford followed household spending after the central bank lowered interest rates. They started by taking the average mortgage payments preceding this lowering of interest rates and then looked at the two years after the interest rate adjustment.

On average, the monthly payments fell by $900, significantly increasing income. This amounted to tens of thousands of dollars over the remaining life of a mortgage! In the wake of this reduction, average monthly car payments increased by 40% and the probability of purchasing a car increased by more than 45%.

In the second study, Parker et al. found that households spent between 12% to 30% of their 2008 stimulus payments on nondurable consumption goods (goods that are used or consumed relatively quickly and have a short lifespan, such as food, beverages, clothing, and personal care items), and another 38% to 60% on purchasing vehicles.

Suppressing rising interest rates is like turning a blind eye to the warning signs of a struggling economy. By intervening, central banks are hindering the necessary correction process and perpetuating a culture of overconsumption and fiscal irresponsibility. It signals to individuals and businesses that it's acceptable to continue their spending habits without caution, despite the underlying economic risks.

Furthermore, this intervention doesn't always unfold as expected. Around the mid-2000s, the Chinese government subscribed to the adage, "if you build it, they will come," and relied on low-interest rates to spur on artificial economic growth. Thanks to the suppressed cost of capital, property developers over-built far beyond what the market could absorb, wasting immense quantities of resources. By 2010, some "65 million properties connected to the power grid were not using any electricity," and estimates suggested that 20% of urban dwellings were unoccupied. That is enough property to house the population of Canada twice over.

This influx of capital into the housing market, driven by artificial means, resulted in an unsustainable overuse of resources and a misallocation of capital. Had the cost of capital accurately reflected the realities of the market, these developers might have reconsidered their investments while, at the same time, reducing the demand and saving large quantities of valuable resources.

The modern-day expansion of global supply chains is another prime example of how monetary intervention adversely impacts our environment. Elongated supply chains place greater demands on resources and consume far more energy to get products into the hands of the end consumer compared to their domestic equivalents.

According to Valentina Bruno et al. in "AEA Papers and Proceedings," modern-day supply chains require "substantial financing needs," which increase non-linearly given the length of the supply chain.[282] Due to the capital-intensive nature of supply chains, "when the cost of borrowing ... falls, multinational companies are inclined to construct longer supply chains."[283]

For example, consider an automobile engine produced in Japan, sent to Mexico for installation on the vehicle's frame, and then sold in the United States. Or on a personal level, during my time at a mountain bike manufacturer, we heard that a Canadian competitor was shipping their locally made handlebars to China for decal addition and then back to Canada. In a scenario with cheap capital, such practices become economically feasible.

In our heavily subsidized world, the average product touches six countries before ending up in the hands of the consumer. This may be convenient for consumers, but the environmental impact of the extensive transportation of consumer goods cannot be overstated. If capital costs accurately reflected the free market, these elongated supply chains would become economically unviable.

In such a scenario, with a higher cost of capital, companies that rely on such supply chains may struggle to compete effectively against their competitors. Competitors, who adopt leaner and more localized supply chains, can benefit from reduced costs, faster response times, and better control over the quality and reliability of their products. Therefore, when capital costs are higher, companies are incentivized to optimize their supply chains, streamline operations, and allocate resources more efficiently. This approach not only promotes competitiveness but also aligns with economic, environmental, and sustainability considerations.

However, it's not just the environmental impact we must worry about. As supply chains have lengthened, nations have become ever more interdependent. This, combined with cheap capital, which fuels artificial growth and consumption, creates a fragile globalized world where a crisis in one locale can have massive ripple effects throughout the world. We are now at a point where global supply chains can quickly cease when economic stressors arise, leading to catastrophe.

A perfect example of this fragility became evident during the COVID-19 pandemic. As countries panicked and laid off workers, global supply chains quickly ground to a halt, creating significant manufacturing disruptions. At the pandemic's peak, manufacturing lead times had increased by over 200%, with some companies seeing their lead times go from 60 days to 18 months.[284] Furthermore, the cost of shipping a container from China to Europe rose from $1,600 pre-pandemic to an incredible $10,000.[285]

If the cost of capital reflected reality, this would push corporations to produce domestically rather than internationally, reducing elongated supply chains and unnecessary expenses and, most importantly, decreasing global interdependency as countries would no longer be as reliant on one another, reducing the risk of global disruptions in the future.

Before wrapping up the topic of environmental impact, it's crucial to emphasize that a sustainable future is not possible in a fundamentally unsustainable system. Our current monetary system severely impacts our planet. Unbridled consumerism and government intervention are distorting the natural flow of capital and depleting vital resources, exacerbating environmental degradation.

Society is full of passionate individuals striving for change, yet, until we recognize that everything is downstream of money and our true adversary is our money, we will continue to spin our wheels, wasting precious time and resources fighting the wrong battles. Therefore, it is vital that we understand the hidden cost of money and how it shapes our lives and the world around us, as only then can we work towards creating a more sustainable future.

CONCLUSION

The problems discussed so far are only a small part of the larger picture. The incentive structures inherent in our system have far-reaching consequences, impacting everything from education to pharmaceuticals, healthcare, and food. Money touches every aspect of society. By distorting the incentive system, you corrupt the outcomes.

However, as, Kudzai, a great writer, and a friend of mine, says:

Most of the world's biggest problems are worsened by attempting to solve them from the same economic system that is responsible for their creation. This is also true at an individual level as well. Knowing the inherent flaws in the design and operation of this monetary order is an important first step in insuring yourself against them.[286]

If I were to summarize the last few chapters in a single sentence, I would borrow a line from the book *The Subtle Art of Not Giving a F*ck,* by Mark Manson: "Emotions are simply biological signals designed to nudge you in the direction of beneficial change."[287]

But in this context, I'd put a twist on Manson's wise words:

These monetary byproducts are simply signals designed to nudge us in the direction of beneficial change.

Just as emotions are biological signals designed to push us, as individuals, in the direction of personal change, monetary byproducts can be seen as signals that give us insight into much-needed economic change. Now we can choose to listen to these signals or ignore them. But if we choose the latter, we shouldn't expect rainbows and unicorns. Well, maybe a few more corporate unicorns.

As we come to the end of exploring money's influence on our behaviour, the parent-child bond, business, government, and our environment, it's time to shift gears and examine the relationship between money and totalitarianism, investigating how money in its current form influences controlling structures.

CHAPTER 9

THE HYPNOTIC TRANCE
OF MASS FORMATION

How Controlling Structures Use
Psychology to Command Change

*"From the totalitarian point of view history is
something to be created rather than learned."*
—George Orwell

....

I n a world built upon perpetual growth, where governments frequently encounter economic challenges and environmental issues, policies of intervention and financial manipulation have become the go-to means of effecting change. However, as we have come to realize, this approach is unsustainable and merely conceals the underlying problems. With the increasing number of economic crises and concerns, those in power must now take bold actions to avert collapse and ensure the continued functioning of the system.

With this in mind, don't be fooled by the notion that totalitarian structures are solely the product of evil individuals. Rather, they often stem from well-intentioned ideologies and the belief that their actions are for the greater good of humanity, even if it means sacrificing individual rights and freedoms.

When we discuss oppressive structures, I refer to the concepts of authoritarianism and totalitarianism. While both systems entail centralized control and restricted individual freedoms, authoritarianism generally allows for certain levels of social, political, and economic autonomy. In contrast, totalitarianism aims to suppress dissent and exert dominance over most, if not all, aspects of society. In this chapter, we will discover how oppressive structures are prone to arise when society is breaking down.

As discussed in Chapter Five, our inherent evolutionary need for connection and attachment is crucial for our survival. However, this desire for belonging can also make us susceptible to external influences. When we experience emotions like loneliness, meaninglessness, anxiety, or frustration, we naturally seek solace and support from others. This yearning for connection and guidance can sometimes lead us to place trust and authority in controlling entities. On a personal level, this can manifest as entering into relationships with controlling and abusive partners or becoming involved with cult-like organizations. Initially, these individuals or groups may appear to offer kindness, understanding, and assistance, but unfortunately, their hierarchical and domineering nature often prioritizes their own interests rather than our well-being. This pattern is mirrored on a larger scale with totalitarian governments as well.

That said, these oppressive regimes don't just materialize out of thin air. They require the appearance of backing from the majority of the population. With this support, these regimes can carry out transformative actions that enable them to advance down the path of greater control and authority.

This widespread support is often referred to as a "mass formation." Only through understanding mass formation can we piece together the rise of totalitarian structures. This exploration in mass formation will also provide a deeper understanding of how individuals may be driven to:

- Sacrifice their sovereignty
- Abandon their personal principles
- Develop an intolerance towards dissenting opinions
- Display extreme obedience to the government
- Unquestionably adhere to the collective narrative, even when it surpasses moral boundaries.

Adherents to oppressive regimes may fear punishment or sincerely believe it is all for the greater good of the collective.

MASS FORMATION

This idea of mass formation, which falls under crowd psychology, is not new or fringe. It has been studied extensively by Sigmund Freud, Gustave Le Bon, Floyd Allport, and many others. However, for a more modern take on mass formations and crowd psychology, I will reference Mattias Desmet's book *The Psychology of Totalitarianism.*[288] Mattias is a Belgian clinical psychologist and professor of clinical psychology at Ghent University and arguably the foremost leading expert in totalitarianism.

A mass formation, in its essence, refers to a large crowd where the group's collective behaviour influences the individuals within it. This phenomenon is often associated with the concept of "mob mentality," although it should be noted that a mass formation does not inherently lead to violent or judgmental behaviours.

A defining characteristic of a mass formation is its extensive *"uniformization."* Those immersed become one with the collective, pushing aside their own ideas, values, and beliefs to align with the crowd. This uniformization creates a total loss of independent thought and the capacity for critical reflection. Even those who are usually highly capable of critical thought can succumb to the pressure of conformity and become engulfed.

Moreover, once immersed in the crowd, people often relinquish responsibility. This is such a well-known issue that emergency respondents are trained to call to specific individuals for any necessary assistance, rather than broadly calling for help, since in a crowd, it is more likely everyone will assume someone else will step up, absolving themselves of the responsibility to assist. And beyond letting go of a sense of responsibility for good behaviour, people are also more likely to give in to impulses normally considered unethical and immoral, such as violence, bullying, and ostracization.

A prime example of people standing by against what seems like a clear moral imperative is the infamous Kitty Genovese case in 1964.[289] Despite over 38 witnesses hearing or seeing parts of the attack, no one intervened as Ms. Genovese was robbed, raped, and stabbed to death outside her apartment in Queens, NY. This tragic event highlights the tendency for people to rely on others to take action rather than taking personal responsibility, even if they disagree with the situation. Psychologists have labelled such behaviour as the bystander effect.

Desmet explains that four societal criteria must be met for a mass formation to emerge. Once satisfied, people willingly do whatever is needed for the perceived benefit of the collective, even if that means a total loss of self-sovereignty.

The Four Conditions for Mass Formation

Condition One - Loneliness

For any mass formation to take place, there must first be widespread loneliness.

Human beings are instinctively wired to seek attachment and companionship for our own safety and well-being, so when loneliness sets in, there is a strong drive to establish connections. Loneliness can deeply affect our emotional well-being, leading us to overlook our other personal needs in favour of fulfilling this inner desire for connection.

It's worth mentioning that loneliness often stems from a host of negative emotions, such as fear, shame, or anxiety, which might prevent us from reaching out and forming bonds. This creates a vicious cycle, as avoiding connection only intensifies the negative feelings we are already experiencing.

Condition Two - Meaninglessness

Loneliness doesn't usually exist in isolation (pun intended). All too often, it is accompanied by a sense of meaninglessness.

When society is facing a widespread lack of companionship and connection, motivation tends to drop[290]. With a decline in motivation, people stop striving to collaborate, learn, and grow. As a result, a sense of meaninglessness often starts to emerge.

There are various reasons why individuals may experience meaninglessness, such as job dissatisfaction, cynicism toward societal norms, or simply boredom.

In such cases, when meaninglessness is present, we start to feel drawn to narratives that provide a sense of meaning and purpose, particularly ones that allow us to contribute to something perceived as beneficial for the collective. After all, what could be more fulfilling than positively impacting others?

Condition Three - Widespread, Free-Floating Anxiety

The third condition necessary for a mass formation is the presence of widespread, free-floating anxiety.

It's important to differentiate free-floating anxiety from fixed anxiety. Fixed anxiety has a specific trigger, such as fear of heights, public speaking, or small spaces. On the other hand, free-floating anxiety, also known as generalized anxiety, lacks a clear source or object to attach to. The meaninglessness of the second condition is commonly accompanied by free-floating anxiety— The sense of meaninglessness often brings about a state of free-floating anxiety, where individuals may experience a pervasive sense of worry about living their lives in the wrong way, finding their purpose, or lacking a clear sense of direction. They may grapple with an underlying feeling that something is amiss, causing stress and a desire to address this elusive dissatisfaction.

The problem with free-floating anxiety is that it is difficult to identify and address. Unlike more fixed anxieties that can be tackled head-on through exposure therapy or rationalization about the true risks and dangers around them, free-floating anxiety can shift from subject to subject so that addressing any one issue does not resolve the underlying sense of instability and fear. As a result, it can lead to feelings of hopelessness and disillusionment. In this free-floating state, individuals actively seek to assign meaning to their anxiety, making them even more susceptible to persuasive narratives. If someone can explain the source of their discomfort and offer a potential solution, they are likely to embrace it eagerly.

Condition Four - Aggression & Frustration

Lastly, the convergence of loneliness, meaninglessness and free-floating anxiety often lays the foundation for widespread aggression and frustration in society.

Individuals troubled by their emotional state tend to become more irritable, restless, and aggressive.[291] In an effort to alleviate this tension and seek meaning, they usually release their frustration on anything that exacerbates their discomfort.

At this stage, anger, resentment, and violence may emerge as a consequence of the built-up tension and frustration. This misdirection of negative feelings was even observed in rats in a study conducted by N.H. Azrin, H.B. Rubin, and R.R. Hutchinson in 1968.[292] The study found that when rats were paired together, and one was subjected to an electric shock, the affected rat responded aggressively towards the other rat, despite the other rat having nothing to do with the electric shock. This highlights the potential for aggressive reactions towards innocent individuals when pain and discomfort are present.

Moreover, the capuchin monkey experiment, commonly known as the "inequity aversion" experiment conducted by Frans de Waal and Sarah Brosnan, may explain why social inequality gives rise to such behaviour.[293] In this experiment, two capuchin monkeys were placed in separate enclosures side by side and trained to perform a simple task. Both monkeys were rewarded with food for completing the task, but they received different rewards: one received a cucumber slice, while the other received a more desirable grape.

Initially, both monkeys were content with their rewards. However, when the monkey receiving the cucumber noticed that the other monkey was receiving grapes for the same task, it became visibly agitated. It began refusing to perform the task, banging the enclosure, and even throwing the cucumber back at the experimenter in frustration. The monkey's behaviour demonstrated a sense of anger and frustration due to perceiving an unfair distribution of rewards.

This experiment provided insights into the emotional reactions of animals, suggesting that they have a sense of fairness and react negatively when they perceive unequal treatment. The capuchin monkey's display of anger and frustration in response to inequity reflects a basic understanding of fairness and a natural tendency to compare oneself to others.

In summary, the four conditions necessary for a mass formation are:

1. Widespread loneliness, where people feel a strong drive to form connections.
2. Widespread meaninglessness, which can arise from economic conditions or a decline in companionship, and leads to disillusionment and a lack of motivation.

3. Widespread free-floating anxiety, characterized by an unidentifiable source triggering anxiety.
4. Widespread aggression and frustration, which arises from the convergence of loneliness, meaninglessness, and free-floating anxiety.

Once all four conditions are met, Professor Desmet describes how a persuasive narrative can take hold:

> If, under the aforementioned circumstances, a suggestive story is spread through the mass media that indicates an object of anxiety ... and at the same time offers a strategy to deal with that object of anxiety, there is a real chance that all the free-flowing anxiety will attach itself to that object and there will be broad social support for the implementation of the strategy to control that object of anxiety.

Comparing these four conditions to historical examples of totalitarianism, such as Hitler's regime in Germany, or Stalin's rule over the Soviet Union, we can confirm that these four conditions have all been met.

However, I would argue one more condition has also been met in all major historical examples; there has been a breakdown or co-opting of the monetary system as a precursor to these totalitarian structures.

In the case of Hitler, Germany had famously just experienced the Weimar hyperinflation. The inflation was so bad that "a loaf of bread in Berlin that cost around 160 Marks at the end of 1922 cost 200,000,000,000 Marks by late 1923."[294] *The country was desperate for a way forward and looking for a saviour.* Hitler gave the populace a reason for their anxiety (namely, the Jewish people) and a glimmer of hope that the future would not be as hard as the present.

If you're fighting for survival, unsure what the future holds or whether you can afford your next meal, this is a perfect springboard from which the four other conditions can emerge. I would, therefore, suggest that a misaligned or broken monetary system is a precursor to the four conditions above. While individual-level loneliness, meaninglessness, anxiety, and frustration can and will exist in any setting, a failing monetary system leads to these issues on a society-wide scale and therefore precedes the "widespread" factor of these conditions.

Condition Zero - Misaligned or Co-opted Monetary System
In a misaligned or co-opted monetary system that inhibits monetary expression, you form the foundation for feelings of loneliness, meaninglessness, and anxiety.

As capital controls or debasement impair monetary expression – directing money where you see fit – a sense of meaninglessness tends to spread as you not only feel as though your voice is not being heard, but you feel financially constrained.

You don't have to look far to see the countless studies on the discomfort that arises from financial stress. For example, a study by Soomin Ryu and Lu Fan titled *The Relationship Between Financial Worries and Psychological Distress* found compelling evidence linking financial stress to elevated levels of depression, anxiety, and psychological distress.[295] These findings emphasize the significant role that financial difficulties can play in undermining one's mental health and overall quality of life.

What's more, when you have a monetary system co-opted by the government and a large portion of the population is reliant on financial aid, not only is this a perfect environment for meaninglessness, but it also means these individuals feel compelled to side with the government. If the government takes a certain stance, they will most likely comply to prevent a loss of support.

Let's now focus on how these mass formations emerge from these five conditions.

The Emergence of Mass Formation

At first, it can be hard to understand why someone would allow their rights and freedoms to be eroded, such as under Hitler or Stalin's regimes. However, it becomes much easier to comprehend once we recognize the immense suffering from the aforementioned conditions.

People who find themselves under all five conditions are simply searching for relief from their distress. The allure of mass formation lies in transforming their psychological state from turmoil to a sense of belonging and a release from pent-up frustration.

The appeal of mass formations, such as those seen under Hitler and Stalin, can be better understood when considering the various ways it meets the needs of society. First, it provides a clear source for the anxiety and suffering that has plagued individuals, offering a perceived escape from their discomfort and an external source of blame. Second, it revitalizes the collapsing society by giving it coherence, purpose, and energy through a shared battle against a common enemy. This turns the fight against the source of suffering into a mission with a higher purpose for the betterment of the collective. Lastly, during the conflict, individuals have an outlet to release their pent-up anger and frustration, targeting those who are victimized by or refuse to buy into the mass formation's narrative.

The benefits of mass formation, including emotional relief and a sense of purpose, create a strong sense of relief and satisfaction. As a result, the priority becomes maintaining the community rather than seeking truth. While in a mass formation, the beliefs and opinions of the individual are suppressed as they strive to fit in with the collective and avoid the fear of rejection. They can't fathom a world where the unanimous voice of their community could be wrong, causing the individual to lose their sense of self and pour their energy into the collective instead.

The power of mass formation lies in its ability to tap into our fundamental need for connection and belonging. By joining the collective, individuals feel a sense of solidarity and fulfillment of their civic duty. Refusal to participate can result in accusations of self-interest, as well as potential public shaming or ostracization/cancellation, and ultimately return members to earlier feelings of isolation. This creates a powerful force toward conformity where those who challenge or threaten the community are seen as enemies, perpetuating the longevity of the mass formation, and making it difficult to resist. As a result, mass formations can have strong staying power, often lasting much longer than one might anticipate.

You can find a perfect example of this described in the book *Atomic Awakening* by James Mahaffy[296]. Mahaffy details how because Hitler wanted to stay true to the narrative he was pushing, he promoted "Aryan physics" while the Jewish understanding and approach to physics was discouraged. However, not only was Aryan physics a classical and outdated approach to physics, but Jewish scientists had developed crucial concepts like relativity and quantum mechanics that Hitler was demanding be disregarded. In the end, "a country that prided itself on technical superiority and innovation stopped its forward motion at the most exciting and important point in history."

These days when controlling structures emerge, supposed experts with impressive titles often dominate social media to defend the reasoning. They may argue this new perspective is supported by data and demonstrated by graphs, which, regardless of the legitimacy of the data or its interpretation, is usually taken as fact. An illustrative example of such behaviour occurred during the COVID-19 pandemic. At first, globally recognized experts like Anthony Fauci claimed that COVID vaccines were 100% effective and capable of halting all transmission.[297] However, as time passed, the reality diverged from these early assertions. The effectiveness of the vaccines dwindled, and there was no discernible impact when it came to lowering transmission rates. This but one such example of individuals in positions of authority employing misleading data and experts to advance a particular agenda.

Since most people do not have a strong sense of what is a well-supported idea in scientific circles and what is fringe—*let alone evaluating or interpreting data*—seeing just one "expert" defending an opinion can give the impression that this *"factual"* narrative is widely accepted. People now question themselves rather than question others.

"The experts and professionals must know best."

"I must be misinformed on my own views."

"That expert wouldn't have said that if it weren't accurate, right?"

Even if you are well-versed in evaluating such claims, cognitive processing and verification demand significant time and energy. Hence, people tend to overly rely on experts and other authoritative figures. As a result, the general population often accepts even the most far-fetched narratives as true without question. Eventually, there exists a sizable number of people who embrace this narrative, and this shared belief bolsters itself in a positive feedback loop.

Furthermore, when monetary intervention makes it increasingly harder to get ahead, people have less time to think critically. In such a scenario, given our time constraints, we limit the number of sources from which we consume content. This minimizes our exposure to a diverse mix of information and opinions, impairing our ability to make informed decisions.

Ultimately, this can lead to the rapid spread of narratives, whether or not they are rooted in fact.

In these dark times, this is where change, which would under other circumstances never be accepted, becomes almost demanded by the populous. To stay true to the collective, the individual is now in a state where they are willing to sacrifice their sovereignty and values for the collective's perceived greater good and cohesion.

One such example of a population under totalitarian rule demanding a change in support of their leader that would sound absurd to outsiders is the "Great Leap Forward" campaign in Mao Zedong's China during the late 1950s.[298] The campaign involved:

- Collectivizing agriculture.
- Encouraging people to form communes.
- Promoting backyard steel furnaces for decentralized industrial production.

However, the campaign's implementation was flawed, leading to disastrous consequences. To meet the unrealistic steel production targets set by the government, the Chinese population, in their fervent support of Mao and the Communist Party, took the initiative to produce steel from scrap metal and household items to meet the ambitious quotas. People across the country, often with limited knowledge of metallurgy and steel production, dismantled household items such as pots, pans, and even farming tools, believing that their collective efforts would propel China to industrial greatness. Unfortunately, the makeshift furnaces produced mostly unusable low-quality steel, and the diversion of resources from agriculture contributed to a severe famine that resulted in millions of deaths.

When we invest our time, energy, and resources into something, we may become emotionally attached to it and fall into the trap of the sunk-cost fallacy.[299] This human tendency makes it challenging for us to abandon a course of action, even when it's clear that doing so would be more beneficial. This can further cement individuals in their trance with the collective, preventing them from making rational decisions that would ultimately benefit them, partially out of fear of admitting their earlier choices were not for the best. With this in mind, the more ridiculous and onerous the totalitarian requirements, surprisingly, the better they foster commitment through sacrifice and the more passionately a particular segment of the populace will accept them.

It's important to note that since mass formations thrive on fear and aggression, the population may recognize the harm they have suffered and revolt if these elements are not constantly present. As a totalitarian system solidifies its grip on power, the ruling elite has a vested interest in preventing the general populace from awakening to reality. This often results in those in power taking steps to control both the flow of information and money. The leaders then use these tools to continually stoke fear, including identifying new sources of fear and employing new strategies to eliminate them, putting the controlling structure into a vicious cycle of self-destruction.

During Stalin's rule, which lasted from the 1920s until his death in 1953, the government employed a system of terror and purges to maintain control.[300]

Stalin's regime relied on creating an atmosphere of constant fear and suspicion among the population. The Soviet government targeted various groups, including perceived political enemies, intellectuals, and members of different ethnic or religious communities, through widespread surveillance, arrests, show trials, and forced labour camps.

However, this system of fear and repression was not sustainable in the long run. The regime had to continuously find new enemies and threats to justify its control and maintain the population's loyalty. This led to a cycle of purges and crackdowns, where new scapegoats were identified, accused of treason or counter-revolutionary activities, and subjected to harsh punishments.

The relentless pursuit of sources of fear and the need to eliminate perceived threats ultimately undermined the credibility and stability of the totalitarian regime. As the population became disillusioned and exhausted by the constant cycle of fear, repression, and violence, the regime's grip on power began to weaken. Eventually, Stalin's regime collapsed after his death, highlighting the inherent instability of maintaining an oppressive structure based on fear. As Desmet points out, "When the [totalitarian] system is no longer able to link anxiety to an object, it loses its raison d'être."

Today, evaluating every choice we make and every piece of information we consume is impossible. If we did, we would never get anything done, but this leaves us susceptible to subtle psychological nudges that can alter our behaviour. Corporations have exploited this vulnerability for decades to maximize profits through advertisement and branding. However, don't think for a second that it is just corporations using such tactics. For example, the Nudge Unit, created by the British government in 2010, uses psychological manipulation and propaganda to influence behaviour and motivate individuals to do what is in the government's best interest.[301] With over 750 projects, 1,000 government workshops facilitated, and 20,000 civil servants trained in behavioural insights, this subsidiary of government is at the forefront of such behaviour.[302] It was the Nudge Unit that was behind the use of "grossly unethical" images during the pandemic, portraying acutely unwell individuals in intensive care units on billboards and television adverts. The British government's constant focus on Covid-19 deaths, without acknowledging mortality from other causes or the fact that around 1,600 people typically pass away each day in the UK under normal circumstances, was also a result of the Nudge Unit.[303] Both of these instances illustrate the Unit's apparent efforts to instill fear and submission in the population.

While most would agree that people should be free to make their own choices without undue influence from the state, those in positions of power are naturally incentivized to exert their influence to ensure the continuation of the system that empowered them. This step of control is crucial. For the ruling elite to continue their reign, they must silence alternate narratives or remove any opposition threatening to expose the truth. As a result, the suppression of truth and control over information and capital flows is vital.

And this is as true today as it was 400 years ago when Galileo angered the Church by speculating that the Earth might not be the centre of the universe.[304] If accurate, this would undermine the foundational tenets of the Church's doctrine and, subsequently, their authority. As a result, the Church forced Galileo to admit he was wrong and that the Earth did not revolve around the sun. He was then "found guilty of heresy and sentenced to house arrest, where he remained until he died in 1642."

As Galileo's experience shows, the most challenging part of being on the opposing side of the mass formation is that:

1. Due to your refusal to participate in the collective, you're seen as antisocial and lacking in solidarity and civic duty.
2. Your reasoning is seen as unjustified, as the general public gives little cognitive or emotional weight to critical reasoning.
3. You're seen as a menace who is threatening the status quo and therefore trying to expose the masses once more to the unfavourable conditions that existed previously (loneliness, meaninglessness...)

A system based on truth welcomes good faith scrutiny, while one founded on falsehood does not.

CONCLUSION

The most glaring issue of all that emerges from a misaligned monetary system is the potential for mass formations, leading to totalitarian structures.

When the five factors (misaligned or co-opted monetary system, widespread loneliness, meaninglessness, free-floating anxiety, aggression, and frustration) all exist in a society, individuals will surrender their beliefs, values, rights, and liberties to just about any convincing narrative that alleviates their suffering. This, in turn, leads to obedience and, subsequently, the emergence of oppressive government structures.

What gives these totalitarian structures power is that they exploit our inherent need for connection and a sense of community, creating a conformist force where those who defy the group are deemed as adversaries. However, these structures are not sustainable. To maintain control, leaders perpetuate fear by controlling the flow of money, information, and resources, causing a vicious cycle of self-destruction.

Creating an enemy conveniently allows us to absolve ourselves of responsibility, so it can be a tempting narrative to give in to. The problem with this approach is that it doesn't address the root cause of the issues. Instead of playing the blame game, let's ask the important question: Why are we facing the issues we are? We can only create meaningful and lasting change by taking responsibility for our actions and exploring the reasons behind our challenges.

Now that we have delved into the mechanisms of mass formation and its potential to give rise to totalitarian structures throughout history, it's time to turn our attention to the present. In the next chapter, we will embark on an examination of our current system, exploring whether the signs and indicators of emergent controlling structures exist.

SIDE NOTE: For years, I found myself asking: How can some individuals in positions of power perpetrate such heinous acts or inflict suffering upon others? I've come to believe that effective parenting plays a crucial role in mitigating controlling behaviours in individuals. As highlighted by Alice Miller in her book Drama of the Gifted Child and echoed by numerous others, those in positions of power, propagating controlling narratives, are often unconsciously reenacting their own childhood traumas.[305] They're striving to pass on the suffering they were unsupported with and could not navigate in their youth. By alleviating the stress induced by our monetary system, parents might find themselves better equipped to meet their children's emotional needs, thereby reducing the likelihood of unresolved trauma leading to authoritarian leaders.

CHAPTER 10

THE ILLUSION
OF FREEDOM

How Unsustainable Systems
Erode Our Rights & Freedoms

*"The ideal subject of totalitarianism is not the
convinced Nazi or the convinced Communist,
but people for whom the distinction between fact
and fiction (i.e., the reality of experience) and the
distinction between true and false (i.e., the standards
of thought) no longer exist." —Hannah Arendt*

....

When an unsustainable system is under immense pressure to maintain economic growth, those in positions of power need to respond with ever-greater measures to keep reality from emerging. As a result, rights, freedoms, and values get pushed to the wayside as the primary focus is to determine how to direct the nation's productive capacity toward prolonging the inevitable collapse.

In this context, totalitarian, controlling structures may be tempting or even necessary to maintain the illusion of security.

As these increasingly stringent structures scramble to prolong the inevitable collapse, they will take advantage of economic, national, and international events as a means to implement greater controls. Furthermore, anything to be perceived as obstructing the system's ability to grow is perceived as a threat and painted as the enemy.

- For Stalin, that enemy was the West and Capitalism, as they exposed the failures of communism.
- For Hitler, that enemy was the Jewish population, as they supposedly betrayed Germany, causing the loss of WWI.
- For Kim Jong Un of North Korea, the enemy is the United States,[306]
- For Christianity in the early 15th century, that enemy was the printing press, as it granted individuals the power to access and interpret the Bible on their own terms.
- And during the COVID-19 pandemic, that enemy was, and still is, anyone questioning the official narrative as they attempted to shine a light on failures in response to the pandemic.

As Adam Curtis succinctly sums it up in his documentary series, The Power of Nightmares, "In an age when all the grand ideas have lost credibility, fear of a phantom enemy is all the politicians have left to maintain their power."[307] In a state of fear, we often regress to a more primal mindset, driven primarily by our emotions. During such times, we find ourselves in need of guidance and support as we navigate the complexities of decision-making. It is precisely in these moments that these controlling structures can seize the opportunity to present themselves as a perceived source of direction and stability. The problem: Totalitarian and controlling structures rarely serve the interests of the people. Instead, they prioritize the sustainability of the system.

In saying that, it's important to note that the suppressive actions taken by these structures are often not deliberately oppressive. Rather, they are seen as necessary when motivated by fear. Those in positions of power may not even be aware that the system *is* unsustainable or collapsing. They may be simply responding to the symptoms of the problem without recognizing the root cause.

This prompts the question...

IS OUR CURRENT SYSTEM AT RISK OF MASS FORMATION?

Before we jump to conclusions and start labelling controlling structures, it's essential to revisit the five conditions that must exist for the formation of such structures to occur. By carefully examining these conditions, we can determine whether we are at risk of such formations or not.

Zero - Do we have a misaligned or co-opted monetary system?

Not to sound too much like a broken record, but I think we can confidently say yes.

While it may seem like our monetary system has not completely broken down, the truth is that as of late 2022, many countries worldwide were grappling with crippling inflation. Shockingly, 81 countries are experiencing double-digit inflation, which accounts for almost half of all reporting countries.[308]

As one specific example, over the past decade, Argentina has experienced an alarming increase in pesos in circulation, from 200 billion in 2012 to 3.234 trillion as of August 2022— a staggering 1,512% rise.[309] This surge in money supply has caused a significant decline in purchasing power, with $100 worth of pesos in 2012 only purchasing $3 worth of goods today, reflecting a 97% reduction in value.[310]

What's more, from July 2009, the tail end of the Great Financial Crisis, until February 2023, the US money supply has increased by 246%.[311] In other words, more than twice the amount of dollars have been printed in the last decade than in the history of the US dollar.

This dire situation raises serious concerns about the sustainability of our current monetary system and its ability to meet the needs of people around the world.

One - Is there a sense of loneliness?
In the so-called age of social media, ironically, we are more socially isolated than ever.[312] Both children and adults increasingly rely on their phones and other electronic devices for social interaction rather than engaging with people around them.

The US Surgeon General, Vivek Murthy, has even declared a "loneliness epidemic," with one in three people worldwide and three-quarters of all Americans feeling a sense of loneliness.[313,314] This problem is particularly prevalent among students aged 16-17 and has only worsened in recent years. The Programme for International Student Assessment (PISA) survey found that twice as many adolescents in 2018 reported experiencing elevated levels of school loneliness compared to 2012.[315]

This trend can be attributed to many factors, including the growing pressure on parents to prioritize their financial needs over spending time with their children. As a result, children may be increasingly looking to technology or their peers for connection.

In today's social media landscape, the platforms themselves often incentivize users to portray an idealized version of their lives, creating a virtual community where reality is masked. This constant exposure to curated profiles can instill a sense of inadequacy and pressure individuals to conform, disconnecting them from their authentic selves. As a result, imposter syndrome may take hold, leading people to believe they are the only ones pretending. This hinders genuine connections and, combined with increased reliance on peers, where to mitigate the fear of rejection, one may suppress one's true self, creates to a perfect breeding ground for loneliness.

If the general population is lonelier than before, let's now turn our attention to meaninglessness and see if the same trend is occurring.

Two - Do we face widespread meaninglessness?

Beyond social media's impact on loneliness, its influence extends to our mental well-being. The societal pressures to portray an idealized life, which can contribute to feelings of isolation, also foster discontentment when our own reality doesn't measure up to the perceived lives of our peers. Comparisons and unrealistic expectations can take a toll on our mental health, creating a sense of dissatisfaction and unease.

There is evidence that this is happening on a widespread level. A poll in the UK found that 89% of 16 to 29-year-olds feel their lives have no meaning or purpose.[316] Job satisfaction is another indicator of meaningfulness, and data from CivicScience, which has been tracking job satisfaction since 2015, reported its lowest recording to date in Q4 of 2021.[317]

Although it is tough to pinpoint the exact reasons why we are experiencing a rise in meaninglessness, a few factors stand out: First, our social media feeds are full of success stories and overnight millionaires. These stories often fail to expand on the difficulty and time these individuals put in to achieve their triumph. This gives us a false sense of reality, where it seems like everyone should be able to see the same success, and we feel like failures if our efforts don't see the same results.

Second, our society, driven by consumerism, places excessive value on material success. We find ourselves constantly seeking validation through the acquisition of goods, mistakenly believing that keeping up with our peers and conforming to societal expectations will bring us fulfillment. However, we fail to realize that true meaning, happiness, and satisfaction stem from within ourselves, not from external possessions. This misguided focus on materialism is evident in the statistics: between 2002 and 2021, while the population grew by 15%, personal consumption expenditure, adjusted for inflation, skyrocketed by over 50%.[318,319]

Lastly, we cannot overlook the significant challenges posed by the increasing cost of living, soaring asset prices, and growing wealth inequality. These factors make it exceedingly difficult to achieve financial stability and progress in life. As discussed in Chapter Four, the impact of these issues on our mental well-being is profound. When combined with the above points, they form the foundation for a pervasive sense of meaninglessness to take hold.

Three - Is there widespread anxiety?

Anxiety and unease have also become ever-more common in our society, with one in three individuals now suffering from anxiety, according to the 2022 US Census Bureau.[320]

Meanwhile, in the UK, a study found that between 1995 and 2014, the percentage of British children diagnosed with mental illness rose by 600%, and those aged 16 to 24 saw a staggering 1,000% increase over the same period.[321]

The relentless pressure to succeed and project an idealized life on social media, the pervasive lack of meaning and purpose in our daily lives, and the mounting financial pressures collectively contribute to a widespread sense of anxiety. Furthermore, countless individuals find themselves trapped in unfulfilling jobs purely to attain this elusive financial security. This leaves them toiling long hours to make ends meet, leaving little time and energy for relaxation and decompression after demanding workdays. The constant stress from a relentless pursuit of productivity makes it increasingly more difficult to engage in comforting activities such as socializing, immersing oneself in nature, practicing meditation, or cultivating other self-care habits that promote emotional well-being.

Four - Are we experiencing inflated aggression & frustration?
You don't have to spend much time on social media to realize that people are more polarized than ever. Although this is a hard statistic to quantify, one method is to look at societal trust, which, according to the US General Social Survey since 1972, has experienced a 46% decline.[322] The timing of this trend, coincidentally, lines up closely with the US's departure from the gold standard.

When approached with a topic which doesn't align with our values, now more than ever, people seem to shut down or respond with increased frustration. There no longer seems to be the ability for individuals to talk it out. Both sides believe they're right.

This polarization is most apparent in the US, where "77% of Americans said the country was now more divided than before the [COVID-19] outbreak."[323] As a result, political parties today are moving away from shared ideas or policy preferences and trying to align with their voters on moralized identities. Professor Cynthia Wang of Northwestern University goes as far as to say that "it's not just that people only trust or associate with their own side, it's that they're contemptuous of the other side, whom they see as 'other' and less moral— an existential threat. This rise in out-group hate is what we find so alarming."

This contempt in the face of polarization is what leads to aggression towards those with opposing views.

During a congressional election, a "landslide county" is a county where the winning candidate beats the losing candidate by 20 percentage points or more, indicating a strongly red or blue political leaning.[324] In the 1976 presidential election, only 27% of Americans lived in such landslide counties, with the remaining 73% residing in more politically balanced counties. However, by the 1992 election, the percentage of Americans living in a landslide county had increased from 27% to 38%, and this trend has continued to rise. In the most recent 2020 presidential election, a record 58% of Americans lived in a landslide county.

In a similar trend towards ideological bubbles, in the book, *Coddling of the American Mind*, the author sheds light on the concerning statistic that in 2017, 58% of college students in the US believed that it was important for their campus community to shield them from "intolerant and offensive" ideas, as opposed to being exposed to diverse perspectives.[325] This may seem like a non-issue, except that polarization has dangerous consequences as it can create a sense of individual superiority. When people start viewing those who disagree with them as less moral, they may feel justified in reacting aggressively or violently. This phenomenon might partly explain the alarming rise in homicides and assault charges in the US over the past decade, which the Centers for Disease Control (CDC) has reported to be a 57% and 79% increase, respectively.[326]

People are frustrated and angry! It seems to be increasingly difficult to engage in vitriol-free discourse. This can further be seen in the tripling of racial and threatening language on social media over the same period.[327] Instead of engaging in healthy and productive discussions, people are quick to resort to censoring or personally attacking one another.

If Professor Desmet's conditions for totalitarianism to emerge are accurate, then you could say, *"Houston, we have a problem."* Given that our global society meets most, if not all, of the conditions mentioned above, one could argue that controlling structures are likely to emerge.

And as we might expect under these conditions, Figures 10.1 and 10.2 from Freedom House's annual report on political rights and civil liberties demonstrate a gradual decline in democracy. Figure 10.1 underscores that we are currently at a critical juncture in history, where controlling structures are increasingly adept at co-opting or circumventing basic rights and freedoms, all under the guise of "serving the greater good." Furthermore, our monetary system enables those in power to favour those with similar interests, exacerbating our societal problems and undermining our civil liberties.

Figure 10.1

16 Years of Democratic Decline

Countries with aggregate score declines in the Freedom in the World report have outnumbered those with gains every year for the past 16 years

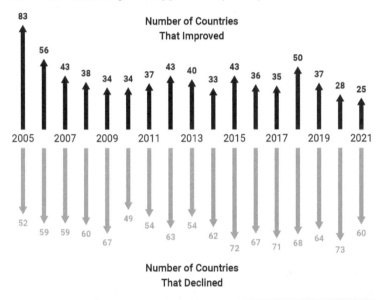

Source: Freedom House, Freedom in the World 2022 report

The first time I saw these charts, I was left speechless. Today, 80% of people live in "partly free" or "not free" countries. Even in so-called "free" countries, our freedoms are in jeopardy.

Figure 10.2

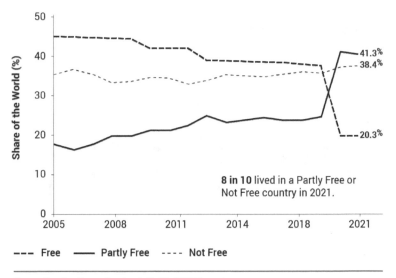

Living in a Less Free World

The share of the world's population living in Free environments has fallen as authoritarian practices proliferate.

Source: Freedom House, Freedom in the World 2022 report

We are the proverbial frog in boiling water, gradually losing our rights and freedoms without even realizing it. It's similar to how inflation can sneak up on us until we compare prices from the past to the present.

It is, therefore, crucial that we examine the narratives and events that are being used to justify changes that ultimately infringe on our freedom of expression.

> **FUN FACT:** *The idea that monetary interventionism leads to tyrannical governments is nothing new. It has a long history, dating back to the fourteenth century and the works of Nicolas Oresme.*[328]

THE RISE OF TOTALITARIANISM & THE ILLUSION OF FREEDOM

Most of us raised in the developed world are taught that we live in an environment that supports free speech and civil rights. That may appear to hold true, until our speech and rights are seen as a threat, at which point they can quickly vanish.

This begs the question: If our rights can be removed when we need them most, did they truly exist in the first place? Similarly, if we are prevented from spending our money as we wish, can we really consider it our money?

What makes modern-day totalitarianism difficult to identify is that, first, it is not always led by dictator-like figures in the vein of Stalin or Hitler but by everyday bureaucrats, Silicon Valley entrepreneurs, and unelected organizations. These individuals nonetheless use narratives that tug at our heartstrings to push for changes that, under alternate circumstances, we would not accept.

Second, contemporary totalitarianism is not limited to explicit rule of law enforced through corporal punishment, as seen in places like North Korea or Afghanistan. It can also manifest in more nuanced forms of coercion disguised as the pursuit of the "greater good" as defined by the ruling leadership.

Lastly, the narratives put forth by those in power are often built upon some kernel of truth in addition to meeting the needs of people's free-floating anxiety. Given these three points, it can be hard to recognize these entities and how they erode our freedoms.

Crackdowns on freedom of expression, whether of action, speech, or spending, reveal that these rights are not "inalienable" as the United States' Declaration of Independence purported. Instead, we are allowed only the illusion of free speech and basic human rights— as long as they do not pose a threat to those in power.

Although countless noteworthy events have illustrated the erosion of human rights, including the Federal Reserve Act and the Nixon Shock discussed in earlier chapters, we'll now turn our attention to a few of the more prominent ones.

THE WAR ON DRUGS

The government-led war on drugs, which began in the 1970s, was purportedly aimed at stopping illegal drug use, distribution, and trade by increasing prison sentences for drug dealers and users. However, what started as an initiative to reduce drug abuse quickly turned into a massive power grab by the police state, allowing them to infringe on civil liberties.

In 2021, the Working Group on Arbitrary Detention conducted a study that found the "war on drugs" led to mass incarceration due to racial profiling, excessive pretrial detention, disproportionate sentencing, and the criminalization of drug users, including pregnant women in some countries.[329] Moreover, the study uncovered widespread human rights abuses, such as illegal detention, treating children and adolescents as "adults," torturing and mistreating them, denying them the right to a fair trial, extrajudicial killings, and the abusive application of the death penalty. Far from successfully treating and reducing the public health issue of addiction, it had a myriad of societal ramifications that continue to harm people worldwide.

Despite comprising only 4% of the world's population, the US accounted for 22% of the world's prison folk in 2016.[330] In the words of writer German Lopez, "the US is out of line not only with its developed peers but also with authoritarian nations like Cuba, Russia, and China."

In the 40 years post the War on Drugs—*and coincidently after the departure from the gold standard*—the US Prison population grew by nearly 700%. In stark contrast, over the 40 years leading up to the War on Drugs, the prison population only grew by 48%.

This alarming expansion of the US prison system shouldn't go unnoticed.

With 8% of the US prison system now privatized and numerous public prison services outsourced to private corporations, the prison system has transformed into big business.[331] Given that the average annual cost per prisoner is $45,771, the prison system most definitely helps boost GDP.[332] As discussed in Chapter Three, our relentless pursuit of economic growth and the need to service mounting debt has led to the monetization of virtually everything around us. One might easily question whether our pursuit of monetary growth in domains where monetary exchange was previously absent or minimal has permeated the prison system.

Sometimes, it can be challenging to grasp the tangible effects of the war on drugs and how it directly impacts our lives, so let me paint a picture. Imagine you want to buy something online, but suddenly, you hit a roadblock— your bank account gets flagged and frozen, and you're unable to complete the transaction. Why does this happen? It's because of the implementation of Anti-Money Laundering (AML) regulations, which have gradually been introduced to monitor all financial transactions as a consequence of the war on drugs.

Additionally, to counter money laundering, Congress enacted the Bank Secrecy Act in 1970. This legislation required banks to submit reports to the government when their customers engaged in transactions exceeding $10,000. At that time, this amount held far greater significance, surpassing the median annual income. Consequently, reporting occurred relatively infrequently. However, this amount has never been adjusted for inflation. Over the past five decades, this failure to account for inflation has effectively reduced the reporting threshold, resulting in an ongoing expansion of government surveillance without the need for further legislative action.[333]

In essence, the war on drugs has led to an erosion of human rights and a proliferation of regulations and surveillance that affect our daily existence. Not only have we experienced the rise of a police state, but now we must navigate through a sea of regulations impacting everyone, from families to financial institutions.

Even the UN has called for an end to the war on drugs.[334] They claim it "undermines health and social wellbeing and wastes public resources while failing to eradicate the demand for illegal drugs and the illegal drug market. Worse, this 'war' has [been] ... to the detriment of national development. Such policies have far-reaching negative implications for the widest range of human rights."

THE WAR ON TERRORISM

Launched after the tragic events of September 11, 2001, the War on Terrorism was aimed at preventing the financing of terrorist organizations around the world.[335] However, the government's response to the threat of terrorism has long had many people questioning its benefit due to its immense economic cost and significant impact on our civil liberties.[336]

While few among us disagree that terrorism should be stopped, the War on Terrorism has not been the answer. This campaign led to the signing of the US Patriot Act, amplifying the surveillance state.[337] This act gave the US Intelligence Community unprecedented funding on an ongoing basis to expand its information-gathering capabilities.[338]

The American Intelligence Community operates largely outside public scrutiny and seemingly without accountability. As former government "special activities" contract pilot Philip Marshall has revealed, they control every armed federal force, including the FBI, CIA, DHS, TSA, DEA, and the Department of Defense.[339] They have nearly one million people on their payroll, including 832,000 employees with Top Secret clearances. And they continue to use the threat of terrorism to expand their reach and influence. As of 2012, they were in the midst of using $3.5 billion of taxpayer's money to build a new headquarters near Washington, which monitors every county sheriff and city police office. But despite wielding immense power and having access to substantial resources, the overwhelming majority of taxpayers remain unaware of the extent to which these entities have infiltrated and influenced every facet of the economy.

Since 9/11, the Intelligence Community has lost a staggering $21 trillion from the Treasury through "phony" accounting "designed to obfuscate ... propelling US military spending higher year after year."[340] To put that number in perspective, US healthcare spending for 2021 was $4.3 trillion.[341]

They have also implemented various surveillance programs under the guise of "preventing terrorism." Among these programs were the NSA and FBI's collection of metadata on millions of Americans, which Edward Snowden exposed to the public in 2013.[342] Snowden revealed that the NSA and its UK counterpart had direct access to the servers of major tech companies like Apple, Microsoft, Facebook, and Google. The exposure of these programs sparked public outrage and raised serious concerns about privacy and civil liberties. Snowden's whistleblowing ultimately led to him being charged with espionage, highlighting the government's displeasure with the public exposure of their surveillance activities.

Another example of this government surveillance can be seen in the Twitter files mentioned in Chapter Seven, which shows that the FBI paid Twitter millions in taxpayer dollars to monitor and ban accounts primarily associated with conservative voices.

Lastly, in the wake of the War on Terrorism, we've seen a significant increase in digital monitoring and a troubling erosion of financial privacy. Pervasive Know Your Customer (KYC) regulations now impact all of us and have made it almost impossible to maintain privacy, let alone control our personal financial information. For instance, you are probably familiar with the hurdles associated with opening a bank account, applying for a loan, or engaging in certain financial transactions? To comply with KYC requirements, you must provide detailed personal information and documentation, including identification documents, proof of address, and sometimes even the source of your funds. The government knows everything about us and our spending habits.

The economic cost, in combination with the consequences and the subsequent erosion of civil liberties that emerged from the War on Terrorism, should not go unnoticed.

THE GREAT FINANCIAL CRISIS (GFC)

As we have discussed at length, one of the more significant economic events in recent history has been the 2008 Great Financial Crisis.

During the GFC, lax monetary policy in the preceding years led to the proliferation of speculative investment vehicles and derivatives, which caused the US housing market to shift from boom to bust rapidly, with widespread financial ramifications across the country.

Subsequently, the government stepped in to "stabilize" the financial markets and provide consumer protections to assist the people. However, this intervention triggered a whole host of additional monetary interventions, which still impact us today. As previously stated, this major economic breakdown ultimately resulted in the evisceration of $65 trillion of wealth, plus $13 trillion in taxpayer-funded bailouts.

At the end of the day, this was not only the largest transfer of wealth from taxpayers to the government and subsidized private corporations, but it also gave the government a perfect excuse to extend its regulatory reach. Following 2008, major regulatory creep ensued. In one of the boldest moves toward greater government power over the financial sector, in 2010, President Obama signed the Dodd-Frank Act.[343] This act shifted government regulation in several ways, including:

1. The government consolidated regulatory agencies, centralizing controls in the hands of a few.
2. It introduced extensive regulations and compliance requirements that disproportionately affect smaller financial institutions, such as community banks and credit unions, and deter new entrants from entering the financial sector, i.e., "instead of 100 new community banks a year, we get three, and sometimes one."[344] These controls have been shown to reduce competition and consolidate power in the hands of a few dominant players.
3. Under Dodd-Frank, the United States established itself as a leader in financial regulation and encouraged other countries to adopt similar regulatory reforms. By emphasizing the importance of coordinating regulations and sharing information with international counterparts to address the interconnectedness of the global financial system, the Act extended the US government's reach globally under "increasing international standards and cooperation."

Moreover, Dodd-Frank reinforced bail-in laws, which grant banks significant authority to cancel debts owed or freeze customer funds if they face insolvency. I'm guessing that if it were up to the general public, whose money bailed out the global economy, those bailout funds would not have gone to the big banks and bonuses of upper management.

This leads us to another recent event that hits home for most of us.

THE PANDEMIC

As we delve into this topic, I acknowledge that it can be a controversial and sensitive issue for many. That said, I encourage you to approach it with an open mind and consider the potential impact on our freedoms and rights, irrespective of personal beliefs.

The COVID-19 pandemic, as most people are aware, is an ongoing battle against the coronavirus disease. Similarly to the narratives and events already covered, the world encountered a threat, and those in power responded.

What began as a few harmless measures to reduce the spread of covid eventually resulted in the digital ID movement, with countless countries issuing health passports, a.k.a vaccine passports. In the words of the government of Canada, the policies around these documents "required [people] ... to disclose personal health information ... in exchange for goods, services, and/or access to certain premises or locations."[345,346] These health passports gave governments immense power, as they could restrict access to public facilities and travel for individuals who did not meet certain criteria.

However, it didn't end there. At least 83 governments worldwide used the pandemic as a pretext to infringe upon the fundamental rights of free speech and peaceful assembly.[347] Governments like the US have monitored online speech in countless countries, with dissident voices facing censorship and punishment.[348] For example, according to research conducted by The Federalist, it has come to light that tax dollars are being utilized to finance the advancement of artificial intelligence (AI) and machine learning (ML) to enable the government to monitor and identify what they deem as "problematic" speech.[349] Then, in conjunction with major tech companies, corporate entities, and media outlets, the government can suppress this speech under the pretext of countering "misinformation" and "disinformation."

As a result, social media posts deemed as "misinformation" have been and are being swiftly removed, and people's profiles are being deleted... even after FaceBook admitted in court that fact-checks are simply opinions.[350,351,352] It even went so far as PayPal proposing a $2,500 fine for "spreading misinformation."[353] Unsurprisingly, that was quickly met with opposition.

In some Western nations, simply participating in a protest could lead to dire consequences such as arrest or having bank accounts frozen.[354] A clear example of this was during the peaceful Freedom Convoy protest in Ottawa, Canada, in 2021. If you were seen donating money to the truckers in support of their right to cross the Canadian/US border unvaccinated against COVID-19, your bank account could be frozen.[355]

However, the most egregious violation was that of the Nuremberg Code, a set of ethical research principles established after the horrifying acts committed against innocent civilians. The Code was devised to protect individuals' rights through informed consent and bodily autonomy.[356] Despite the lack of long-term data on experimental vaccines, individuals worldwide were and still are being pressured to accept immunization or face job loss. It is concerning that those in power today have felt it necessary to override this ethical research code, which was put in place to prevent crimes against humanity in the wake of the Nazi regime's actions during World War II.

We're now at the point where the US government is currently pushing a bill that would impose severe penalties for utilizing a virtual private network (VPN) to access prohibited applications or information.[357] If caught, individuals could potentially face a "minimum 20-year sentence plus a $250,000 fine." And Australia's recently proposed legislation looks to establish a ministry of truth.[358] Under this legislation, the Australian Communications & Media Authority would assume the role of the "arbiter of truth" with the power to censor any content on social media that contradicts the official government narrative.

This blatant disregard for our civil liberties and right to free speech should raise significant concerns for everyone.

CLIMATE CHANGE

Given how prominent the subject has been in media over the last couple of decades, most people are aware by now that climate change is the long-term shift in temperatures and weather patterns. You are getting no argument from me about whether we are experiencing climate change. The climate has been changing since the dawn of time— whether or not climate science is settled remains a separate topic. But we must ask ourselves, does climate change give those in positions of power the right to infringe on our rights and civil liberties?

Just like the examples above, climate change is now driving a new era of monetary monitoring and regulation. In Western countries, credit cards incorporating carbon tracking capabilities have emerged, allowing for spending restrictions if a predetermined carbon footprint limit is exceeded.[359] We are also seeing the rise of the Environmental, Social, and Governance (ESG) movement and agendas such as Net Zero (cutting greenhouse gas emissions to zero by 2050)[360] on corporate and nation-state levels. These movements are supposed to help steer individuals, countries and companies toward socially responsible behaviour. However, they are rapidly transforming into tools for enforcing compliance and allocating capital based on arbitrary standards.[361]

For example, in an effort to achieve capricious emissions targets, the Scottish government is considering measures that could restrict homeowners from selling their properties unless they switch from gas boilers to heat pumps.[362] These heat pumps currently cost, on average, four times that of traditional gas boilers and are many times not even fully compatible with older houses lacking modern insulation, which constitutes a significant portion of residences.[363] The projected cost of converting all homes amounts to a substantial £33 billion. To provide some context, this figure represents approximately 20% of Scotland's GDP, which stood at £168 billion in 2021.[364] To further illustrate the scale, Scotland's education expenditure for the same year amounted to just £6 billion.[365,366] Furthermore, starting April 2024, gas boilers will be prohibited in new homes. Essentially, amidst the uncertainties of current scientific understanding, the government is advancing an environmental agenda, favouring select industries and imposing needless financial burdens on homeowners.

Moreover, certain corporations and Western nations, driven by the desire to present an appealing facade to satisfy their voter base and counterparts, have resorted to naively outsourcing their food and energy production to foreign countries in order to meet arbitrary ESG goals. Rather than prioritizing domestic production, these entities opt to create an illusion of being a more environmentally friendly nation by attributing emissions from their energy and food production to countries that are not actively working towards meeting ESG guidelines. This approach undermines the true intent of ESG, as it neglects the core principles of sustainability and responsible resource management, instead favouring optics and short-term gains.

On the food front, three notable instances include Sri Lanka, Ireland and the second-largest global food exporter, the Netherlands.

Sri Lanka

Sri Lanka has relied on foreign fertilizers and pesticides in their farming practices for many decades. However, to meet ESG standards, the Sri Lankan government decided to push an organic farming action plan.[367] While this initiative may seem promising, one of the first action steps was a ban on fertilizers and pesticides, which around 90% of farmers depend on. As a result, crop yields have plummeted, and prices have soared. In 2021 alone, the cost of food rose by 33%, placing a significant burden on consumers. Meanwhile, 85% of farmers expected reductions in their harvest, with over half fearing declines of up to 40%.

Ireland

The Irish government has set a target to reduce farming emissions by 25% by 2030. Recent media reports have indicated that one potential measure being contemplated involves decreasing the national dairy herd by 10%, resulting in the culling of approximately 65,000 cows per year for a duration of three years.[368] The estimated cost of implementing this plan is $217 million (£170 million) annually.

Netherlands

To align with the emissions reduction targets set by the European Union, the Dutch government has formulated plans to purchase and close approximately 3,000 productive farms, which account for a staggering 25% of all farms in the country. [369,370] This initiative, scheduled to commence in 2022, introduces the possibility of forced buyouts for farmers who do not willingly sell their farms. Not only does this amplify their dependence on foreign food imports, leading to increased emissions, but it also results in significant job losses and disruption to the global food chain.

And here are two cases of ESG taking its toll on European energy.

Germany

In 2011, Germany decided to close down all its nuclear power plants by 2022, aiming to move away from nuclear energy and towards more renewable sources.[371] However, in doing so, they faced an increased reliance on natural gas, which at times made up 37% of their energy mix.[372] Consequently, Germany became more dependent on Russian natural gas, with 55% of its gas supply coming from Russia.[373]

Due to escalating tensions over the war in Ukraine, Russia reduced natural gas supplies through the Nord Stream 1 pipeline to only 20% of capacity, which serves as Germany's primary source of natural gas.[374] This reduction resulted in a destabilization of Germany's energy grid. Ironically, this "green" shift away from nuclear power led to Germany's reliance on less sustainable imported fossil fuels, which led to energy grid instability and concerns about long-term energy security.

Europe

European countries are shifting away from traditional energy sources and turning to biomass (wood energy) to meet their commitments under the Paris climate agreement. Every year, millions of tons of wood are extracted from US forests and transported across the Atlantic to be burned in power plants in countries such as the UK and the Netherlands, all in the name of climate change.[375] As a result, biomass has grown to account for over 60% of Europe's renewable energy in 2022, up from 40% in 2014.[376] This is because, in 2009, the EU pledged to achieve 20% renewable energy by 2020, and biomass was included on the list of renewable sources.

As discussed in Chapter One, Goodhart's law warns that "when a measure becomes a target, it ceases to be a good measure." In this case, focusing on meeting arbitrary targets has led to environmental damage in other, potentially more harmful ways. Scientists estimate that the world would need to double its commercial logging to generate a measly 3% increase in global energy demand using wood. This would have serious ecological consequences. By simply targeting "renewable energy" use rather than thinking holistically about environmental health, these countries have lost sight of the greater goal.

This misguided belief that the path to prosperity is through outsourcing energy, production and manufacturing to other nations and that ESG, intervention and financialization are the way forward, comes at a cost. As the consequences of these tactics emerge over time, corporations and nations will be forced to realize that true value does not arise through virtue signalling or intervention but through value creation. Which, in our present-day system, is in short supply. No matter how much governments intervene or central banks print money, they cannot create value, such as energy, food, and commodities, out of thin air. But that doesn't stop them from trying.

As governments increasingly restrict traditional means of food and energy production and rely on monetary intervention to direct change, we must consider the fundamental laws of supply and demand: When demand outstrips supply, prices inevitably increase until equilibrium is reached. So, if we don't change course, there's only one direction for prices to go: up! And suppose we cannot keep the bigger picture in mind. In that case, we'll face catastrophic environmental destruction as we transition toward alternate, less effective, but "socially acceptable" means to achieve the same output.

With all this in mind, we must question ESG and plans such as Net Zero. Removing fossil fuels that currently power more than 80% of the world's energy supply within a span of less than 30 years is not only unworkable but also catastrophic for the majority of the global population, primarily developing countries.[377,378] Moreover, while minimizing human-caused environmental degradation is critical, it is important to distinguish this from climate change. The scientific understanding of climate change is far less settled than mainstream media portrays.[379] The causal relationship between temperature and CO2 levels remains a topic of ongoing debate. Therefore, it is crucial to approach this situation with objectivity and rationality rather than succumbing to fear-mongering and heavy-handed tactics.

Looking back at the history of climate predictions, our track record is not strong. In 1971, climate scientists, such as Dr. Murray Mitchell of the National Oceanic and Atmospheric Administration, predicted an impending ice age by 2000.[380] And in 1989, a senior UN environmental official warned that "entire nations could be wiped off the face of the Earth by rising sea levels if the global warming trend is not reversed by the year 2000."[381] These are merely two examples among numerous predictions that never came to fruition. Nevertheless, we must acknowledge these past inconsistencies and exercise caution in our approach.

CONCLUSION

Totalitarian regimes like Nazism and Stalinism were characterized by their constant reorganization, with their power lying in their ability to adapt and change. This dynamic nature is a defining feature of totalitarianism, as new threats and challenges require new responses, leading to a constant stream of new regulations, directives, and decrees.

However, in a world where central banking reigns supreme, it is not only dictators and elected officials we need to be cautious of but those who govern our central banks and monetary systems. These individuals possess the authority to employ monetary policy that debases our currencies, granting them access to virtually unlimited capital. As a result, they have the power to shape events and narratives, fostering conditions that persuade individuals to compromise their beliefs, values, and freedoms in the name of a perceived greater good. Without this sacrifice, these systems cannot continue to operate as they are.

Each of the events discussed in this chapter increased the control of those in power, whether through the flow of information (limiting our emotional expression) or the flow of money (limiting our monetary expression). While the government may not have directly caused the crises that led to its expansion of power, it arguably took advantage of these situations. As Winston Churchill famously advised: "Never let a good crisis go to waste."

I want to clarify that I am not discrediting the abovementioned events, as many are indeed based on significant truths. However, we must question whether those in positions of authority simply responded to the circumstances they faced or exploited their power to impose more extensive controls and advance their personal interests.

The power of these anxiety-directing narratives lies in their universality. Each one has the potential to impact every person, making them relatable and applicable to all:

- Climate change affects us all,
- Covid can strike anytime,
- Terrorism threatens everyone,
- And drug use touches the lives of many.

This universality makes these narratives highly effective at instilling fear on a grand scale, which those in power can exploit to mobilize the population toward change. They can use this fear to herd the masses into a conformist force that can then be leveraged to create unconscionable change that impacts our ability to express ourselves authentically emotionally and monetarily. And every new event gives leaders another reason to slowly encroach and infringe on our rights and freedoms.

At what point will people stop and say, enough is enough?

We are now witnessing a world where regulation, capital controls, and censorship are becoming expected, where it is normal for your emails, online banking, and web hosting to be monitored.[382] The recent failures of centralized corporations like the cryptocurrency exchange FTX have prompted US senators to propose even more regulatory measures.[383,384] These new bills would make it incredibly difficult for US citizens to acquire sovereign assets, further limiting capital flows and keeping people tethered to the current monetary system.

What's even more alarming is that expressing certain views, such as protesting against government overreach or sharing information deemed "disinformation" on social media, is increasingly being labelled as an act of domestic terrorism, leading to further restrictions on free speech and civil liberties.[385,386]

The current state of affairs should ring alarm bells for anyone who values their civil liberties. Although one may argue that the Western world is not under totalitarian rule, it's important to highlight that totalitarian regimes come in many shades, from notorious Nazi Germany, Soviet Union, and communist China to more subtle forms of oppression we're experiencing today. We, therefore, should not ignore the many aspects of society that demonstrate controlling tendencies.

For those who may be skeptical, it's important to acknowledge that while these infringements may not currently be debilitating, these policies and practices add up over time, and normalizing them could be dangerous. By observing the world around us, it is evident that many signs of control percolate through society:

- Surveillance is now the norm, not just in CCTV but on all digital devices,
- Increased censorship through the filtering of misinformation, disinformation, and the silencing of opposing views is the new normal,
- Regulatory hurdles inhibiting capital allocation,
- World leaders ruling by force rather than basic democratic principles,[387]
- Regulatory creep leading to the monitoring of all financial transactions (i.e., KYC and AML practices),

- Government agencies who are meant to be there to protect us are in intruding on our private lives,
- Or monetary and fiscal intervention alongside financial repression, decimating our purchasing power.

These regulations, capital controls, and infringements impede our capacity to express ourselves freely, ultimately distorting capital flows and our ability to reach well-considered conclusions.

With the debt burden growing ever larger, we are at a tipping point where oppressive structures will increasingly become commonplace if we do not defend freedom for all people. This carries the potential for us to lose touch with individuality— the core of being human. As our rights and freedoms gradually erode, our ability to freely express ourselves diminishes, ultimately making us mere appendages of the state, indistinguishable from one another.

To wrap things up, with the awareness of some of the primary narratives that have infringed on our human rights and civil liberties, I feel it is important to mention that I am not in a position to say what is right or wrong. That said, I also believe that no one should have the sole authority to claim right from wrong or label certain speech as either misinformation or fact. Such power only limits us in accessing and disseminating information, impeding our ability to make informed decisions based on a diverse range of perspectives and viewpoints.

We should be mindful of restricting capital flows, free speech, and access to information based on present-day ideologies and beliefs. Case in point, classifying dissent as "misinformation" during the pandemic has only hindered our ability to adapt to changing circumstances. Had we known that vaccines do not halt the spread of COVID-19, masks do not prevent transmission, and natural immunity offers great protection, our approach to the pandemic might have been different.[388,389,390]

Instead of limiting monetary and emotional expression, we should strive to reduce friction by allowing capital and information to flow freely. Only then can we more effectively decipher the world around us.

Now that we have a glimpse of how controlling structures are slowly infiltrating our daily lives, it's time to take a step back and observe these structures on a nation-state level. As we zoom out, notice how they impact entire countries, particularly those unable to fend for themselves.

CHAPTER 11

BEHIND CLOSED DOORS

How Unelected Organizations Govern Global Finance

"In the long run, ... paper money ... must either collapse in hyperinflation or force the government to adopt a policy of increasing control, and eventually total control, over all economic resources. Both scenarios entail economic disruptions on a scale that we can barely imagine today." —
Jörg Guido Hülsmann, The Ethics of Money Production

....

As economic events increasingly ravage the world, central banks are lavishing in the limelight.[391] However, this isn't without cost. As we will explore, with the oversight and control of central banks growing by the year, there is a corresponding rise in the influence and capital flows directed towards unelected institutions. Institutions that operate behind closed doors and wield incomprehensible authority.

Under the pursuit of unsustainable, endless economic growth, immense power is placed in the hands of these soon-to-be-discussed institutions. All in an attempt to maintain the status quo of continued expansion regardless of the limiting factors of reality.

In the previous chapter, we explored how this power dynamic has led to those in the position of power slowly infringing upon the rights and freedoms of its populace. However, this infringement extends far beyond the borders of any single country, with smaller nations often finding themselves subject to the will of larger, more powerful ones.

In this chapter, we will examine three such examples where our monetary systems have enabled not only the emergence of controlling structures on the personal level of citizens but also on a nation-state level. To this end, we will investigate:

1. The International Monetary Fund and the World Bank,
2. The relationship between the French Treasury and the Central African Franc (CFA),
3. The Bank of International Settlements.

THE WORLD BANK & THE INTERNATIONAL MONETARY FUND (IMF)

In 1944, at the tail end of WWII, the World Bank and the International Monetary Fund were established by 44 founding member countries to create a framework for international economic cooperation and to reduce poverty worldwide.

On the surface, these appear to be noble causes with the potential to bring immense benefits. However, the reality is far from what was promised. In his thought-provoking article, "Structural Adjustment," Alex Gladstein, Chief Strategy Officer at the Human Rights Foundation, sheds light on how the IMF oppressed emerging nations and channelled their resources to richer ones.[392]

Although the IMF and World Bank purport to "foster sustainable economic growth, promote higher standards of living, and reduce poverty," rather than supporting the local populations they claim to help, the infrastructure funded by these entities often serves to facilitate wealth and resource extraction.[393] As a result, the well-being of local habitats and communities is often ignored in favour of corporate interests.

As we will explore, when the IMF steps in to aid underprivileged nations, it doesn't seem to assist the nation in long-term recovery but rather prevents them from going bankrupt with a cash infusion in the form of loans. This ensures that the country remains indefinitely in debt to the IMF, perpetuating the cycle of poverty and leaving it vulnerable to the organization's influence.

Without the IMF's intervention, these nations would face the painful but necessary consequences of their government's actions, bankruptcy. Which, in turn, could lead to the removal of corrupt leaders and the emergence of new politicians with values aligned with the needs of their people. This turmoil is destabilizing but necessary to create change and alter course.

With this in mind, let's explore two frequent IMF and World Bank intervention outcomes.

Decimation of Resiliency

When supporting a struggling nation, these organizations typically provide financial assistance. This sounds harmless, except these support packages often come with a stringent set of conditions to which the recipient must agree to qualify for aid.

For instance, the loans provided by the IMF and World Bank may come with a set of instructions that encourage the borrowing nation to focus on exporting raw materials, such as "oil, minerals, coffee, cocoa, palm oil, tea, rubber, cotton, etc." Then they are "pushed to import finished goods, foodstuffs and the ingredients for modern agriculture like fertilizer, pesticides, tractors and irrigation machinery."
This strategy serves three purposes:

1. It channels cheap resources to Western nations, supporting their economic growth and consumption

habits by enabling the manufacturing of goods at prices that would otherwise be unachievable.

2. It increases the nation-state's reliance on the IMF and exporting countries. By narrowing its focal point of production to a few key raw materials, the local community no longer produces the goods and services necessary for self-sustainability. Instead, they must look to other exporting countries to import the goods they no longer produce.

3. Western corporations' benefit by obtaining cheap raw materials and selling finished goods back to these nation-states, which can no longer produce many of their necessities.

If these countries grew their own food and created finished products, they would not require foreign aid. In a state of sustainable independence, "poor countries wouldn't be buying billions of dollars of food per year from rich countries, whose economies would shrink as a result." *So rather than guiding struggling countries to sufficient production to meet their own needs, they are directed toward ongoing dependency.*

These debt relief packages also often require the recipient nation to sell off valuable assets, including public businesses, vast swaths of lands, and national resources. These assets are then auctioned off to international corporations. The IMF further negotiates with these nations to provide legal protection and exemption from local taxes and laws for the winning corporations. In this way, the countries receive a short-term windfall to stave off bankruptcy but lose a source of ongoing wealth or tax income.

Ultimately, these aid packages perpetuate the recipient's debt reliance and further contribute to the loss of sovereignty as these nations become reliant on the IMF and the World Bank.

Transfer of Wealth

In addition to the unfavourable trade terms, these loans inherently transfer wealth away from the countries they're supposedly helping. As is standard of most loans, borrowers are generally required to pay back more than the principal amount borrowed in the form of interest payments. Since nations in need of support are made to pay interest on all financial aid borrowed, the repayment of this loan is effectively a continual extraction of capital back to the West.

The period between the collapse of the gold standard and the onset of the Great Financial Crisis, spanning from 1970 to 2007, saw developing nations pay a staggering $7.15 trillion in debt service payments to wealthy nations.[394] Moreover, if you total the flow of capital from 1960 to 2017, $62 trillion was extracted from the developing world.[395] To put that in perspective, the UK has a GDP of just over $3 trillion. Twenty times the size of the UK moved from the developing to the developed countries. By comparison, in 2012 alone, $1.3 trillion flowed into developing countries via income, aid and investment. That same year, $3.3 trillion flowed out. A net loss of $2 trillion. And in anthropologist Jason Hickel's article "Aid in Reverse," he reveals that since the '80s, "for every $1 of aid that developing countries receive, they lose $24 in net outflows."[396]

The IMF and World Bank were created with the goal of aiding impoverished nations to achieve self-sufficiency and resilience while also addressing their financial constraints. However, as Gladstein points out, the evidence suggests the opposite has occurred.

This is where totalitarianism doesn't just fall on the individual. Nation-states, whether by fault of their own or not, end up giving up their rights, freedoms, political power, and natural resources, all for the future glimmer of prosperity the IMF pushes.

To understand the scale of what we are talking about, we can look at a few examples of the IMF and World Bank intervention during the 70s and 80s.

Peru underwent IMF structural adjustment between 1977 and 1985; as a result, Peruvians' average per capita income plummeted by 20%, while the rate of inflation shot up from 30% to 160%.[397]

Since 1982, Ghana's currency has suffered a cumulative devaluation of 38,000% under pressure from the IMF, all while the IMF also encouraged the extraction of the country's natural resources. Shockingly, out of the $5.2 billion worth of gold extracted from Ghana between 1990 and 2002, the government received a mere $87.3 million, with foreign investors pocketing 98.4% of the earnings.[398]

The Philippines underwent IMF structural reforms in 1984 and 1985. Within a year, real incomes declined by 46%, which meant the Gross National Product (GNP) per capita fell to the same level as in 1975.[399]

After ten rounds of structural adjustment, the number of malnourished Brazilians increased from "27 million (one-third of the population) in 1961 to 86 million (two-thirds of the population) in 1985."[400]

From 1975 to 1984, Bolivia followed the IMF's directives, and as a result, the average person had to work five times more to purchase the same 1,000 calories of food than they would have had to a decade earlier.[401]

And lastly, in the 1980s, Mexico implemented structural adjustment programs under the guidance of the IMF, which resulted in a decline of over 75% in real wages for Mexican workers. Meanwhile, the government was paying out $27 million per day in interest to its creditors.[402]

The examples mentioned here are just a few among many others, highlighting the IMF's and World Bank's not-so-rosy structural reform and aid packages for developing nations.

It's also important to note that in addition to the IMF, the Chinese operate along similar lines with their "Belt and Road" initiative[403], which includes encouraging raw material exports, importing finished goods, and gaining control over national assets. One study has found that 35% of Chinese Belt and Road Initiative projects were embroiled in scandals involving corruption, environmental problems, or labour violations.[404]

While these countries' results appear damning, it is fair to ask, "are these examples cherry-picked?" Gladstein's rebuttal to this query is that "on average, every year from 1980 to 1985, there were 47 countries in the Third World pursuing IMF-sponsored structural adjustment programs, and 21 developing countries pursuing structural or sector adjustment loans from the World Bank."[405] These countries were predominantly in Latin America and Africa, and meanwhile "during this same period, 75% of all countries in Latin America and Africa experienced declines in per capita income and child welfare." This suggests that the regions looking to these organizations to improve their conditions overwhelmingly saw declines instead.

To summarize, the IMF and World Bank were established to promote international economic cooperation and reduce poverty. However, their results paint a much darker picture. Their policies have facilitated wealth and resource extraction, benefiting Western corporations at the expense of impoverished nations.

As a result, these recipient nations have seen their rights, freedoms, political power, and natural resources decimated, and their debt reliance, poverty, and vulnerability grow under guidance from the IMF and the World Bank.

THE FRENCH TREASURY AND
THE CENTRAL AFRICAN FRANC (CFA)

Did you know that the French Treasury still controls the currency of fourteen French-speaking African countries?

Countries like Senegal, Ivory Coast, Niger, and others have more than 183 million inhabitants, over twice that of France, and cover 2.5 million square kilometres of territory. Although the French began decolonization in 1956, these territories remain under French monetary control.

During its height in 1680, the French colonies covered four times the landmass of the current CFA nations, and they reaped significant benefits from these territories for centuries. These colonized territories even provided crucial military support in both World Wars and were a rich source of valuable natural resources. It was not until the end of WWII, when global colonization was declining, that France created a currency for its African territories. Initially, this currency was called the "franc of the French Colonies of Africa," however, now it is simply referred to as the Communauté Financière Africaine (African Financial Community), CFA franc for short.[406]

Given that the definition of colonialism is "the policy or practice of acquiring full or partial political control over another country, occupying it with settlers, and exploiting it economically," it could be argued that this financial influence over these African nations was an effort to transition France's colonialism to a more palatable form in an era when many territories were gaining their sovereignty.[407]

In addition to the examination of the IMF, Alex Gladstein has some valuable insights on the CFA system, particularly in his article, "Fighting Monetary Colonialism with Open Source Code."[408]

The CFA franc is a tool by which the resources and productive capacity of the nation's underpinning the currency are continuously siphoned off to enrich the French. As Gladstein describes, even though the CFA system has undergone changes since its establishment, and although this exploitation has evolved from harsh slavery regimes, it still very much exists but in a more refined covert method that ensures the developing nations are under political and economic subjugation.

The CFA franc, which was first introduced in 1945, had an initial value of 1.7 French francs, with the French Treasury determining its value. This value was later revised to two French francs in 1948, which is a step in the right direction.[409] However, by the time the CFA franc was pegged to the euro at the end of the 1990s, it had lost 99.5% of its value, with one CFA franc purchasing just 0.01 French franc. With each devaluation of the CFA franc, France increased its purchasing power in its former colonies while simultaneously making it more difficult and expensive for these nations to import essential goods.

Furthermore, Gladstein states that "in 1992, the French people were able to vote on whether or not to adopt the euro through a national referendum. The CFA nationals were denied any such right and were excluded from the negotiations that would peg their money to a new currency," clearly demonstrating the self-governance and freedom being denied to these nations.

The fourteen CFA nations are currently served by three central banks:

1. The Banque Centrale des États de l'Afrique de l'Ouest (BCEAO),
2. The Banque des États de l'Afrique Centrale (BEAC),
3. and The Banque Centrale des Comores (BCC).

These central banks hold the foreign exchange reserves, or national savings, of the individual nations in their respective regions. These nations must always keep a staggering 50% of their reserves with the French Treasury. It's also important to point out that this percentage, although outrageous, is the result of historical negotiations, as the former colonies were originally required to keep 100% of their reserves in France.

Moreover, the CFA nations have no authority over or insight into their bank reserves in France. On the other hand, the French see precisely where and how each CFA nation directs its capital.

If that wasn't enough, France produces all the banknotes and coins used by the CFA nations, charging roughly €45 million annually for this "assistance." And France still holds 90% of the CFA countries' gold reserves, some 36.5 tons.

Additionally, France has significant power over international trade with these countries through the right of first refusal on imports and exports. If you are a zinc miner in Burkina Faso, you must offer your products to France before reaching out to other nations. Similarly, if you're working on a major infrastructure project in Niger, you must offer the contract to the French before anyone else.

With this in mind, the CFA system benefits the French government in several ways. First, the French can access CFA reserves and use them as they see fit. Second, they control a large multinational market where they can export expensive goods and import cheaper resources. Third, they benefit from preferential loans when the CFA nations are in surplus while also offering favourable interest rates to them when they are in debt. Finally, there is a "double loan" arrangement where when a CFA nation borrows money from France, the terms and conditions often require the borrowing country to use the funds to contract goods or services from French companies. This requirement creates a dependency on French companies, as the CFA nation may face limited options for sourcing goods and services from other countries. This limits the economic autonomy and diversification of CFA nations, as it hinders their ability to explore alternative trade partnerships and engage in fair competition on the global market.

It's no wonder that according to the United Nations, 10 out of the 14 CFA countries are classified as "least developed countries."

Given the parallels between France's "support" of these countries and the IMF's aid to developing nations, it should come as no surprise that "the World Bank and the International Monetary Fund have historically worked in concert with France to enforce the CFA system, and rarely, if ever, criticize its exploitative nature."

In one such instance of France and the IMF partnering, in the early 1990s, France was pressuring the Ivory Coast to devalue their currency. The Ivory Coast was putting up resistance, so in response, the IMF withdrew its lending support to the Ivory Coast, presenting an ultimatum of sorts: Either the country repaid its debts to the IMF, or it must accept devaluation.

Ultimately, by the end of 1994, the Ivory Coast and other CFA nations accepted devaluation. In this and many other cases over the years, France and the IMF were able to get their way regardless of the wishes of these ostensibly self-governing nations.

If you're interested in learning more about the injustices of our present-day monetary systems in developing countries, I cannot recommend Gladstein's work more highly. He provides valuable insights that can help shed light on some of the issues we face.

THE BANK OF INTERNATIONAL SETTLEMENTS (BIS)

We live in a world where the majority of leading countries are supposedly democratic, yet at the heart of these democratic nations is an institution shrouded in secrecy— an institution so powerful it governs the world's monetary systems. This institution is the Bank of International Settlements, often called "the central bank of central banks."

In his eye-opening book, *The Tower of Basel,* Adam LeBor explores this little-known institution that controls the majority of the world's monetary networks.[410] What immediately stands out upon reading the introduction is that its members back in 2013 were effectively a who's who of global finance, including "Ben Bernanke, the chairman of the US Federal Reserve; Sir Mervyn King, the governor of the Bank of England; Mario Draghi, of the European Central Bank; Zhou Xiaochuan of the Bank of China; and the central bank governors of Germany, France, Italy, Sweden, Canada, India, and Brazil."

The Bank for International Settlements (BIS) was established by an international treaty in 1930 and has been granted significant legal protections under a 1987 Headquarters Agreement with the Swiss government. These protections are similar to those granted to the headquarters of other international organizations, such as the United Nations and the International Monetary Fund, as well as diplomatic embassies. As a result, the BIS is exempt from Swiss taxes, and the authorities require the permission of the BIS to enter the bank's premises.

And it's not just the BIS that benefits from these legal protections. Its employees do not have to pay income tax— and their salaries, paid by the taxpayer, are far from inconsequential. In 2011, the general manager earned the equivalent of $825,000 in Swiss francs, while department heads were paid $634,000 plus allowances. The BIS's legal privileges also extend to its staff and directors, who are granted special status similar to that of diplomats. For example, BIS officials have lifelong immunity under Swiss law for acts carried out during the service of their duties, and their bags cannot be searched during work-related travel.

Every month, the members of the BIS convene to discuss crucial topics concerning the global financial system, payment systems, and international markets, and all the members present are guaranteed complete confidentiality, discretion, and the highest levels of security. As LeBor notes, as far back as 1930, the Bank for International Settlements (BIS) has been known for its strict culture of secrecy. A *New York Times* reporter was once denied entry to the BIS boardroom, even after the directors had left.

To further safeguard the bankers, the BIS does not release, let alone take, any minutes, agenda, or attendance list. While the bankers may jot down their own notes, the details of these discussions remain inaccessible to the public, and this tradition of privileged confidentiality has stayed true since its inception.

Through all these measures, the BIS fiercely protects its core activities, that is, "control[ing] monetary policy in the developed world." To this end, "they manage the supply of money to national economies. They set interest rates, thus deciding the value of our savings and investments. They decide whether to focus on austerity or growth." In short, as LeBor puts it, "their decisions shape our lives."

As such, the discussions among central bankers at the BIS are highly political in nature. Not only are they ultimately the ones largely behind the monetary intervention discussed in this book, they evaluate policies, exchange opinions, and ultimately make important decisions that direct our global economy. These decisions have far-reaching consequences that affect everyone on this planet. Yet they have no oversight or democratic influence.

Without jumping to conclusions, it is reasonable to ask: Have they proven to be responsible, given their immense power?

Unfortunately, within the first decade of its existence, the BIS had already given the world reason for pause. During World War 2, when Nazi Germany annexed Czechoslovakia, it turned to the BIS to assist in taking control of the nation's gold reserves. Before the occupation, the Czechoslovakian National Bank had hastily transferred "most of its gold abroad to two accounts at the Bank of England: one in the name of the BIS, and one in the name of the National Bank of Czechoslovakia itself." This move left a mere 6,337 kilograms of gold still in Prague out of the original 94,772 kilograms.

However, the Czechoslovakian's faith in the BIS turned out to be misguided. In 1939, Berlin ordered Prague to transfer 14.5 tons of gold to back the German currency, and the BIS complied, handing over the money that had been safeguarded under their name.

One month later, a Reichsbank official threatened the directors of the National Bank of Czechoslovakia with death, ordering them to instruct the Bank of England to transfer almost 27 metric tons of gold held in the National Bank of Czechoslovakia's account to their BIS's gold account. They were then tasked with informing the BIS to transfer 23.1 tons of that Czechoslovakian gold to the Reichsbank BIS account. After the bank's general manager spoke to London and the governor of the Bank of France, the BIS processed the transfer with a view that "as long as the paperwork was in order, the monies must go through." As LeBor remarks, "with London, Paris, and Basel's [BIS] compliance, Nazi Germany had just looted 23.1 metric tons of gold without a shot being fired."

In the end, the BIS helped Nazi Germany in its crusade across the Eastern bloc countries by ensuring that they could freely transact and had access to significant capital.

However, this was not a lone incident. Throughout the BIS's 90 years of existence, they have participated and assisted in countless unconscionable situations. More recently, when Argentina declared bankruptcy in 1991 after defaulting on $81 billion worth of debts, the BIS stepped in.

First, the BIS supported Argentina by offering its creditors a paltry "thirty-five cents on the dollar." By contrast, "previously bankrupt countries had offered fifty to sixty cents." Although many of these creditors accepted the terms, a portion demanded a higher payout. That portion was sixty thousand Italians, which included many individuals who had bought these bonds to fund their retirement and investment funds.

But more alarming, the Argentine bank was allowed to transfer its reserves to the BIS to escape its creditors, as its legal structure provided a "safe haven for a country fleeing its creditors." This is only possible given that the BIS has immunity, and their assets remain untouchable under international treaty.

Eventually, the Italian investors fought their case against the Argentine Central Bank through the International Centre for Investment Disputes. However, unfortunately, in 2012, "the Swiss Federal Council (the Swiss federal government) confirmed that the funds cannot sequester any of the Argentine deposits held at the BIS."

The core problem is that the BIS has a serious conflict of interest in its foundation. It is trying to oversee the whole world, but to do so it must balance central banks' interests against each other, effectively choosing which party will come out on top.

CONCLUSION

Given their ability to benefit some countries over others, we should seriously consider the power that centralized banks like BIS, the World Bank, and other unelected organizations currently hold. Minimizing their control would not only promote fiscal responsibility and give power to the free market but also better democratize the global financial system.

Unfortunately, the BIS, IMF, World Bank, and other similar institutions have little incentive to provide the public with transparency and accountability, even though they are funded by the taxpayer. Therefore, unless we act swiftly, it's unlikely that the situation will change. Nevertheless, we should continue to advocate for greater transparency and accountability in the global financial system. The exploitative and manipulative practices that currently plague our system affect us all.

All four examples described in this chapter emerged from periods of financial ruin when the global economy was in shambles and people were desperate for stability and solutions. The Bank for International Settlements was founded in 1930 during the Great Depression to help Germany pay off war reparations, the International Monetary Fund and the World Bank were established in 1944 at the end of World War II, aiming to stabilize the international monetary system and monitor world currencies, and the CFA franc emerged in 1945 as the French franc was deteriorating, and, in each instance, we can identify a breakdown of monetary systems, a sense of loneliness and meaninglessness, and deep anxiety and frustration. As discussed in Chapter Nine, the conditions were ripe for the emergence of controlling structures.

In light of everything discussed, the influence of central banking reaches beyond the mere management of money. Central banking directly or indirectly governs the world around us— and just as governments can give way to totalitarian tendencies, so too can our financial systems. As a result, these institutions' practices, built around intervention, have paved the road for major economic events from which other controlling structures have emerged at both the personal and nation-state levels.

As we've uncovered, handing over a nation's currency means handing over power, leaving citizens at risk of exploitation and abuse. And even when the country we reside in appears to have control over its currency, we're still at the whim of organizations with limited to no oversight and who do not fall under the purview of the traditional democratic process.

By understanding these examples, we can begin to see the urgent need for us to re-examine our current monetary systems. But even when we see the flaws in the way things are today, it can be hard to imagine them otherwise. How else would we structure a global economy? In the next chapter, we'll embark on a new journey by reimagining what a monetary system that promotes truth, integrity, and freedom of expression might look like.

CHAPTER 12

REALIGNING INCENTIVES

What a Monetary System Built on Truth May Look Like

"There are two types of healing, whether it is physical healing or otherwise. One is removal of cause, which is good. The other is removal of symptom, which merely postpones the reckoning." —Peace Pilgrim

....

I t may be a cliché, but more often than not, a problem is simply an opportunity in disguise. But how can we seize this opportunity if we can't accurately identify the problem? Achieving true healing—*whether mental, physical, emotional, or economic*—requires seeing reality as it is. Focusing on immediate needs without looking to the root of the issue only masks underlying problems, allowing them to fester.

Up until this point, I have done my best to paint an unvarnished picture of the world we live in. However, considering the weightiness of the topics we've explored, I am wary that it can be easy to fall into a cycle of despair. So, let's take a break from the side effects or "symptoms" of a misaligned monetary system and go back to the drawing board. How do we build a new system from the ground up, one that realigns incentives and promotes truth, integrity, and freedom of expression? In crafting such a proposal, I will employ a first principles approach, deconstructing the complex problems we've encountered into fundamental truths and devising solutions rooted in this newfound understanding.

REALIGNING INCENTIVES

In theorizing a better system, I must build from some precepts that I hold true. First among them is an acknowledgment that value is subjective! What one person values, another person may not. Value is based on an individual's perception, needs, and preferences. It is shaped by personal experiences, cultural norms, beliefs, and social influences.

You've probably noticed that your own values change over time based on how your shifting circumstances and experiences shape your attitude. You may learn new information or develop new attachments that shift your priorities and, therefore, your sense of value. This subjectivity makes it difficult to determine any objective measure of value and highlights the importance of individual freedom in determining what is valuable to each person.

Along these same lines, my views, values, and beliefs may not always, or even often, align with the majority. The same is true for all people and, therefore, also true for those in positions of power.

With this complexity in mind, I have asked myself: What does a monetary system look like that allows for freedom of expression and enables the varied values of the populace to shine through?

In our present system, where expression is impeded, there is no way to disseminate fact from fiction. Even if those in power have the population's best interests at heart, we still face two significant challenges:

1. Our economy is one of the most complex, multifaceted systems in existence. To accurately assess what is needed—

with limited human biases and avoiding conflicting interests steering those in power astray—is a near-impossible task.

2. The transience of political power. Even if the individuals in power manage to accurately diagnose the correct plan of attack and execute it, all their hard work can quickly evaporate when the political tides turn.

The goal is to create a stable system, one that can account for and reflect the variety of needs and values that a society holds. Humanity cannot grow in a system that masks supply and demand and leans on changing our monetary environment when problems arise. The variable resulting in the problems discussed throughout this book is us and our desire to use the monetary lever to create change.

In the following two chapters, let's examine potential transformations our monetary system could undergo to better reflect societal values and create a more just society that realigns incentives, fostering productive and sustainable behaviour.

The Core Tenets

Before examining the intricate workings of such a system, we must ask ourselves: What core tenets must be present to support the functioning of such a system? Drawing from my ongoing personal exploration of the intricate puzzle that constitutes our monetary system, I have arrived at the belief that **creative destruction** and **accountability** are indispensable elements for a system to operate in a just and productive manner.

Creative Destruction

It is innate for leaders and individuals alike to believe in and champion whatever it is that they value, whether misguided or not. However, as we have seen, when individuals with misguided values have overwhelming power, this has resulted in some not-so-healthy situations.

In a climate of enhanced financial and personal freedom, we would possess the ability to channel our emotional and monetary resources more easily towards the causes we deem meaningful. Within such a framework, leaders and politicians are at liberty to support their own goals and values, but they would be limited in their ability to rule through force or suppress the varied values and beliefs of the populace.

If someone or something does not offer value in the eyes of the populace, then limited to no capital will flow toward what they are doing. If capital no longer flows to areas of the economy that do not offer value— creative destruction can take hold. Within this context, the practice of artificially sustaining unproductive behaviour would struggle to exist, i.e., counterproductive businesses would be allowed to fail instead of being artificially propped up during challenging periods, making room for new enterprises that offer greater value.

Accountability

Not only do we have to ensure healthy competition so that natural selection in value creation can take hold, but we must ensure those in power (whether in government or business enterprises) feel that taking responsibility is a necessity.

Under a system that prioritizes freedom of expression, where undue capital can no longer flow to areas of the economy deemed unproductive, governments and individuals must be accountable for their actions and adapt to their environment, rather than attempt to alter their environment to suit their needs.

If they fail to offer value, they must accept their shortcomings, adjust course, and acclimate to the world around them. We should move away from interventionist practices whereby we try to create a world that fits our interpretation of what's right.

Instead, we should entrust the free market to determine what is of value, allowing it to communicate through capital flows and natural price discovery.

In a system that prioritizes creative destruction and accountability, we enhance humanity's capacity to flourish by confronting our shortcomings and challenges directly, rather than ignoring or concealing them. Instead of merely papering over economic difficulties through continuous monetary interventions, we are compelled to scrutinize our actions and their impact on society. This approach fosters a deeper understanding of our individual and collective contributions to the betterment of society as a whole.

Given the inherent challenges of making informed decisions within a manipulated monetary system that enables the obfuscation of problems, let's examine the necessary attributes of a system that can, at the very least, alleviate, if not solve, these issues.

The Alteration of Money

To better understand what this improved monetary system may look like, we must first understand the three fundamental functions of money. With this foundation in place, we can identify the key traits required to establish truth and integrity in a financial system, ensuring a reliable and clean medium of expression that speaks to its user's authentic needs and desires.

Store of value
This money should maintain its purchasing power over time.

Money is an integral part of value exchange and creation, so people must have trust and faith in its ability to store value. Otherwise— *whether conscious or not*—they will be pressured toward choices based not on their natural instincts but on the threat of loss in their held currency.

In our present system, as we rely on growth and inflation, currency holders experience a constant reduction of purchasing power. With our purchasing power declining from one day to the next, we must dedicate more of our productive capacity to receive the same benefits as we previously did with less.

As already outlined, such a system disincentivizes saving and encourages spending. To realign our spending to calmer, more intentional levels, our money must:

1. Store value over time so the general populace is incentivized to save and spend as much as they feel called to by their own needs and desires. Our money supply should, therefore, be built around scarcity so that our purchasing power captures technological advancement and productivity. As a result, the cost of many goods and services will decline, reflecting reality as these things become more efficiently created or performed. In this scenario, as productivity increases, we would experience the liberation of time, alleviating the need to continually extend working hours. Our money would align with our largely deflationary world.

2. Be easily stored and impervious to coercive and controlling structures. That is money that can't easily be taken by force. This ensures our money can act as an effective store of value over time without risk of unexpected loss.

Medium of exchange

This money should be recognized as a viable intermediary for exchange.

For this money to be a workable alternative in the age of technology, it must be digitally native, easily divisible and with minimal fees to meet the varied needs of the population. Therefore, we must be able to transact seamlessly in a digital manner.

Under such a system, we are minimizing trade friction, allowing capital to flow wherever we would like. If someone wants to send money overseas, transact in small amounts, or remit money back to their family, nothing should prevent or impede them from doing so.

Unit of account
This money should be widely accepted in trade.

To maximize accurate decision-making, we must have a precise ruler to guide our actions. Take a builder, for example. If their ruler's measurements change every time they use it, you can't expect whatever they build to be structurally sound. The same is also true for money: Money is a form of measurement. It measures the value of time.

In our present system, we are trying to make economic decisions based on a unit of measurement, i.e., our currency, which is constantly changing due to capital controls and monetary intervention.

With this in mind, I will use Gresham's law and Thiers' law as a means to describe why the removal of legal tender laws – where the currency is designated by the state and must be accepted as payment for goods and services – inhibit money as a effective unit of account, as well as a store of value.

Gresham's law, named after Sir Thomas Gresham, a 16th-century English financier, states that when legal tender laws exist, "bad money drives out good." This results from people tending to spend the bad money (the legal tender) and hoard the good money (That which holds value over time), causing the good money to disappear from circulation.

On the other hand, Thiers' law, named after Adolphe Thiers, a 19th-century French statesman and historian, asserts that "the market is the best guardian of values." According to Thiers, the market is more effective at determining the value of money than any central authority or government. When no legal tender laws exist, the market, through supply and demand, will always accurately reflect a currency's value. Therefore, "good money drives out bad," as people are unwilling to accept a weaker form of money when a more sought-after one exists.

In short, intervention is not conducive to a productive and sustainable monetary system. Without legal tender laws, the market will favour stronger currencies, gradually eliminating weaker ones. In contrast, legal tender laws have the opposite effect. Inferior currencies are given preference in trade over superior ones, as people tend to hoard good money when the law permits the use of weaker currencies.

This emphasizes the importance of removing government intervention and allowing the market to determine the value of money. By removing money from the state and allowing money to be selected by the market, our money will improve over time.

Considering the above laws and that money is arguably our most important channel through which we gain insight into society's diverse needs and preferences, we should not only prioritize the accuracy of such money through scarcity but maximize freedom of expression by preventing intervention. To do so, we should limit, if not remove, all third parties and intermediaries (governments, corporations etc.) from the issuance and transaction process. This thwarts anyone from inhibiting our ability to transact or altering the flow of capital to where it wants to go, something impossible under a decentralized, trustless and permissionless system. In an alternate system that removes the necessity for intermediaries, no third-party trust or permission is required meaning alterations to the system are built on consensus over powerplay.

Lastly, recognizing the significance of freedom of expression within a monetary system, it is essential not only to accurately convey our needs and values in the present but also to maintain a historical record of our monetary expressions. Such a record would enhance our ability to make informed decisions, increasing humanity's chances of survival. Therefore, it is worth giving thought to the construction of this monetary system on a public ledger, ensuring a transparent and precise record of transactions accessible to all participants. This approach would provide a comprehensive chronology of capital flow, both past and present, empowering us to make more informed choices. I like to refer to this idea as "Proof of Expression."

With a clear understanding of the potential characteristics of a revised monetary system, including:

1. **Store of value**: This money should maintain its purchasing power over time, be easily stored and impervious to coercion, and be built around the tenet of scarcity.
2. **Medium of exchange**: This money should be digitally native, easily divisible, and have minimal fees to seamlessly integrate into the modern digital economy and serve as an efficient and practical medium of exchange.
3. **Unit of account**: This money should exist independently of the state and, as a result, not rely on trust and permission from any centralized authority. This would enable it to function as a precise unit of measurement for decision-making and enable freedom of expression.

Money & Its Effect on Behaviour

A new monetary system that implements the changes described above would naturally result in different behaviours than our current one. Some of these shifts are outlined below.

Time-Preference

Under a monetary system built around scarcity, one that aligns with the inherent deflationary aspects of technology, our purchasing power will most likely increase over time as efficiency improvements from technological advancement enable us to produce more with less resource or labour expenditure. No more inflation from monetary expansion!

For instance, the advent of LED bulbs showcases the impact of technological advancements in the lighting industry. LED bulbs consume 85% less energy compared to halogen bulbs. Considering the average home has around 37 lightbulbs, switching from halogen to LED can yield annual savings of up to $237.[411] Our money goes further when technology drives down the cost of everything around us, from lightbulbs to cars, solar panels to smartphones.

Under such a system, simply holding the currency, such as in the days of gold, becomes a primary method of capital allocation as our purchasing power will grow from one day to the next. Instead of consuming debt, investing in high-risk assets to outpace inflation, or indulging in lower-quality goods in the present, the act of **saving** itself becomes a source of motivation to defer immediate gratification. Furthermore, as our purchasing power continues to increase over time, there is a disincentive to take on debt for unproductive purposes, as it would swiftly become a burden.

By altering the characteristics of money, we create an incentive for a reduced time preference. Unlike the current paradigm, where immediate gratification is often rewarded, this proposed system encourages a long-term perspective, where delayed gratification is recognized and incentivized. The benefits of low time preference thinking, both economically and mentally, are substantial:

- **Enhanced Self-Discipline and Well-being:** Low time preference thinking cultivates self-discipline and the ability to resist impulsive behaviours, resulting in improved personal well-being and a stronger sense of self-control.[412]
- **More Productive Capital Allocation:** As simply saving currency becomes a viable option for building future security, we observe a reduction in capital flowing into unproductive investments driven solely by the pursuit of yield or appreciation. This means that investments must prove their worth to attract capital inflows.
- **Thoughtful Decision-Making:** Low time preference thinking promotes conscientious decision-making, empowering individuals to consider the long-term consequences of their actions and make more informed choices.[413]
- **Increased Financial Stability:** By prioritizing long-term financial planning and saving, individuals can enhance their financial stability and resilience to economic uncertainties.

Compassion & Altruism

When the currency serves as a reliable savings instrument, it particularly benefits those in the lower socioeconomic strata. As discussed in Chapter Two, historically, wages have often lagged behind inflation. However, in a scenario where the currency's purchasing power is consistently rising, the opposite could occur. As our purchasing power increases over time, while wage adjustments happen less frequently, our effective real wages would experience growth rather than decline. This has the potential to partially alleviate financial pressures for the lower and middle classes, who rely heavily on cash, and provide them with enhanced clarity, security, and predictability regarding future prospects.

Fear and anxiety often narrow our focus and limit our capacity for awareness. When individuals are grappling with financial hardships, it becomes challenging to prioritize the needs of others or contribute to charitable causes. However, in a future where we're no longer battling against the tides of currency debasement, people may find themselves with greater resources and emotional capacity to extend support to others. This newfound stability and confidence may inspire increased acts of kindness and generosity, i.e., volunteering, support for charitable organizations, or assisting friends and family in times of need.

Therefore, the financial stability and security brought about by a currency built around scarcity, whose purchasing power increases over time, has the potential to cultivate the conditions for people to be more inclined toward acts of compassion and altruism.

That said, it is not solely inflation that hampers our capacity to contribute and give back. In numerous instances, the conventional financial system exacts a significant toll on our purchasing power through transaction processing fees. To illustrate, picture being born and raised in Tonga. While you hold a deep affection for your home country, you quickly realize the limited job opportunities within your local community. Consequently, you make the challenging choice to leave Tonga and relocate to a country offering greater employment prospects. This enables you to provide better support for your family by sending a portion of your earnings back home.

This is a reality for billions worldwide, particularly those in Tonga. Astonishingly, as of 2021, remittances, the act of sending money back home to loved ones, accounted for a staggering 45.5% of Tonga's GDP.[414]

Now, you might wonder, what's the issue with this situation? The problem lies in the costs associated with sending money overseas through services like Western Union. It is not free; in fact, it incurs significant charges. Sending $100 US to Tonga costs $12.61, and an additional $8.60 is lost due to unfavourable exchange rates.[415] This means that more than 21% of the total amount sent ends up in the hands of Western Union, a multinational corporation, rather than in the deserving hands of Tongan families.

Imagine the tremendous benefits of having an extra 21% added to your income. Moreover, considering Tonga's GDP was $469 million in 2021 and remittances constituted 45.5% of it, the exorbitant fees imposed for sending money home deprive Tonga of an additional $45.2 million.[416] Tonga could enjoy a 9.6% increase in GDP if not for these fees.

Tonga's situation underscores the urgent necessity for a fairer and more accessible system, like the proposed digital solution, that eliminates burdensome transaction fees. Such a system would enable a larger portion of hard-earned money to remain in the hands of those who have worked hard.

It's worth acknowledging that financial security and stability are just one of many factors that can influence compassion and altruism and that many people exhibit these qualities regardless of their financial situation. Nevertheless, financial stability has the potential to provide individuals with the resources and peace of mind to place greater focus on the needs of others and their community.

Meaninglessness & Motivation
In Chapter Four, we discussed how, in our present-day system, we have a reverse robin-hood effect taking place, thanks primarily to two practices:

1. The unilateral dilution of our purchasing power
2. The redirection of this purchasing power from one area of the economy to another

These seemingly innocuous traits of our present system have the capacity to shift our locus of control externally, whereby when it comes to the extent to which we have control over the events and outcomes in our life, we feel they are primarily influenced by external factors rather than our own actions and decisions. This is not conducive to promoting a motivating and meaningful environment.

These above points, combined with impaired monetary expression due to capital controls or restrictions, as outlined in Chapter Ten, have the potential to intensify any feelings of meaninglessness and diminish motivation. When we are unable to freely express our values through financial transactions, it raises the question of why one should strive to contribute value to society if the means to express and support those values is restricted.

Moreover, the current system of intervention designed to avert collapse, wherein unproductive behaviour is rewarded, establishes a fallback mechanism that discourages many businesses and individuals from taking responsibility. Instead of promoting accountability, our existing system nurtures a culture of reliance and the deflecting of blame onto external factors.

On the flip side, by removing centralized entities from the issuance and governance of money, we establish a stronger connection between our livelihood and our actions. In this scenario, the risks of monetary debasement, capital redirection, or currency controls are significantly reduced, leading to the lessening of many of the byproducts outlined throughout this book.

The idea of "reaping what we sow" refers to the concept that our actions have consequences and that the results we experience in life are tied to the choices and decisions we make. If we plant the seeds of good behaviour and hard work, we will reap the rewards in the form of success and satisfaction. On the other hand, if we engage in unproductive behaviour, we can expect consequences to follow. This is a powerful motivator because it has the potential to shift our locus of control internally, providing a sense of control and agency over our lives. When we understand that many of the outcomes we experience result from our choices and efforts rather than external factors dictating what we can and cannot do, we are more likely to take ownership of our circumstances and take proactive steps to create the life we want.

This sense of control and responsibility can be incredibly empowering, fueling our motivation and unwavering focus on achieving our goals, even when confronted with obstacles and setbacks. In practical terms, within a system with limited fallback mechanisms and one that incentivizes value creation, we consistently turn inward and ask ourselves: If I'm not offering value, what adjustments do I need to make? Failure to create value would result in mounting challenges, as capital would cease to flow toward us. This impetus drives us to work diligently, treat others with kindness and respect, and make choices that align with our values and aspirations.

With all this in mind, it is worth highlighting the numerous extensively studied and documented benefits associated with an internal locus of control. Some of these benefits include:

- **Increased Mental Resilience:** Individuals with an internal locus of control tend to exhibit higher levels of resilience, allowing them to cope more effectively with stress, setbacks, and challenges.[417]
- **Improved Emotional Well-being:** Having a belief in personal control over one's life is associated with higher levels of self-esteem, confidence, and overall emotional well-being.[418]
- **Greater Motivation and Achievement:** Individuals with an internal locus of control tend to display higher levels of motivation, initiative, and perseverance. They are more likely to set ambitious goals, take responsibility for their

actions, and persist in the face of obstacles, leading to greater achievements.[419]

- **Enhanced Physical Health:** Research suggests that having an internal locus of control is associated with better physical health outcomes, including improved cardiovascular health, lower levels of stress-related illnesses, and better overall health behaviours.[420]

CONCLUSION

Authentic healing in all forms—*mental, physical, emotional, and economic*—requires a clear understanding of reality. However, our current monetary system is misaligned with public values and undermines freedom of expression, making it difficult to distinguish truth from fiction and address issues effectively.

To overcome these challenges, we must revamp our monetary system, prioritizing creative destruction and accountability. By doing so, unimpeded monetary expression will enable the free market to determine genuine value, and unproductive areas of the economy will gradually fade away.

Under a system that shifts our time horizons toward saving, promotes value creation, and pushes individuals to take responsibility for their actions, the benefits to our economy could be unfathomable.

Next up, let's investigate the potential impact of a monetary system that values freedom of expression and realigns incentives. We'll examine how it can promote environmental sustainability, transform government and politics, drive innovation in business, and strengthen the family unit.

CHAPTER 13

MONEY REIMAGINED

How This Revamped Monetary System May Benefit Us

*"If the American people ever allow private banks to control
the issue of their currency, ... the banks and corporations
that will grow up around them will deprive the people of
all property until their children wake up homeless on the
continent their Fathers conquered ... I believe that banking
institutions are more dangerous to our liberties than standing
armies ... The issuing power should be taken from the banks
and restored to the people, to whom it properly belongs." —
Thomas Jefferson, Third President of the United States*

....

M oney has a profound impact on every aspect of our lives, from
the choices we make as consumers to how our governments
function, the way businesses operate, and how families interact.
Our money shapes our world in ways we may not even realize.
So, what happens when money is re-designed to better align with
our values and priorities?

This chapter will explore the far-reaching effects of our
reimagined money, discussed in the previous chapter, on our
environment, government and politics, wealth inequality,
businesses, and family units, and delve into the monetary options
currently available to us.

Let's dive in, starting with how this money may play a hand in reducing wealth inequality.

Wealth Inequality

Wages have long been stuck in neutral while inflation roars ahead, leaving the majority of people struggling to keep up. Given the stickiness of wages mentioned in Chapter Two, asset prices and the cost of living continue to outpace, driving wealth inequality.

But as we mentioned in the previous chapter, if the stickiness of wages held true while our purchasing power increased over time, the tide would turn in favour of wage earners. As our currency strengthens, wages may decline but lag behind deflation, transferring wealth toward the currency holders and those who work for a living.

And with the power of a unified currency and seamless transactions, why settle for paying someone in a developed country far more than someone of equal calibre abroad? A decentralized unified currency with near instantaneous settlement and minimal transaction fees creates a natural leveller. In such a scenario, money will flow to developing countries. But not just any money, money far superior to their local fiat currency, which is prone to debasement. This means over time, these individuals who are currently at the whim of overreaching governments will have a method to opt into a much more beneficial system.

What about the affordability of housing and other financial assets?

Chapter Three exposes the harsh reality that our monetary system does not align with our deflationary world, where technological progress is growing at a rapid clip. This advancement leads to price declines, but unfortunately, these declines are never realized due to interventionist monetary practices and inefficient capital allocation. As a result, many people pursue ownership of assets that offer scarcity and the potential to mitigate the effects of inflation. Whether people are directly aware of how savings will lose value as time passes, conventional wisdom instructs them to invest their money for greater security over time.

This is where the challenges emerge. Assets like real estate, farmland, and commercial property provide value beyond their monetary worth, serving as homes, storefronts, and agricultural fields that contribute to society. However, when investment-oriented demand outweighs practical use, prices rise, making it difficult for those seeking assets for their intended purpose to afford them. This trend can lead to a reduction in productive capacity within the economy. As people increasingly acquire these assets as a hedge against inflation rather than for their productive value, their original purpose becomes secondary, shifting towards primarily serving as an inflation hedge.

Figure 13.1

The Deterioration of Cropland Feasibility

Ratio of per-acre cash rent for cropland to per-acre value of cropland, 1967 to 2011

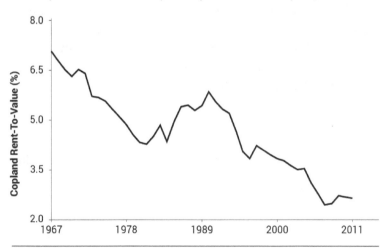

Source: USDA-NASS Quickstats & USDA-ERS

The impact of this phenomenon is evident in the cropland rent-to-value ratios. Over the past 50 years, farmers have faced a 60% decline in farming feasibility as land values have skyrocketed, directly resulting from declining interest rates and the appeal of debt consumption. Figure 13.1 highlights this shift in a striking visual.

This can also be seen in real estate, whereby monetary intervention exacerbates the already pressing issue of housing shortages in desirable locations. With the wealthy seeking refuge from inflation by buying up properties for investment purposes rather than rental purposes, it's taking many residential dwellings off the market.

In London, estate agents Barrows and Forrester disclosed that in 2022 there were 80,295 empty properties totalling £41bn, a 12% increase from the previous year.[421] In Whistler, a staggering 61% of homes are left unoccupied, while the limited availability is causing newcomers to pay $4,000 a month for a tiny studio apartment.[422] Meanwhile, in New York, LendingTree reports 955,437 empty homes, while rental rates in areas such as Brooklyn have skyrocketed by 27% due to limited supply.[423,424]

Moreover, real estate isn't the only asset receiving capital flows, given that saving is no longer viable due to inflationary pressures. Today, many individuals find mutual funds, index funds, or exchange-traded funds (ETFs) easily accessible investment vehicles, as they offer diversified holdings across various companies and sectors. Unfortunately, as money loses value, capital increasingly flows into these investment products, setting in motion a self-reinforcing performance and centralizing mechanism. The influx of capital into these funds bolsters their performance—*furthering the divide between the haves and have-nots*—and attracts even more capital, granting significant control to the centralized entities managing these investment products.

When you buy an ETF, you typically become a shareholder of the ETF itself, not the individual underlying companies held within the ETF. As a result, you do not retain direct voting rights for the individual companies in the ETF's portfolio. Instead, the ETF issuer holds these voting rights.

As of November 2020, the "big three" issuers—*Blackrock, State Street, and Vanguard*—receive a staggering 82% of all capital flowing into investment funds.[425] Combined, these three funds constitute the largest owner in 88% of the S&P 500 corporations. Blackrock alone "holds a 5% or greater stake in more than 97.5% of the S&P 500 companies." In the words of former Securities and Exchange (SEC) Commissioner Robert Jackson, "A few large institutions today vote millions of American families' money in corporate elections that will help decide our economic future."

A currency with a fixed supply cap could provide a solution to these problems. With the limited supply, its purchasing power would increase as the economy grows and technology advances. At the current rate of technological advancement, doubling every two years, it's not out of the question for prices of non-scarce goods and services to decrease by 10-15% annually.

The appeal of real estate and financial products as inflationary hedges would also decrease with a stronger currency. Currently, real estate appreciates at around 8.6%, equities at 10.1%, and farmland at 12.2% annually.[426,427,428] But with a currency whose purchasing power is increasing at 10-15%, saving would once again become viable. Investors would no longer need to seek refuge in these assets, incentivizing the movement of capital back into the currency. This could cause real estate prices to drop, making them once again accessible for everyday people looking to contribute to society by using these assets for their intended purposes. Furthermore, such a development has the potential to diminish the concentration of power held by major financial players such as the "big three" listed above.

Lastly, with rapid advancements in AI and robotics, job redundancy is becoming a larger threat. This can pose a significant challenge in a system characterized by interventionist inflation.

As purchasing power decreases, people are forced to work more to make ends meet.

However, by aligning our monetary system with the natural progression of technology, as purchasing power is on the rise, people are able to work less as the cost of living decreases. This gradual shift may alleviate some of the potential issues in the job market due to technological advancements.

All in all, our current inflationary system is leaving the majority of people struggling to keep up with the rising cost of living. In conjunction with increasing asset prices and inflation, the stickiness of wages is causing growing wealth inequality.

But by aligning our monetary system with our deflationary world and technological advancement, we may be able to reverse this trend and create a more equitable and just economy for everyone.

Business

In the current economic landscape, businesses often prioritize boosting stock prices to attract investors and meet the shareholders' expectations, often relegating genuine value creation to a secondary or even optional role.

As Siddharth Kara, an expert on modern-day slavery and child labour, explains, shareholder value is tied to net profit, calculated by subtracting expenses from total revenue.[429] Since labour is the largest cost component for most businesses—accounting for upwards of 70% of a business's expenses, pursuing low-cost labour becomes a means to maximize profit and shareholder value.[430]

Siddharth highlights a troubling consequence of this situation: labour conditions, brought about by penny-pinching, often violate human rights. For instance, an alarming 74% of global cobalt production occurs under unethical and abusive circumstances, despite its widespread use in batteries, including smartphones (with over 8 grams) and electric cars (with 10 kilograms).[431] Moreover, the United States Department of Labor records hundreds of millions of dollars in wage theft owed as back wages each year, and this only accounts for companies with reported labour law violations.[432] Surprisingly, this pervasive exploitation affects us all and receives limited attention in mainstream media.

Access to cheap labour and materials is vital to fueling growth in a debt-based system. Therefore, when faced with a choice between declining shareholder value or using unethical labour, many companies will prioritize shareholder value over ethical concerns.

Siddharth claims that through regulation, this issue can be solved. However, I would argue that the puzzle piece Siddharth is missing is that this is not a problem with regulation or even greed. It is a problem with our money. When debt is cheap, we see:

- Increased consumerism
- Lengthening supply chains built on cheap capital
- Corporations incentivized to locate the cheapest possible labour to maximize return to investors.

As a result, environmental and humanitarian values are, at best, afterthoughts to profit. And if one company is not willing to supply cheap products, then another will. This creates a race to the bottom since the cheapest option is favoured by companies whose top goal is to keep costs low rather than to produce the best possible product. The market becomes flooded with poor quality products made from unsustainably sourced resources, built on underpaid labour, often infringing on human rights, all fueled by cheaply borrowed capital.

However, in a world where the purchasing power of money grows, equities face a new challenge. While shareholder value will remain a key consideration, equities no longer benefit from the current level of capital flows from inflation-evading investors. The portion of investments motivated purely by a desire to grow wealth at a rate exceeding inflation will diminish as simply holding currency offers a viable and safe way of building wealth.

In such a scenario, people may be more inclined to invest not primarily as a means to build wealth but in order to support companies they believe in. As personal values come more and more into play in access to capital, companies must align with potential investors' values to acquire and retain capital. If a company fails to do so, individuals may choose to divest their holdings and save their money instead or support a competitor that better aligns with the impact they wish to have in the world. This trend will likely result in a growing demand for sustainable and ethical business practices, reducing the emphasis on maximizing shareholder value.

Another significant influence on business behaviour arises from the existence of a buyer of last resort: the central bank. In times of economic adversity, the government and/or central bank usually intervene by acquiring assets from struggling institutions and infusing capital into the economy to alleviate financial challenges. The expectation that the government or central bank will intervene often fosters complacency and risk-taking and results in the misallocation of resources. This lack of fiscal responsibility causes excess capital, intended as a safety-net financial buffer, to be utilized for further profiteering instead. For instance, during the COVID-19 pandemic in Canada, companies of all sizes were eligible for a wage subsidy covering 75% of expenses if they saw just a 15% decline in revenue.[433] Following the taxpayer-funded subsidies, corporations achieved record profits as a direct consequence.[434]

What does this tell businesses? "There is no need for fiscal prudence. If you find yourself in a bind, don't worry. We got your back!"

In contrast, if the government and central banks are limited in their capacity to bail out businesses experiencing setbacks, fiscal responsibility becomes a necessity.

A fiscally responsible government may still have surplus capital from tax revenues, so it still has the freedom to support businesses financially. But with limited capital, the government is more likely to seek out truly vital and beneficial companies that offer maximal value. This, tied with increasing purchasing power, means corporations and individuals alike will only take out debt when they're confident that the benefit of an immediate infusion of cash outweighs the burden of debt.

In this environment, from a research and development standpoint, individuals and corporations will be inclined to put more skin in the game (that is, investing their own capital rather than external financing) to prove viability from the outset. The deflationary environment will encourage a culture of mindful spending. The resulting competition for consumption dollars will drive a higher flow of capital toward innovative and promising ideas, reducing the misallocation of capital toward unproven, "fairy tale" technology. And finally, with more costly debt and greater rewards for saving, people and corporations will be less likely to part with their cash. In turn, it'll be far harder for charlatans to sucker individuals into Ponzi schemes.

In short, our money has the power to revolutionize business behaviour.

Government & Politics

Money's influence on government and politics is where we really start to see change happen.

By deceiving people with the idea that they can receive something for nothing, i.e., stimulus checks, it becomes effortless to manipulate people for personal gain, such as politicians, in the pursuit of votes. However, this illusion of a free lunch is simply funded by debasing the currency already in circulation. It's akin to robbing Peter to pay Paul.

On the other hand, our reimagined money supports a fundamental truth: there's no such thing as a free lunch. To enhance one's life, one must offer something of value. Similarly, politicians must provide tangible value if they want to obtain votes.

With this in mind, the first and most obvious difference is that when money is separate from the state, we now have a system that promotes value creation and cooperation between the state, corporations and the populace.

Separating money from the state forces individuals and nations to adapt to our ever-changing environments rather than trying to alter the environment through monetary intervention. This is natural selection at work. The people and nations that are able to adapt will thrive and succeed, while those that don't wither away.

A secure, permissionless, and trustless store of value is a strong incentive to adapt or risk catastrophic failure.

In this structure, as the state can no longer fund operations through monetary intervention, the only way to obtain capital is to offer value to society, creating an environment where the populace willingly wants to contribute. In such a scenario, the government has to act as a fiscally responsible organization, just like businesses do.

One such example would be that governments would be far more restricted in their ability to use the monetary system as a tool for funding unelected entities such as the BIS, IMF, and World Bank. Without the ability to manipulate the monetary supply, governments lose a significant funding source and must find alternative means of financing their operations. This shift away from government-controlled money has the potential to lead to a more sustainable and efficient financial system as entities are forced to compete on a level playing field and operate within the constraints of market forces rather than relying on unproductive government subsidies.

Additionally, misguided governments, or those that act self-interestedly, will eventually see their population flee and experience a redirection of capital away from them. This shifts power away from the misaligned government and back toward the populace. It also opens the door for another political party that does have the interest of the public at heart to rise up.

Conversely, governments that offer favourable environments will attract people and capital, further enabling sustainable growth and prosperity and incentivizing integrity, honesty, and transparency.

Further, since capital is limited, governments will be required to carefully consider their spending decisions and prioritize long-term outcomes over quick fixes. This is not the case in our current system. As an illustration, here are four examples of such behaviour:

- The Canadian government introduced the ArriveCan app during the pandemic to facilitate the preparation of customs and immigration documents for travellers entering the country. However, the initial \$80,000 development costs for the app ballooned to over \$54 million by early 2023. A significant portion of these expenses were attributed to "indirect costs associated with the project, including employee benefits, accommodations, and payments to other government departments."[435]
- The US Government Accountability Office (GAO) reported that major defence acquisition programs— the purchase and development of military equipment, systems, and technology, exceeded their original cost estimates by an average of 27% and experienced schedule delays of 2 years.[436]

- During testimony before the US Senate, Harvard Professor David Cutler highlighted that an estimated 15-30% of the healthcare budget is allocated to administrative expenses, which could be more effectively utilized to improve patient care and health outcomes.[437]
- In Toronto's west end, the community sought the construction of a set of seven stairs to improve access from the main street to a park. The government estimated the cost to be over $150,000. In outrage, a resourceful 73-year-old retired mechanic took matters into his own hands and built the staircase himself for $550. Sadly, the municipal government subsequently demolished it.[438]

These examples perfectly illustrate the tendency of government projects to encounter cost overruns and inefficient resource allocation. The availability of deficit spending allows governments to shift the burden of costs onto taxpayers through financial intervention. Consequently, the present monetary system lacks the necessary incentives for long-term thinking and responsible management of resources, ultimately fostering a cycle of escalating capital consumption that is unsustainable in the long run.

In a system where rules take precedence over rulers, those in positions of power face financial constraints when attempting to run deficits without the populace's support, as they cannot resort to currency debasement. This incentivizes them to exercise caution in spending, carefully manage budgets, and optimize capital allocation. Moreover, a decentralized digital ledger enables greater accounting transparency, simplifying verification and enhancing overall government accountability.

This shift in focus toward sustainability reflects a heightened awareness of the consequences of fiscal irresponsibility. No longer can governments "lose" billions of dollars, outcompete the private market in wages or afford to bail out struggling corporations in an attempt to ease immediate economic pressures. Instead, they must look toward more sustainable and strategic solutions.

Lastly, money, as the lifeblood of a nation's economy, has the power to shape the nation's future in ways we can barely imagine. And when it comes to war and politics, the impact of money can be especially profound. Money in its current form allows governments to pursue their agendas without true support from the people. This allows the government "to tap the property of its people without having obtained their consent, and in fact, against their wishes," which not only undermines the very principles of property rights, it enables governments to fund wars that lack support.[439]

Currently, when a country finds itself in an untenable military situation, the traditional course of action has been to devalue the currency to bolster operations, which was the case with countless wars such as World War I, World War II, and the Vietnam War— the expense of which, as mentioned previously, triggered President Nixon to leave the gold standard in 1971.

When money is decoupled from the state, and governments are limited in their supply of capital, this has two primary benefits:

1. **Governments must be mindful of resource allocation:** No longer can they finance wars through currency devaluation and sacrificing citizen well-being. This makes war less likely and, if it does occur, more limited in scope and destruction, given the constraints on available capital.
2. **Governments are incentivized to rethink their approach to war:** When fighting a losing battle, withdrawing from such conflict is now the most viable option available, leading to shorter and less damaging wars.

Furthermore, in a decentralized digital money system, individuals have the ability to maintain self-custody of their assets, making it inherently more difficult to seize compared to traditional centralized assets that are subject to a single point of control. Historically, asset seizure has been a significant motivator for conflict and war. With the reduced possibility of seizing assets, the allure of engaging in warfare diminishes.

Ultimately, in such a system, the government's capacity to proceed without support is restricted, shifting the focus away from power acquisition through fear and war. Instead, value creation emerges as the most effective avenue for obtaining power.

As the age-old saying goes, "money talks," which speaks volumes about a nation's priorities in this scenario. With the focus on value creation, military spending falls down the list of essentials, and nations are incentivized to think twice before entering into conflict. Although wars will likely exist long into the future, they would be limited in scope under such a monetary system. In short, a monetary system that values creation over destruction has the potential to bring greater peace and stability to the world.

In these ways separating money from the state allows for an environment of consideration, creation, and cooperation. With a secure and trustless store of value, citizens are empowered, while governments are held accountable for their actions and their fiscal management. This shift in power towards the public incentivizes governments to act with greater transparency, honesty, and integrity.

Environmental Impact & Consumption

Nick Szabo's "Shelling Out" is a thought-provoking article highlighting the concept of symbiosis in nature.[440] He describes how some small fish that swim in and out of the mouths of larger carnivorous fishes remove parasites and clean bacteria to maintain the health of their mouths. This is a vivid example of symbiosis in action— the small fish feed on the parasites, while the large fish receive a thorough cleaning service, improving their health.

The larger fish could choose to wait for the cleaner fish to finish their job and then consume them, but they choose not to. This is because consuming the cleaner fish could deplete their population and jeopardize the essential services they provide. Due to the costs associated with finding new cleaner fish and the potential decline in the quality of their work, the larger fish are motivated to maintain a harmonious relationship with the smaller fish.

We, humans, should take inspiration and learn from this symbiotic relationship. We should strive to live in harmony with each other and our planet. However, it is unfortunately clear that our monetary system is obstructing this effort. As the currency is losing value from one day to the next, we're incentivized to consume. There is little regard for our planet and future generations when building security against life's struggles resulting from monetary intervention is at the forefront of our minds.

This doesn't have to be the case.

Under a decentralized digital monetary system built around scarcity, sustainability emerges as a paramount concern. As mentioned earlier, when our purchasing power increases over time, the desire to bring forth future spending through the use of debt is disincentivized, as unproductive debt can quickly become a burden. This does three things:

1. Sustainability is held in much higher regard, given the costs associated with unnecessary consumption and the advantages of saving within such an environment.
2. Reduced debt use for consumption purposes contributes to a decline in overall consumption levels.
3. Individuals are incentivized to spend their money only when the advantages of consumption surpass the benefits of saving.

This shift in mindset makes persuading people to part with their funds increasingly more difficult. Manufacturers are compelled to elevate their standards to meet this reduced demand, as consumers, recognizing the benefits of delayed purchases, now seek higher-quality products that offer greater value and make consumption truly worthwhile.

In adventure sporting gear, we can observe examples of companies prioritizing quality and sustainability. Brands like Patagonia and Arc'teryx have established a strong focus on crafting sustainable, well-made products, recognizing the demand for environmentally conscious outdoor gear.[441,442] Another notable example is TenTree, which goes beyond product quality and commits to planting ten trees for each item purchased.[443] While currently catering to niche market segments with higher disposable income, in a monetary system that enables genuine expression of our values, we would likely witness a rise in companies finding innovative ways to achieve greater sustainability. As consumption levels decrease, competition among businesses to devise innovative approaches for achieving greater sustainability increases.

Considering that it's not out of the realm of possibility where corporations are compelled to adopt sustainable practices given the demand, we have the potential to establish a more symbiotic relationship with our planet— we extract and consume resources more on necessity rather than undue consumption, allowing us to align our actions more harmoniously with the constraints of the environment.

Under a system built on suppressed interest rates, the temptation for individuals, corporations, and governments to borrow beyond one's means to alleviate short-term stress is all too real. However, under a system built around scarcity, taking a short-term gain is akin to the larger fish devouring the cleaner fish— in the long-term, you would be harming yourself, as your debt burden will quickly grow under a monetary system with increasing purchasing power.

Another significant benefit of this reimagined monetary system is that disconnecting money from the state and allowing market forces to dictate prices reduces the risk of depleting vital resources.

The current system, where governments provide subsidies to artificially lower energy prices when prices rise, perpetuates unsustainable consumption habits. As subsidies suppress the price of energy, preventing price from reflecting supply and demand pressures, individuals and governments blindly consume beyond their means, with little understanding of the knock-on environmental consequences. This vicious cycle must be broken to promote responsible resource usage and a sustainable future.

As Knut Svanholm explains in his book *Everything Divided by 21 Million*, "deflation is always advertised as a bad thing by those who run the money printers. This is the greatest lie ever told. In truth, a deflationary monetary base layer is the only thing that can save humanity from itself. By giving people an incentive to save rather than spend, we stop the vicious cycle of consumerism."[444] While shifting culture will never be as simple as flipping a switch, creating a system that allows for deflation will at least gently press the brakes on our accelerating pace of consumerism.

When the state no longer controls the money, governments are limited in their ability to manipulate the economy through monetary intervention. With limited resources, they must carefully consider their spending, including subsidies that could artificially lower the price of energy. This incentivizes them to make fiscally responsible decisions rather than artificially propping up prices, as they cannot rely on the ability to freely print money to cover their expenses.

As a result, energy prices, free of monetary subsidies, naturally adjust given supply and demand. If demand for a resource rises and supply stays constant, prices rise. In such a scenario, those who can no longer afford the resource must now look for alternative solutions.

This does three things:

1. It sparks ingenuity and creativity as people who can no longer afford the raw material look for other means of achieving the same result.
2. As prices rise, unnecessary consumption pressures subside as it becomes costly to live a wasteful existence. Given that a substantial portion of the Gross Domestic Product (GDP) is derived from consumption (68% for the United States)[445], promoting saving and reducing consumption can significantly decrease the resource demands that our current consumer-driven society has put on our planet. Moreover, the rise and fall of prices offer everyone information on the current conditions of any resource.
3. Energy and resource companies are rewarded adequately for their work, which allows them to dedicate more money to research and development, driving efficiency and technological advancement.

To summarize, the current monetary system incentivizes consumption and disregards the impact on the planet and future generations.

On the other hand, a decentralized digital monetary system based on scarcity can incentivize sustainability and encourage individuals to reduce consumption, directing more of their money towards essentials and saving. This could lead to a demand for higher-quality products and sustainable practices from corporations.

Furthermore, by disconnecting money from the state and allowing market forces to dictate prices, we reduce the risk of depleting vital resources and incentivize governments to make fiscally responsible decisions.

With an understanding of the impact of money on the environment and consumption, let's now look at how it might support the family unit.

Family Unit

In Chapter Five, we shed light on the financial challenges parents currently face in supporting their families, which may impair child development and weaken the family unit over time. This has resulted in a trend of postponing parenthood and limited quality time for those who do have children. Simultaneously, we confront the expanding presence of the welfare state, which increasingly assumes responsibilities that families traditionally shouldered, such as education, childcare, and elderly care. This, as we explored in Chapter Seven, results from the private sector being unable to compete with the public sector.

The financial strains and transfer of responsibilities from families to the government have profound and enduring effects on the family unit. Combined, we have witnessed:

- Heightened stress levels during pregnancy and critical developmental years, potentially compromising children's social, emotional, and physical well-being.
- Diminished opportunities for children to engage with parents and elders, leading to negative impacts on their emotional resilience and authenticity.

This arrangement, while seemingly convenient, is not only detrimental to the family unit but also inefficient from an economic standpoint. As the welfare state operates through large bureaucracies and lacks the incentive of free market fiscal responsibility, let alone meeting the unique needs of these children, the result is an excessive waste of otherwise productive capital. The reliance on taxes and monetary intervention to fund the welfare state highlights its inability to compete with families in a fair market.

What's more, with the availability of taxation and monetary intervention to fund welfare programs, the upfront costs of these services appear minimal, although taxpayers ultimately bear the costs through taxes and debasement. This dynamic creates an uneven playing field where families and the private market struggle to compete, resulting in increasing government control over the provision of these services. The untameable growth of the welfare system presents potential risks to the parent-child bond and the well-being of future generations as the government gradually assumes roles that families have traditionally fulfilled.

I want to emphasize that my intention is not to criticize the concept of providing welfare services through the government or the importance of such services. Instead, my focus is on highlighting the negative consequences of monetary intervention on the expanding welfare state, resulting in the erosion of essential roles traditionally held by the family unit, which has a greater capacity to cater to the diverse and specific needs of children and the elderly.

On the flip side, by decoupling money from the state, the power dynamics would shift back to the family unit. With limited access to capital, the government would have to compete with families on an equal footing in the free market. This fiscal constraint would require the government to be more mindful of the boundaries of the welfare state and prioritize essential services.

And arguably, most importantly, if our currency's purchasing power increases over time, we should witness a reduction in our cost of living and daily expenses and a rise in future security. With lower parental stress during children's crucial developmental years and reduced financial burdens, parents would have the opportunity to decrease their working hours and dedicate more time and attention to nurturing the parent-child connection. As families reclaim their role in providing familial services, the parent-child bond is poised to strengthen, promoting greater authenticity, emotional resilience, and overall well-being in children as they grow and develop. Furthermore, the increased resources and time available to families from rising purchasing power could result in higher-quality care and support, fostering a stronger and more supportive community. All in all:

Reduced financial pressures → Less adverse childhood experiences → Supported neurodevelopment → Social, emotional, and cognitive development → Reduced likelihood of adopting health-risk behaviours → Greater resilience against diseases, disabilities, and social problems

Tying everything together, decentralized money, separate from the state, has the potential to:

- Lessen the global disparity in wealth,
- Limit government overreach and incentivize international cooperation,
- Promote value creation and ethical practices in business,
- Greatly reduce the environmental impact of consumerism and resource extraction,
- and strengthen the family unit.

These benefits cannot be overstated!

Overall, such a monetary system has the potential to improve the financial health and well-being of individuals, businesses, and society as a whole.

AVAILABLE OPTIONS

Now that we've delved into some of the essential characteristics of money required to incentivize productive and responsible behavior, we are now better positioned to explore and assess the various options available, identifying the one that best aligns with our objectives.

Let's start with the timeless and coveted metal that has fascinated humanity for centuries: gold.

Gold

Are you wondering why we don't just return to a gold standard after reading all of this? Many have pondered the possibility of going back to the commodity that served us for centuries.

Gold was foundational in the evolution of money and has played an important role in the exchange of value throughout history. For thousands of years, gold has been recognized as a valuable and precious commodity. Its rarity, durability, and malleability have made it an ideal medium of exchange and a store of value.

During the Middle Ages, gold coins were used widely throughout Europe as a medium of exchange. In the 17th century, the development of paper money allowed gold to be used as a backing for national currencies, and the gold standard was born. For much of the 19th and early 20th centuries, major economies used the gold standard to stabilize their currencies and facilitate international trade since it had universally recognized value.

To this day, gold's unique properties have made it an enduring symbol of wealth and prosperity. For over 2600 years, it has not only given many currencies purchasing power stability but also given individuals an ungoverned, somewhat trustless method of storing value.[446] For instance, refugees often turn to gold jewelry as a reliable form of wealth preservation, readily accepted in their new country, especially when foreign currency poses challenges to hide, let alone exchange. This stability and universality, in addition to its glimmering look, is what gives gold its allure. But is it still as useful as it once was?

As nice as it is to have a physical store of value, this characteristic is bittersweet in the age of technology. Given that gold requires physical custody for its safekeeping, this poses a problem. Gold struggles to keep up with the rigours of modern-day life.

Let me explain...

Trust

One of the primary reasons for the mess we are in today is the ease of abuse we faced during the gold standard. Money issuers took advantage of gold because they realized that currency holders rarely, if ever, looked to exchange their money for the gold it laid claim (as discussed in Chapter One). As a result, issuers printed beyond their means, unknowingly creating the first fractional reserve system, whereby there was more money in circulation than gold in reserves. This system became a ticking time bomb, as money issuers were at risk of becoming insolvent if everyone suddenly wanted to redeem their gold.

This raises an important question: Would history repeat itself if we were to return to a gold standard?

While a gold standard could provide a stable framework for the monetary system, it is susceptible to exploitation. As gold is physical in nature, we must either take on the arduous task of storing our gold ourselves or place our trust in a third party, hoping that they have our best interests at heart. This makes for a central point of failure or, worse, a central point of control.

Some may raise the idea of a gold-backed cryptocurrency, but this only transfers the responsibility of maintaining the gold peg to another party. Placing faith in that party still carries the risk of moving towards a fiat currency system once again.

The issue of trust may seem trivial, but history has shown us that those in power can quickly abandon their commitment to a gold standard if they lack support or the capital to fund operations. This has often led to de-pegging from gold and a devaluing of the currency or, at times, a total banning of gold altogether, as with Executive Order 6102. Hence, we will most likely find ourselves in a situation similar to what we have today, where the system is vulnerable to abuse and instability.

But let's just say we can trust the money issuers and that they all agree to maintain our currency's gold backing. Even then, we still have another issue...

Dilution & Manipulation

With the emergence of central banking also came a deterioration in transparency, particularly regarding gold reserves. As it stands, there is an estimated 201,000 tons of gold above ground, with more than 17% of that being held in central banks.[447] But how can we be sure they hold that much? We can't!

The problem lies in the fact that central banks are not required to provide detailed information about their gold holdings. They do not differentiate between physical gold and gold swaps, such as lending, leasing or where gold is temporarily exchanged for another financial asset. This means that we cannot be sure about the exact amount of physical gold that central banks possess.

Take, for instance, the UK post World War I.[448] Due to the country's previous history of printing money beyond its means, after returning to the gold standard in 1925, the public was skeptical about whether the government had enough gold to back its currency. So, rather than risk being behind the curve if the banks fell short, many people began to exchange their money for gold.

Faced with this dilemma, the UK government had to act quickly. They established a $200 million gold bullion swap line with the US Federal Reserve, intended to give the impression that the Bank of England was financially secure and could honour requests for gold redemption. But ironically, this move reveals that not only did the UK lack the resources to fulfill its gold obligations, but now the Federal Reserve was also in a precarious position, as rather than physical gold, it had a $200 million IOU for gold. Essentially, these were accounting maneuvers designed to create the appearance of fiscal responsibility while still functionally operating through fractional reserve rather than total backing of currency.

Although the swap line provided temporary relief, giving the UK the appearance of being on the gold standard, the UK eventually folded and abandoned the gold standard altogether in 1931 due to economic pressures.

And today, this type of accounting trickery still takes place.

During the 1960s and 1970s, central banks began to realize that they could generate a return on their non-interest-bearing gold assets by leasing them out. This led to an increase in gold swaps between central banks and gold miners, as the miners sought to hedge their gold production by locking in prices, and the central banks sought to profit from the leasing arrangement.[449]

However, these transactions were not transparently disclosed on the central banks' balance sheets. Instead, when a central bank leased out its gold, the resulting IOU was counted as part of the bank's physical gold holdings.[450] If the counterparty of this IOU sold this borrowed gold into the market, it effectively doubled the perceived amount of gold in circulation, as it now existed both on the bank's balance sheet and in the market. And this duplicitous practice is still legal today.

By seemingly doubling the gold leased out, this illusory increase in supply exerts significant downward pressure on the price of gold, suppressing its value in addition to calling into question the accuracy of central bank gold holdings. This raises new concerns about whether or not a gold standard is even possible, as we have no idea what the unadulterated price of gold is.

And to add fuel to the fire, in 2005, a declassified document emerged from the US State Department, exposing the fact that by promoting the gold futures market, the government could increase price volatility and reduce the price of gold.[451]

Digitization

Another drawback to returning to the gold standard is that, as a medium of exchange, gold struggles in a globalized digital world because of its inherent physical properties. In a digital, web-based economy, people expect remote and *almost* instantaneous transactions, which require a medium of exchange that can be easily transmitted and verified electronically.

Gold, on the other hand, must be stored and transported, which adds significant cost and complexity to digital transactions. Additionally, verifying the authenticity and purity of gold can be difficult and time-consuming, slowing down transactions and increasing costs.

Moreover, in a global digital economy, a medium of exchange must be highly divisible to efficiently facilitate transactions of varying values, which is a challenge for gold.

In summary, while gold has historically been a widely accepted medium of exchange and has paved the way for thousands of years, in the age of technology, it struggles to meet the strenuous demands of our digital economy due to its reliance on trust, its physical nature, the difficulty in verifying its authenticity, and limited divisibility.

So, if gold isn't a great option, what alternatives exist?

Central Bank Digital Currencies (CBDCs)

According to data from the Atlantic Council CBDC tracker, over 20 countries are set to launch a CBDC pilot in 2023.[452] Among them are Japan, UAE, Australia, Thailand, Brazil, India, South Korea, and Russia.[453] Modern society needs a digital form of money that meets the rigorous demands of our interconnected planet, so how would central bank digital currencies work as a potential solution?

Central bank digital currencies may provide a more efficient and cost-effective means of transacting, but this comes at a cost. By prioritizing ease of use and transaction efficiency, we open the door to multiple threats on our monetary expression, such as a loss of financial privacy through increased surveillance by central authorities and the potential for capital controls that put time restrictions on our savings or prevent us from spending in certain areas of society.

And suppose CBDCs were to be combined with social credit, not to be confused with credit scores? This scenario could grant the issuer the authority to impose limitations on individuals' spending choices, restrict access to specific services, and even affect their eligibility for mortgages based on their societal standing, all in the name of security.

This may sound far-fetched, but Agustin Carstens, the head of the BIS, made a similar observation of this potential:

> For our analysis on CBDC in particular for general use, we tend to establish the equivalence with cash, and there is a huge difference there. For example, in cash, we don't know for example who is using a hundred dollar bill today; we don't know who is using a one thousand peso bill today. A key difference with a CBDC is that the central bank will have absolute control on the rules and regulations that determine

the use of that expression of central bank liability. And also, we will have the technology to enforce that.[454]

If we simply take the words Carstens said at face value, the intention behind these currencies and how they will be regulated is pretty explicit.

And this risk of outsized manipulation of people's spending through digital currency restrictions is not just theoretical. In 2021, the Chinese government introduced a prototype CBDC that allows the government to set expiration dates on money.[455] This effectively pressures citizens to spend the currency within a set timeframe or lose it, preventing them from saving or building wealth. In October 2022, Bo Li, the Deputy Director of the IMF and former People's Bank of China (PBoC) deputy governor, remarked that "by programming CBDC, money can be precisely targeted for what kind of people can own and what kind of use this money can be utilized."[456] Furthermore, the Chinese have combined their social credit system with their CBDC. They can now:

1. Constantly monitor and surveil individuals.
2. Grant people access to exclusive benefits based on behaviour.
3. Blacklist individuals and restrict essential services such as travel, career advancement, property acquisition, and even enrollment in private schools.

To top it all off, if you disagree with these tactics, they are publicly exposing non-conforming individuals at movie theatres, displaying their personal details and addresses.[457]

The ascent of CBDCs is already underway, and policymakers are not hesitant about declaring their implications for our financial autonomy.

And even if these were acceptable risks, there's no guarantee CBDCs will solve the issues we face, considering the direction governments have already taken on money over the past 200 years. While CBDCs may offer advantages in terms of ease of use, they do not address the fundamental issues raised in this book. The existing monetary system does not incentivize productive, fiscally responsible behaviour, and the introduction of CBDCs would only exacerbate these issues by extending centralized control over our monetary system to unprecedented levels.

Therefore, we should approach the implementation of CBDCs with immense caution and carefully consider their potential implications on financial stability, privacy, and monetary expression.

So, if gold or CBDCs are not viable, are there other forms of money that meet the stringent characteristics laid out in the previous chapter?

Bitcoin

Although many individuals and nations have tried to achieve a fair and equitable monetary system, none come as close to meeting the rigorous demands as Bitcoin. Despite being viewed by some as a speculative and volatile asset, when we push aside our preconceived ideas, a closer examination reveals its capacity to fulfill the essential criteria of a sovereign monetary system, which could transform the world as we know it.

How can Bitcoin play a role in reshaping society?

Ross Stevens, founder of Stone Ridge Asset Management, aptly describes Bitcoin as a "monetary system governed by rules instead of rulers."[458] Bitcoin is the first truly decentralized digital currency in history that meets the characteristics of money laid out in the previous chapter and bridges the gap between money and our inherently deflationary world.

It also represents a peaceful revolution, one that has the potential to bring about significant and lasting change in almost every sector of our economy. By breaking away from government control and empowering individuals to control their own financial resources, money, such as Bitcoin, has the power to realign incentives and bring about positive change on a societal level.

Unlike fiat currencies, which are subject to devaluation through expansion and controlled by central entities, Bitcoin is:

Permissionless

Bitcoin's peer-to-peer nature ensures that no one is prevented from using it, as no gatekeepers or intermediaries' control who can or can't participate. This allows for truly inclusive and decentralized access to the world of digital finance.

Trustless

The absence of intermediaries or gatekeepers in the Bitcoin network eliminates the need for trust in centralized entities, creating a decentralized, trustless system.

Open-Source

Bitcoin's source code is freely accessible to everyone, allowing for transparency and collaboration. Anyone can review, suggest changes, duplicate, or distribute the codebase and public ledger of transaction history, promoting a more open and democratic system.

Transparent Blockchain

Given Bitcoin is built on a globally distributed public ledger. Anyone can audit the network to ensure that all participants are following the same rules set by the community. This transparency offers a level of accountability and trust that is not present in the current system.

Fungible

With Bitcoin, all coins are equal and interchangeable, regardless of their previous ownership or use. This eliminates the need for anyone to worry about the history or origin of the coins they hold.

Divisibility

At present, Bitcoin can be divided into eight decimal places, allowing for transactions as small as $0.0003028 USD. However, suppose the price of Bitcoin rose significantly, necessitating greater divisibility for smaller transactions. Its digital nature allows for increased divisibility based on the community's perceived need.

Fixed Supply

Bitcoin eliminates the fear of devaluation caused by inflationary monetary policies. With a fixed supply of 21 million coins, while there is ever-increasing demand and continuing advancements in technology and productivity, there is only one direction for Bitcoin's purchasing power to go... up!

To quote Twitter user @BitBaggins:

> Bitcoin is the only currency on earth that guarantees a finite supply. Because this allows a fixed denominator, all numerators (prices) will decrease proportional to the increase in goods and services added to the economy. A finite currency respects the worker— who has a finite amount of time & energy to provide to others.[459]

Combined, these features make Bitcoin a game-changer in the financial landscape and a beacon of hope for a fair and equitable monetary system.

With Bitcoin offering a decentralized global record of truth, with no need for trust in third parties or permission to use, in the age of censorship, you could argue that Bitcoin is the ultimate evolutionary adaptation to free speech.

Paraphrasing Julian Assange of WikiLeaks, history can be easily deleted or rewritten in the digital realm.[460] And even without the intent to delete, undocumented history starts disappearing. Of what history remains, it is very much centralized in museums under lock and key. Those who control these historical records have the capacity to alter how history is portrayed. As George Orwell once said, "He who controls the past controls the future. He who controls the present controls the past."[461] Historical monetary data and freedom of monetary expression are critical to ensuring that the past, present, and future cannot be altered through false narratives by centralized entities.

Bitcoin offers a solution to the challenge of disappearing history by providing an immutable record of every transaction through its transparent and secure blockchain technology. A history that cannot be rewritten or changed, thanks to mathematics and cryptography. This gives us not only verifiable proof of past events but also a reliable means of expressing ourselves in the present. As a result, it becomes increasingly difficult for centralized entities to manipulate the truth and control the narrative. *This cannot be overstated.* We now have an accurate record of past transactions stored in a trustless, permissionless blockchain where anyone can access or verify its authenticity. If Bitcoin were widely used, this record would allow us to access accurate information on supply and demand, leading to more sustainable economic growth, increased innovation, and improved error correction— all while providing individuals with a sense of security as their savings are protected from debasement and other forms of monetary intervention.

Moreover, in natural systems, there is no such thing as exponential or required growth. That which consumes beyond its means eventually withers away. Bitcoin is the closest thing we have to a natural system. It puts control back into the hands of the community and has scarcity, like many resources. As a result, it allows us to tap back into our sense of self, to grow in concert with our planet rather than as a result of our planet.

It'll be fascinating to follow the experience of early adopters like El Salvador, which embraced Bitcoin as a legal tender in 2021. In the first year alone, their tourism increased by 30%, and within the first eight months, 1.9% of remittances were conducted in Bitcoin, saving El Salvadorians $4 million in fees.[462,463] This is equivalent to adding 1,100 average annual incomes to the small country. The progress of other nations and jurisdictions, such as the Central African Republic and Madeira, who have embraced Bitcoin, will also be intriguing to observe in the years ahead.[464,465]

That said, irrespective of whether we eventually transition to a global economy built upon Bitcoin, the digital currency offers individuals:

1. **Empowerment:** Bitcoin grants autonomy in a world where our rights and freedoms are increasingly under pressure, as it gives people the ability to save for the future, direct capital according to their preferences, and take control of their funds without relying on intermediaries.

2. **Jurisdictional Neutrality:** Bitcoin serves as an asset that remains indifferent to jurisdictional boundaries. Whether you're located in America or the Congo, as long as you take ownership of your Bitcoin, i.e., do not leave it on an exchange, your stored wealth remains beyond the reach of undue control. This stands in contrast to any other asset throughout history, which are all either physically located and subject to seizure (real estate, gold, commodities, cash...) or digital and held by a third party in a jurisdiction controlled by an entity with overriding authority (equities, bonds, digital cash...).

Given these attributes, Bitcoin is a viable option to foster prosperity on an individual level, regardless of where you are in the world or whether we witness widespread nation-state adoption or not.

You may wonder why traditional fiat currency has maintained its dominance over Bitcoin despite its numerous shortcomings. While Bitcoin offers decentralization, security, and scarcity, transitioning to a new currency, especially one that may seem complex to the uninitiated, is challenging. The initial surge in Bitcoin's value raised concerns of a speculative bubble, making some skeptical of its long-term viability. Additionally, our preference for short-term convenience often outweighs the potential long-term benefits. Fiat currency, benefiting from extensive capital investment and established infrastructure, holds an advantage in terms of ease of use. However, this gap is quickly closing. Nevertheless, it is crucial to recognize that the convenience of traditional fiat money comes at a significant cost. Fiat is vulnerable to manipulation, guaranteed to lose purchasing power, and increasingly used to infringe upon our rights and freedoms.

It's also important to note that individuals who do not *yet* see themselves as oppressed may show less inclination to adopt an alternative monetary system. However, countless people from developing nations have come to appreciate the extraordinary utility of Bitcoin, given their first-hand experience with oppressive government systems. These individuals understand the growing toll of using fiat currencies on their wealth, health, and communities, making them more receptive to embracing Bitcoin.

Lastly, you may have encountered the meme "Bitcoin fixes this." Although this may sound pithy, this meme is simply trying to shed light on the fact that at the root of most of our problems lies a common denominator— our money. Posters of this meme are highlighting that Bitcoin can serve as a sound monetary system, independent of government control, and this has the potential to address many of the challenges we face today. *But... it is only through understanding the costs and repercussions of the fiat system can one truly grasp the benefits of sovereign sound money such as Bitcoin.*

....

SIDE NOTE: *The notion that Bitcoin and gold are too volatile to serve as a stable store of value or units of account overlooks a crucial factor: their valuation is currently tied to fiat currency. The volatility experienced by these assets stems from the inherent instability of the underlying unit of measurement, in this case, the dollar or some other currency. As noted by Lawrence White in his book Better Money, price fluctuations primarily arise from people seeking a hedge against inflation.[466] White further points out that historical evidence demonstrate greater price stability during the UK gold standard of 1821-1914 compared to the fiat money era of 1971-2022. Considering this, it is misguided to judge the volatility of assets like gold or Bitcoin based on their price behaviour under a fiat standard. In reality, all you're really highlighting is the volatility of fiat.*

....

CONCLUSION

As society grows and technology advances, we have been increasing productive capacity, which has the potential to translate into rising purchasing power. However, the monetary system determines who is the benefactor of this increased productivity.

In a debt-based inflationary system, the benefactors of this increased productive capacity are those who control the monetary printers, as they get to direct capital wherever they see fit. Although purchasing power could increase and prices decline, currency holders never experience this as productive capacity is re-distributed towards rising asset prices, debt service payments and inefficient social agendas.

Our current monetary system is similar to playing the childhood favourite "floor is lava" game. Individuals are increasingly incentivized to scramble over one another in an effort to protect their wealth. But despite these efforts, our purchasing power continues to decline. Paraphrasing Jeff Booth, trying to escape monetary debasement through strategic money management is much like rearranging deck chairs on the Titanic. It's still sinking!

In contrast, a sound money system like Bitcoin would be akin to receding "lava." Money would then not only serve as a medium of exchange and a unit of account but also as a store of value— a crucial function of money missing in our current system.

Rather than governments and the wealthiest asset-holders benefiting from our inherently deflationary world, the currency holders would benefit. This creates a situation where meeting immediate needs becomes easier, leading to a focus on cooperation and value creation.

Lastly, a decentralized and cryptography-backed form of digital money, such as Bitcoin, eliminates any central point of control or physical location, giving it greater immunity to seizure or coercion. The intangible and decentralized nature of such a monetary system levels the playing field, preventing any single entity or nation-state from having an unfair advantage over others.

This shift towards cooperation as the primary means of obtaining capital transforms the incentive structure, promoting value creation and collaboration over coercion and forceful extraction. The result should be a more peaceful and harmonious society.

While the history of money has too often been one of exploitation and manipulation, all hope should not be lost. The future holds great promise with the advent of decentralized, scarce forms of money like Bitcoin. This is an exciting moment in history where, for the first time, we have the opportunity to initiate a peaceful revolution that returns power to the people. Let us not squander this chance to shape a brighter future.

When all the king's horses and all the king's men cannot put the monetary system back together again, that is when a free market sound money will thrive, and deflation in the form of declining prices will be king.

As we wrap up our journey exploring the possibility of a decentralized monetary system, it's time to confront some of the key challenges and objections that have been raised against this revolutionary idea.

SIDE NOTE: This chapter has only lightly scratched the surface of the benefits of sound money, like Bitcoin. Therefore, I highly encourage everyone to continue exploring its possibilities and, more importantly, to pay attention to how money impacts you and those around you.

CHAPTER 14

REBUTTING MAINSTREAM BELIEFS

Why Capitalism Isn't the Problem & Regulation or Taxation Are Not the Answer

"Democracy and socialism have nothing in common but one word, equality. But notice the difference: while democracy seeks equality in liberty, socialism seeks equality in restraint and servitude." —Alexis de Tocqueville

....

When I was a little whipper snapper growing up in New Zealand, I had my eye on a scooter at the local toy store. I thought, "If I could just get that scooter, it would fix all of life's problems!"

After three endless months of diligent saving, I finally had saved enough. I wandered down to the store with my father and two brothers, and following much deliberation over which colour to go for, I had made up my mind. As we walked up to the till, my excitement quickly turned to disappointment when my dad suggested it was unfair that I was to get a scooter while my brothers went without. By the time we left the store, I had paid for my scooter, while my dad had purchased one for each of my brothers. Despite finally having the scooter I longed for, I felt bitter and disillusioned.

I left the store that day with a sour taste in my mouth. Although my father claimed this was in the name of fairness, the world felt unfair to me. "What about all the extra chores I had shouldered, the candy I had sacrificed, and the energy I had dedicated to saving up for that scooter?" I thought to myself. "My brothers hadn't contributed anything, yet they enjoyed all the candy and the ultimate reward of the scooter." This unfairness weighed heavily on me, creating immense resentment in my young mind.

Looking back, what I find fascinating is that this experience may have unknowingly been the catalyst that sparked my interest in monetary intervention, starting the journey that led me here, writing this book.

If I took one thing from this experience, it is that monetary intervention misaligns incentives. When people receive money through channels outside the traditional realms of work or trade, it severs the link between the act of work and the pursuit of what we desire. This can lead to disastrous consequences, such as normalizing the exploitation of others' labour for personal gain. This is true whether we're talking about a child's allowance, a government stimulus package, or a housing subsidy.

But, of course, not everyone sees things this way. For example, my brothers lean towards a socialist approach to society, strongly supporting government intervention. *Hmm... I wonder why.* They might argue that the problems we face are not the result of government overreach but rather:

1. unregulated capitalism,
2. insufficient regulation,
3. inadequate taxation,
4. or lack of social support from the welfare state.

While I respect that everyone is entitled to their own beliefs, I'd like to push back on these four common left-leaning beliefs to round out this book.

Capitalism

You don't have to browse social media for too long or read the news to see that people want change. People are starting to speak out about the issues within our society: wealth inequality, rising house prices, the relentless increase in the overall cost of living, systemic malinvestment, and the great concentration of monopolies. However, it can be challenging to decipher the root cause of the issues we face, so we see several conflicting opinions even when the problems themselves are clear.

Countless millennials feel disconnected from previous generations as they will be the first generation to be poorer than their parents.[467] The middle class, once a symbol of stability and prosperity, is becoming disillusioned as traditional markers of middle-class life, such as owning a home, are increasingly out of reach.[468] Frustration and dissatisfaction are driving individuals to seek alternatives and explore solutions to escape this predicament. And, unfortunately, capitalism and its lack of governance appear to take the brunt of the blame. As a result, in recent years, people have been more drawn to regimes such as communism or socialism that purport to promote liberation and equality (40% of Americans have a favourable view of socialism, up from 36% in 2019).[469] This growing portion of the population sees capitalism as the foundational issue plaguing society. But is capitalism really to blame?

With capitalism seemingly focused on private enterprise and profit, it is not hard to understand why capitalism appears flawed compared to communism or socialism. However, if history is any representation of the future, the communist and socialist facade of liberation, equality and a focus on the people could not be further from the truth. Here are a few historical examples[470]:

- **Mao Zedong, China, 1943–1976 (Socialism):** 70,000,000 died by mass murder and government policies (largest death count in history).
- **Joseph Stalin, Soviet Union, 1922–1952 (Communism):** 28,000,000 died by war, genocide and famine (second largest death count in history).
- **Adolf Hitler, Germany, 1933–1945 (Socialism):** 12,000,000 died by war and genocide (third largest death count in history).
- **Kim Jong-Il, North Korea, 1993–2011 (Socialism):** 2,500,000–3,500,000 (10–19% of the population) died during the 1990s famine partly caused by government policies.[471]
- **Pol Pot, Cambodia, 1975–1979 (Communism):** 1,700,000–1,900,000 (21–24% of the population) died of government policies and famine.[472]
- **Provisional Military Administrative Council (Communism), Ethiopia, 1974–1987:** 1,200,000 died from famine partly caused by government policies.[473]

It quickly becomes apparent that many of the significant genocides, famines, and wars were all under communist and socialist regimes. These coercive structures have repeatedly failed to fix the problem.

We have an inherent desire to want to help others. This can be seen throughout history in the countless organizations that have been set up to assist the underprivileged. However, forced capital reallocation from the haves to the have-nots is not the answer. Stealth taxation measures, such as financial repression or monetary intervention to redistribute capital, only short-circuit our natural tendency to want help by creating expectations on behalf of the have-nots and distaste in the mouths of the haves. This leads to tension and social unrest.

Capitalism tends to be the scapegoat for many of our issues since:

1. Most of these issues we face revolve around the monetary system,
2. For many, they see money as the driver behind wealth inequality, given that our money is increasingly purchasing less.

The reality is that the victims of so-called capitalism are, in fact, the people who have lost capitalism due to increasing governance, regulation and control. In other words, the more control government is given, the more these issues are exacerbated, as should now be evident. As Hyman Minsky wrote in his 1986 book, *Stabilizing an Unstable Economy,* "Every time the Federal Reserve protects a financial instrument, it legitimizes the use of this instrument to finance activity. This means that not only does Federal Reserve action abort an incipient crisis, but it sets the stage for a resumption in the process of increasing indebtedness— and makes possible the introduction of new instruments."[474]

Capitalism is not undermined by debt per se, but rather by stabilizing the economy by socializing losses during a collapse, eroding capitalism's foundation of creative destruction.

Instead of reducing debt during the 2008 global financial crisis, the world's debt has increased by nearly 50%, surpassing three times the size of the global economy.[475] Without government intervention, our current unnatural economy would collapse. And if Hyman Minsky's theories are accurate, we can continue to expect further intervention and increased turmoil as the problems we face are merely deferred.

Capitalism is the natural process of using ingenuity to increase productivity, with those offering value outperforming those that don't. Arguably, since the dawn of time, capitalism has existed. Cavemen used ingenuity to create tools to increase hunting efficiency and reap more food rewards.

On the flip side, the emergence of communism and socialism can be seen as a response to perceived issues within the capitalist system. While these ideologies criticize capitalism for exploiting workers and concentrating wealth, I would argue that these ideologies emerged out of distrust and resentment towards those perceived as true value creators. This can be seen as the artificial economic structures inherent in communism and socialism restrict freedom of expression and rely on coercive and extractive wealth redistribution. This does a few things:

1. It undermines the "reap what you sow" principle and fosters an "us vs them" mentality, pitting value creators against those relying on support. Rather than promoting collaboration in value creation, these systems have often created widespread distrust.[476]
2. This redirection of resources towards centralized planning and state-controlled sectors limits the ability of market forces to allocate resources efficiently, leading to inefficiencies and the erosion of productive sectors in the economy. As capital is redirected away from economically productive individuals and sectors, overall economic growth and innovation are often hindered.

Given the above traits of these structures, combined with an emphasis on collective ownership and shared resources, they tend to erode individual agency and foster a culture of dependency on government or centralized authority for aid and support.

Have you ever noticed how, during an airplane's safety demonstration, the flight attendant emphasizes the importance of securing your own oxygen mask before helping others in an emergency? This analogy draws a compelling connection to capitalism, in which both capitalism and putting on your oxygen mask first indirectly prioritize the well-being of the collective. Although socialism places the collective above all else, capitalism recognizes that by prioritizing the autonomy and strength of the individual, the system creates a foundation for individuals to support and uplift others. Regimes prioritizing the collective without valuing individual autonomy risk deterioration, as they lack the individuals capable of stepping up and providing the necessary support in times of trouble.

Regarding point two above, innovation doesn't tend to come from large, centralized powers. Instead, it emerges on the fringe. It is through the free flow of information that creativity and innovation thrive. When we restrict competition, impede the flow of capital, and silence dissent, we severely inhibit innovation and creativity. We prevent factual data contrary or divergent from the mainstream messaging from percolating to those who can use this information meaningfully.

But what about monopolies? Aren't they large, centralized powers that are a product of capitalism? To answer this, it's first worth noting that monopolies can be broken into two categories.

An economic monopoly, just like capitalism, can be a naturally emergent structure. This type of monopoly occurs when a company or entity controls the market for a particular good or service because of the unique value it offers. If a company's product is innovative enough to outstrip competition that they dominate the entire market, you might see a natural monopoly formed. Although economic monopolies have the potential to restrict competition, they are limited in what they can do as there is nothing impeding competition. While it may be challenging to dethrone their dominance in the industry, another company can still do so by better meeting the consumer's needs in their own product or service.

On the other hand, a legal monopoly is an unnatural structure as it is created through government intervention and legislation.

They arise when the government grants a single company or entity the exclusive right to provide a particular good or service. This exclusive right is often granted in return for some public benefit, such as the construction of infrastructure or the provision of an essential service. For example, the US Postal Service has a legal monopoly on delivering first-class mail.

Economic monopolies, in a general sense, are not inherently detrimental to society. They only become problematic when they restrict growth and hinder innovation by suppressing competition to preserve their monopoly. This suppression of competition is a defining feature of legal monopolies.

In a free market, an economic monopoly is in its position because it adds value to society. Consumers have chosen to buy their goods and services, leading to their growth and expansion. However, in a healthy, competitive free market environment, when these monopolies stop offering value and/or a superior product or service comes to market, consumers will transition to a new brand that offers greater value.

Unfortunately, this is not the case in our current system. Adversarial monopolies in our current system are not a naturally emergent structure. They are a product of manipulation.

Due to the lobbying environment in most democratic nations, monopolies can donate large sums of money to those in power to sway regulation to their benefit. This regulation aids these monopolies by increasing entry barriers and thus reducing competition— transforming once economic monopolies into legal monopolies.

For example, five big banks dominate and control 45% of the assets in the current banking environment.[477] Since the 1960s, the US has experienced a decline from around 37,000 banks to below 11,000 banks today (Figure 14.1). This is due to legislation like Dodd-Frank, as discussed in Chapter Ten, or the recent expansion of FDIC deposit insurance that exclusively benefits select commercial banks.[478] As a result, depositors are incentivized to shift their funds from small banks to larger ones, perceiving them as more secure. These regulations promote consolidation and mergers, posing significant challenges for smaller banks that must navigate numerous obstacles to remain competitive.

Figure 14.1

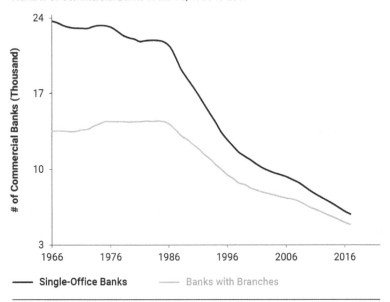

50+ Years of Banking Sector Consolidation
Number of Commercial Banks in the US, 1966 to 2017

Source: Federal Deposit Insurance Corporation

All in all, while the free market of value creation may not always guarantee the best ideas rise to the top, it is far superior and more equitable than relying on any centralized entity to decide what is valuable and what is not. Centralized decision-making is vulnerable to various incentives and biases that distort the selection process. In contrast, the free market encourages diverse perspectives and allows society's collective intelligence to determine the most valuable ideas. This ongoing process of discovery, adaptation, and growth is what enables the economy to advance and grow over time.

SIDE NOTE: Although I may lean towards a free market-based system, it is my belief that no one system is perfect and wholly capable of meeting the varied needs of the population. Therefore, in pursuing a better world, we must refrain from conflating the vehicle—be it capitalism, socialism, or communism—with the destination: improved quality of life, community, and solidarity. Clinging mindlessly to ideologies only hinders progress as we're confined to how things "should be," held hostage by the very camps meant to liberate us. To grow, we must be willing to explore beyond the familiar and embrace alternative paths that embody our shared ideals.

This leads us to the next popular attribution for our economic problems: insufficient regulation.

Regulation

Many would argue that we do not do enough on the regulation front and that the issues we face, such as environmental destruction, pervasive greed, and excessive risk-taking, result from poor regulatory environments. People taking this line of thought tend to see the solution to our problems as tighter regulation to inhibit undesirable behaviour.

However, what this belief doesn't consider is that:

1. In politics, the majority of the public values the appearance of action, even if it leads to suboptimal solutions that create further issues down the line.
2. Heavy-handed regulation to restrict behaviour in our chaotic and complex world often leads to unintended consequences.
3. Regulation is generally a short-term fix that masks underlying issues, inhibiting our ability to alter behaviour and fix the root problem.
4. Imposing regulation doesn't guarantee *good* regulation. Who will regulate the regulators? Thus, regulation often becomes a game of whack-a-mole, attempting to resolve dysregulation from past regulations.
5. Regulation isn't free. We, the taxpayers and businesses, foot the bill through taxation and elevated prices, diverting resources away from value creation.

Pure free market capitalism, in contrast, is frequently associated with a total absence of regulation. However, that is not entirely accurate. In fact, the main factor contributing to the success of free market capitalism is regulation. In a capitalist society, rules are determined by the market rather than by politically driven bureaucrats.

In this sense, the free market has an innate ability to self-regulate, making overbearing regulation unwarranted. In a free market, people chase profits and act in their own self-interest. While self-interest may strike people as a negative concept, I would argue in this setting, it's a good thing! Their behaviour contributes to what the market deems valuable, and profits indicate that an entrepreneur successfully created value— they produced something more valuable than the sum of its combined parts.

This value creation raises everyone's quality of life.

On the flip side, if someone attempts to produce goods or services but ends up making a loss— their end product is worth less than the sum of its parts. The market will force them to either improve quality or efficiency. If not, they will either be driven out of business or acquired by a rival who is better at satisfying customer needs.

When the government plays a heavy hand in regulation, bailouts, subsidies, loan guarantees, or otherwise steps in to socialize private risk, they stimulate behaviour which may have otherwise been avoided. Meanwhile, free market features like free-floating interest rates can serve as natural deterrents to fiscal irresponsibility and malinvestment. When capital costs rise during economic stress, poor choices become costly, limiting capital flows, and providing immediate consequences for behaviour that damages economic health.

When a system lacks self-regulation and starts to break down, heavy-handed regulation often seems necessary. But it is only necessary to redirect capital to areas crucial for the continuation of the unsustainable system. It is true that without this regulation, the system would no longer function. Yet increasing regulation, in this scenario, only exacerbates the issues by ignoring the underlying problems that caused the unsustainability in the first place. For instance, by artificially suppressing interest rates and making debt cheap to ease the burden of debt, we see the proliferation of zombie companies, malinvestment, and ineffective capital allocation, which all require further regulation.

Instead of engaging in a never-ending game of cat and mouse, attempting to squash misaligned behaviour through regulation, first, we should step back and reflect. Would this behaviour exist regardless of the environment, or is it a byproduct of our system? And second, we should acknowledge the free market's capability to self-regulate through incentivizing positive behaviour, where companies strive to raise their standards because it pays to.

Personally, my perspective on regulation is not one of extremes. Rather, I see it as a spectrum spanning from minimal regulation to heavy-handedness. While I generally favour minimal regulation, I also believe that a certain level of regulation is necessary to safeguard the interests of people, businesses, and the environment. The critical question we must ask ourselves is, how much regulation is too much? As this book has highlighted, I would argue that we currently lean heavily towards the "too much" side of the spectrum.

Taxation

The third source that is often mistakenly blamed for the problems in our economic system is insufficient taxation. Folks with this mindset argue that our problems are a product of greed and that the rich are not being taxed enough.

This misdirected view overlooks that our already progressive income tax rates (I.e., your tax rate increases as your wage income rises) inhibit economic productivity.

Everyone is varied in their ability to create value and generate capital. However, we have a system whereby those who have shown to create significant economic value are generally taxed far more than those with a lesser capacity to create value. A progressive tax system ultimately discourages productivity, as higher tax rates are imposed on the ones creating value. In the United States, the top 1% of income earners contribute 42% of the total tax revenue, despite proving to be the best value generators.[479]

We are removing capital from productive means and redistributing to areas of society that are struggling.

Although this seems reasonable initially, we are perpetuating failure and economic destruction. We reward those who fail to allocate capital effectively with lower tax rates and penalize those who create value.

As previously discussed, when a significant portion of one's earnings are forcibly taken in taxes to fund inefficient social spending, it fosters resentment in taxpayers and raises expectations in those seeking support.

If high tax rates were the answer, one would expect California to be one of the more favourable places to live, considering they have the highest tax rate of all the US states.[480] Yet:

- Half of the US's homeless population lives in California.[481]
- California has the most unreliable power grid. "According to data by Eaton Corporation, the state leads the US in power outages every year, with more than double the outages of any other state over the last decade." [482]
- Despite a nearly $100 billion surplus in 2022, California faces a $25 billion budget deficit for 2023.[483]
- California ranks as the state with the lowest quality of life compared to all other 50 states.[484]

As a result, California saw the largest population outflow of any state in the last few years, with 101 thousand families moving elsewhere.[485]

And whilst California is just one state in the US, the reality is that California, in terms of GDP, would be the 5th largest nation in the world, just shy of Germany.[486]

With this in mind, effective capital allocation, not high tax rates, determines the quality of life. Rather than looking to increase tax revenue from the wealthy, we should think very consciously about taxation, and its effects on economic value creation, as our current system is not favourable to sustainable, productive growth.

One potential solution could be implementing a simple flat tax system, where everyone pays the same tax rate regardless of income level. This would contrast with the current complex progressive tax system, which features numerous exemptions, deductions, and credits, incentivizing various special interest groups to seek favourable treatment. By eliminating the ability of any group to manipulate the tax system for their benefit, a flat tax would reduce the influence of lobbyists on government officials and lawmakers. Furthermore, such a system would reduce the government's ability to prioritize certain sectors of the economy through favourable taxation.

Additionally, implementing such a system would significantly reduce bureaucratic overheads and eliminate preparation costs, including fees paid to tax professionals. As a result, more than $14.4 billion, the total spent on tax preparations in 2023, would remain in the hands of the general population, fostering increased financial empowerment.[487]

Welfare State

Self-interest, typically associated with pursuing personal ambitions and prioritizing individual needs and desires, has led to criticisms of free market capitalism's ability to address the needs of marginalized individuals and those facing disadvantageous circumstances. The question arises: How can a system built on self-interest adequately support those who are unable to fend for themselves or have been dealt an unfair hand in life?

Within the confines of this conventional definition, capitalism may indeed seem limited in its capacity to address this pressing concern. However, it is important to recognize that this simplified view doesn't account for the fact that essentially every action we make can be traced back to self-interest.

Consider, for instance, when we support our children financially or emotionally. While it may appear selfless on the surface, an underlying self-interested desire exists to propagate our genetics and ensure our lineage's continuity. Similarly, when we support and assist an elderly parent, we tap into our instinctual desire to love, support, and nurture those dear to us.[488]

Volunteering at a local charity organization may also serve as a testament to self-interest. We are often driven by the desire to contribute to a cause to make a positive impact, or there is an acknowledgment that such efforts can bring social capital and networking opportunities, enhancing our personal growth and connections. What's more, giving back to the community or engaging in acts of altruism is not devoid of self-interest. It may align with our moral and social values, reinforcing our sense of purpose and belonging within society.

It is self-interest that makes the world go round! Recognizing the complexities of self-interest allows us to explore the possibilities of harnessing self-interest as a force for positive change and better understand how and why free market systems function.

Simplifying the free market as devoid of social support or concern for the collective or any other slurs against such a system overlooks the intricate nature of human behaviour and the dynamics of society. As we shift our focus inwards from the broader context of our nation to our local communities and, finally, our immediate families, our behaviour undergoes a transformation.

While someone may strongly support free markets and reduced government intervention at the national level, they can also be actively involved in social, collaborative endeavours on a community level. Since my teenage years, I have volunteered my time to assist vulnerable youth, providing them with essential resources such as food, shelter, and support. Additionally, I've created and conducted countless free financial talks to empower those struggling with society's pressures. I share these experiences not to seek praise but to emphasize that despite my firm beliefs in free markets, such beliefs shift as my circle of influence draws nearer.

Where our present-day system falls short is that, firstly, it places immense pressure on individuals to fend for themselves, impeding their ability to thrive and fulfill their potential. Chapter Four highlights how this pressure drives individuals to prioritize basic physiological needs like food, clothing, and shelter above other more nuanced forms of self-interested behaviour, such as supporting loved ones or contributing to their local community.

Secondly, given the individuals limited time and resources, the state progressively assumes these responsibilities that individuals and communities would otherwise manage. This shift creates a sense of isolation and loneliness for those reliant on the welfare state as their personal agency and connection to their local communities diminishes.

That said, under a system where the government operates with limited capital, primarily obtained through taxation, the welfare state does not simply disappear. However, such a system compels the government to be more conscientious about how it allocates capital, emphasizing the importance of long-term planning and sustainable solutions rather than short-term fixes.

While the government can still fund war above and beyond social support, if the population disagrees with its allocation of resources, it will likely withdraw its support in the form of votes. This dynamic incentivizes the government to listen to the concerns and preferences of the voters, fostering an environment where the government's actions reflect the desires of its constituents.

Through this lens, I envision a more thoughtful and conscientious allocation of capital, moving away from excessive military funding and towards social agendas that prioritize long-term sustainable practices. Moreover, capital limitations serve as boundaries to expanding the welfare state, compelling the government to carefully consider resource allocation to ensure society's long-term health and well-being.

I hope this chapter has highlighted that the pursuit of prosperity and a more equitable economy will not be achieved through increased regulation, taxation, or socialization. Instead, it requires a monetary system that realigns incentives and promotes value creation and accountability. Only then will we see a more conscious approach to capital allocation and a reduction in overbearing government. By unleashing the power of a decentralized sovereign monetary system, we can empower individuals and create a more productive and sustainable society that better meets the varied needs of everyone involved.

FINAL WORDS

"It always seems impossible until it's done."
—Nelson Mandela

....

In 1965, Martin Seligman was researching classical conditioning in dogs, the process by which an animal or human creates associations between different stimuli.[489] In these experiments, Seligman would ring a bell and then briefly shock the dog. After a while, the dog began to anticipate the shock by reacting after hearing the bell but before being administered the shock.

Then something unexpected happened.

These dogs were placed into a crate with a dividing wall running down the middle. The floor was electrified on one side but not on the other. This wall was also low enough that the dog could see or jump over it if desired. Seligman then placed these dogs on the electric side, briefly shocking them. He anticipated the dog would leap over the divider to the non-shocking side. Instead, the dogs sat down. They appeared to have given up on escaping in the second portion of the experiment, having realized in the first section of the trial that there was nothing they could do to stop the shocks. Seligman labelled this state as "learned helplessness." When we repeatedly encounter a difficult situation and struggle to influence or alter the situation, we give up even when there is potential for change.

As we end this book, I want to leave you with one final thought. Like the dogs in Seligman's experiment, we, too, can become conditioned to accept our circumstances, even if they are uncomfortable or detrimental to our well-being. But we just must jump over the proverbial divider to a new system: a system that realigns our actions toward what's best for humanity.

But it won't be easy. We have become so accustomed to wealth inequality, fiscal mismanagement, deterioration of the family unit, and other horrors that plague modern society that we have developed learned helplessness when it comes to our money. We've just accepted it as this thing that only exists through the state and is simply a means of transacting, nothing more.

It is up to us to choose a different path, prioritizing long-term stability over short-term gains and aligning our incentives with the health and well-being of our planet and its inhabitants.

Just as our mind and emotions are inextricably linked to our body, and what we fail to express will show itself in the form of illness or disease, problems in our monetary system will make themselves heard one way or another. Everything in modern society is downstream of money, even deeply personal experiences like how we connect with our families. When our monetary system is "sick," nothing escapes the repercussions that ensue.

By changing our perspective, we can realize that the hurdles and challenges our current system attempts to eliminate or hide are simply signals that give us insight into what's working and what's not. From this, we can choose to implement change and grow, or we can ignore reality. However, as aptly articulated by Ayn Rand, "We can ignore reality, but we cannot ignore the consequences of ignoring reality."

If we were to redirect a fraction of the time and energy we have invested in:

- going to war,
- financial handouts,
- pillaging nations,

- misallocating capital,
- or propping up failing institutions,

on rebuilding the monetary system, I believe that many of the challenges we face today would alter course and trend toward resolution.

Although there is no perfect panacea, and every system has its drawbacks, revising our monetary system to align our incentives will bring us closer to an environment where people look to create value and cooperate simply because it is in their best interest.

And more importantly, if we can realign our money to enable accurate and transparent expression, we will be in a position to gain deeper insight into society's collective aspirations and desires. Armed with this understanding, we will be better equipped to make informed economic decisions, enhancing prosperity and, ultimately, improving humanity's chance of survival.

Lastly, I want to reiterate that no one has all the answers. I definitely don't, but neither do those in positions of power. With this in mind, we must start recognizing how important an effective monetary system is, one with the capacity to give us clearer answers. Democracy, let alone a free market, cannot coexist with a state-controlled monetary system. When the government controls our money, it holds immense power over us, the people. Only by separating money and state can we ensure that the government truly represents the voice of the people, and that power remains in the hands of the populace.

It's about time we realign our monetary system. If we can work together to build a better system, I truly believe the future is bright!

Thank you for taking the time to read this book! Have questions or thoughts? Reach out anytime— I'd love to hear from you. And if you found value in this book, please consider leaving a review on Amazon. Your feedback helps me grow as an author and helps readers discover this book. Thanks again!

LIST OF FIGURES

All sources listed were accessed between December 2022 and October 2023.

Chapter One

1.1   Myers, J. (2023, January 8). Deflation vs. Inflation. https://www.onceinaspecies. com/p/deflation-vs-inflation-a-response

1.2   Statista. (2023a, May 2+2). U.S. minimum wage: real and nominal value 1938-2023. https://www.statista.com/statistics/1065466/real-nominal-value-minimum-wage-us/#:~:text=U.S.%20minimum%20wage%3A%20real%20and%20nominal%20value%20 1938%2D2022&text=Although%20the%20real%20dollar%20minimum,2022%20 of%207.25%20U.S.%20dollars.

1.3   Federal surplus or deficit [-]. (2023, March 15). https://fred.stlouisfed.org/series/ FYFSD

1.4   M2. (2023, June 27). https://fred.stlouisfed.org/series/M2SL

1.5   Net saving as a percentage of gross national income. (2023, June 29). https://fred. stlouisfed.org/series/W207RC1Q156SBEA

1.6   Frank, S. (n.d.). US Debt to GDP - 232 Year Chart | LongtermTrends. https://www. longtermtrends.net/us-debt-to-gdp/

1.7   Hoisington Investment Management Company - Economic Overview. (n.d.). https:// hoisington.com/economic_overview.html

1.8   Goldchartsrus. (n.d.). 200 Years of the Dow/Gold Ratio. http://www.goldchartsrus. com/chartstemp/DowGoldRatio.php

Chapter Two

2.1   Bhutada, G. (2021, April 7). Purchasing Power of the U.S. Dollar Over Time. Visual Capitalist. https://www.visualcapitalist.com/purchasing-power-of-the-u-s-dollar-over-time/

2.2   https://www.google.com/finance/quote/.INX:INDEXSP?sa=X&ved=2a hUKEwiKvMilk9T7AhWCMDQIHey6CswQ3ecFegQIMxAg & Pk. (2023). Historical US Home Prices: Monthly Median from 1953-2023. DQYDJ – Don't Quit Your Day Job. . . https://dqydj.com/historical-home-prices/ & TRADING ECONOMICS. (n.d.). United States Average Hourly Wages - June 2023 Data - 1964-2022 Historical. https://tradingeconomics.com/united-states/wages

2.3   Share of Total Net Worth Held by the Top 1% (99th to 100th Wealth Percentiles). (2022, June 29). https://fred.stlouisfed.org/series/WFRBST01134 & Share of Total Net Worth Held by the 50th to 90th Wealth Percentiles. (2023, June 16). https:// fred.stlouisfed.org/series/WFRBSN40188

2.4   Mack, A. (2019). A Cross-Country Quarterly Database of Real House Prices. In Federal Reserve Bank of Dallas. https://www.dallasfed.org/-/media/documents/institute/wpapers/2011/0099.pdf

Chapter Three

3.1   Anil. (n.d.). Gumroad. https://anilsaidso.gumroad.com/

3.2   Market & Financial Insights, Research & Strategy - BofA Securities. (n.d.). BofA Securities. https://business.bofa.com/en-us/content/market-strategies-insights.html

Chapter Five

5.1   Monaco, A. P. (2020). An epigenetic, transgenerational model of increased mental health disorders in children, adolescents and young adults. European Journal of Human Genetics, 29(3), 387–395. https://doi.org/10.1038/s41431-020-00726-4

5.2   Government of Canada, Statistics Canada. (2016, May 30). The rise of the dual-earner family with children. https://www150.statcan.gc.ca/n1/pub/11-630-x/11-630-x2016005-eng.htm

5.3   Jones, R. S., & Seitani, H. (2019). Labour market reform in Japan to cope with a shrinking and ageing population. OECD Economics Department Working Papers. https://doi.org/10.1787/73665992-en

5.4   Ingraham, C. (2020, January 21). Millennials' share of the U.S. housing market: Small and shrinking. Washington Post. https://www.washingtonpost.com/business/2020/01/20/millennials-share-us-housing-market-small-shrinking/

5.5   File:US consumer debt.png - Wikimedia Commons. (2016, December 20). https://commons.wikimedia.org/wiki/File:US_consumer_debt.png

Chapter Six

6.1   Wealth Management | Morgan Stanley. (n.d.). Morgan Stanley. https://www.morganstanley.com/what-we-do/wealth-management

6.2   Today's Unicorns Have Bigger Cumulative Losses than Amazon, Lost Money far Longer than Amazon, Still No Turnaround | Wolf Street. (2021, July 5). https://wolfstreet.com/2021/07/05/todays-unicorns-have-bigger-cumulative-losses-than-amazon-had-lost-money-far-longer-than-amazon-still-dont-show-a-turnaround/

6.3   Tabarrok, A. (2019, August 16). Are Health Administrators To Blame? - Marginal REVOLUTION. Marginal REVOLUTION. https://marginalrevolution.com/marginalrevolution/2019/08/are-health-administrators-to-blame.html

6.4   Hamtil, L. (2018). The Annoying Capex vs Buybacks Narrative. Fortune Financial Advisors. https://fortunefinancialadvisors.com/blog/the-annoying-capex-vs-buybacks-narrative/

ENDNOTES

All sources listed were accessed between December 2022 and October 2023.

1   Statista. (2023, June 2). U.S. population share by generation 2022. https://www. statista.com/statistics/296974/us-population-share-by-generation/

2   Ingraham, C. (2020, January 21). Millennials' share of the U.S. housing market: Small and shrinking. Washington Post. https://www.washingtonpost.com/ business/2020/01/20/millennials-share-us-housing-market-small-shrinking/

3   Casais, E. (n.d.). US household income distribution. © 2008 Areppim AG. https:// stats.areppim.com/stats/stats_compxgrowth_us.htm

4   Schneider, R. (2023, January 19). The average car price the year you were born. Cheapism. https://blog.cheapism.com/average-car-price-by-year/#slide=63

5   Pk. (2022). Average, Median, Top 1%, and all United States Individual Income Percentiles. DQYDJ – Don't Quit Your Day Job. . . https://dqydj.com/average-median-top-individual-income-percentiles/#:~:text=adjusted%20for%20inflation.-,What%20was%20the%20median%20individual%20income%3F,up%20from%20%2444%2C225%20in%202021.

6   Gitlin, J. M. (2023, January 12). You're not imagining it—new cars really have gotten much more expensive. Ars Technica. https://arstechnica.com/cars/2023/01/the-average-new-car-price-reached-49075-in-december/#:~:text=The%20average%20transaction%20price%20of,to%20factors%20like%20dealer%20markups.)

7   Lee, B. (2021, August 19). China's capital controls: here to stay? Central Banking. https://www.centralbanking.com/central-banks/currency/7860946/chinas-capital-controls-here-to-stay

8   Board Members. (n.d.). https://www.federalreserve.gov/aboutthefed/bios/board/default.htm

9   Fed announces massive cash injection to relieve U.S. debt market. (2020, March 12). POLITICO. https://www.politico.com/news/2020/03/12/fed-announces-massive-cash-injection-to-relieve-us-debt-market-127284

10   Romm, T., Meyer, T., Caldwell, L. A., & Sotomayor, M. (2023, May 28). Biden, McCarthy reach 'agreement in principle' to raise debt ceiling as default looms. Washington Post. https://www.washingtonpost.com/business/2023/05/27/debt-ceiling-talks/

11   DeParle, J. (2021, July 18). Stimulus checks substantially reduced hardship, study shows. The New York Times. https://www.nytimes.com/2021/06/02/us/politics/stimulus-checks-economic-hardship.html

12   What it takes to build a solar farm | Arcadia. (n.d.). Arcadia. https://www.arcadia.com/blog/how-to-build-a-solar-farm

13   How gold is mined | Gold mining process | World Gold Council. (n.d.). World Gold Council. https://www.gold.org/gold-supply/gold-mining-lifecycle#:~:text=Gold%20Mine%20Exploration%3A%201%20-%2010%20years&text=It%20requires%20significant%20time%2C%20financial,lead%20to%20a%20productive%20mine.

14   Reuters. (2023, May 3). EU okays $1.61 billion for Dutch government to buy out farmers, reduce nitrogen. Reuters. https://www.reuters.com/world/europe/eu-okays-161-bln-dutch-govt-buy-out-farmers-reduce-nitrogen-2023-05-02/

15   Robert Breedlove. (2021, November 23). The Ultimate Macro Framework with Raoul Pal (WiM078) [Video]. YouTube. https://www.youtube.com/watch?v=i9TXVjYBM3U

16   World Population Clock: 8.0 billion people (LIVE, 2023) - Worldometer. (n.d.). https://www.worldometers.info/world-population/#:~:text=World%20Population%20 Clock%3A%207.98%20Billion%20People%20(2022)%20%2D%20Worldometer

17   Canada 2020 and Beyond | Demographic Trends | Environics Analytics. (2020, February 28). Default. https://environicsanalytics.com/en-ca/resources/blogs/ea-blog/2020/02/28/canada-2020-and-beyond

18   Desk, W. (2021, October 1). China's population could halve in 45 years, says study. The Week. https://www.theweek.in/news/world/2021/10/01/chinas-population-could-halve-in-45-years-says-study.html#:~:text=China's%20population%20could%20 halve%20in%20the%20next%2045%20years%2C%20a,per%20woman%20as%20 of%202020.

19   What the 2020 census will reveal about America: Stagnating growth, an aging population, and youthful diversity | Brookings. (2022, March 9). Brookings. https:// www.brookings.edu/articles/what-the-2020-census-will-reveal-about-america-stagnating-growth-an-aging-population-and-youthful-diversity/

20   Wilt, C. (2022). The government will pay you to have babies in these countries. Money. https://money.com/government-pays-have-a-baby-low-birth-rate/

21   Is U.S. currency still backed by gold? (n.d.). Board of Governors of the Federal Reserve System. https://www.federalreserve.gov/faqs/currency_12770.htm

22   Meredith, S. (2023, June 21). History of U.S. circulating Coins | U.S. mint. United States Mint. https://www.usmint.gov/learn/history/us-circulating-coins#:~:text=Coinage%20Act%20of%201792&text=The%20Mint%20delivered%20 the%20nation's,%2C%201793%3A%2011%2C178%20copper%20cents.

23   Gold Standard - Econlib. (2023, April 14). Econlib. https://www.econlib.org/library/ Enc/GoldStandard.html#:~:text=The%20United%20States%2C%20though%20 formally,passed%20the%20Gold%20Standard%20Act.

24   White, L. H. (2021, May 20). How U.S. Government Paper Currency Began, and How Private Banknotes Ended. CATO AT LIBERTY. https://www.cato. org/blog/how-us-government-paper-currency-began-how-private-banknotes-ended#:~:text=Private%20commercial%20banks%20issued%20banknotes,and%20 semi%E2%80%90%E2%80%8Bgovernmental%20issues.

25   Myers, J. (2023b, January 8). Deflation vs. Inflation. By Jesse Myers. https://www. onceinaspecies.com/p/deflation-vs-inflation-a-response

26   Elwell, C. K. (2011). Brief History of the Gold Standard in the United States. Congressional Research Service. https://sgp.fas.org/crs/misc/R41887.pdf

27   The Fed explained. (n.d.). https://www.federalreserve.gov/aboutthefed/the-fed-explained.htm

28   Mullins, Eustace (2021, March 15). The Secrets of the Federal Reserve

29   WSJ.com News Graphics. (n.d.). A century of inflation. WSJ. https://graphics.wsj. com/annotation/?slug=inflation&standalone=1

30   Hudson, M. (2003). Super Imperialism - New Edition: The Origin and Fundamentals of U.S. World Dominanc. Pluto Press (UK).

31   Wikipedia contributors. (2023). Executive Order 6102. Wikipedia. https:// en.wikipedia.org/wiki/Executive_Order_6102

32   Wikipedia contributors. (2023b). Bretton Woods Conference. Wikipedia. https:// en.wikipedia.org/wiki/Bretton_Woods_Conference

33   Federal reserve actions to support the flow of credit to households and businesses. (n.d.). Board of Governors of the Federal Reserve System. https://www.federalreserve. gov/newsevents/pressreleases/monetary20200315b.htm

34 Kenton, W. (2022). What is Nixon Shock? Definition, what happened, and aftereffects. Investopedia. https://www.investopedia.com/terms/n/nixon-shock.asp

35 Contributor, A. J. P. O. (2023, May 10). The Hill. The Hill. https://thehill.com/opinion/finance/575722-the-us-has-never-defaulted-on-its-debt-except-the-four-times-it-did./

36 Marron, D. (2013, October 8). Actually, the United States has defaulted before. Forbes. https://www.forbes.com/sites/beltway/2013/10/08/actually-the-united-states-has-defaulted-before/?sh=535eba906021

37 12-month percentage change, Consumer Price Index, selected categories. (n.d.). https://www.bls.gov/charts/consumer-price-index/consumer-price-index-by-category-line-chart.htm

38 Staff, D. H. (2023). US banking system nursing over $600,000,000,000 worth of unrealized losses, warns macro guru Lyn Alden. The Daily Hodl. https://dailyhodl.com/2023/03/15/us-banking-system-nursing-over-600000000000-worth-of-unrealized-losses-warns-macro-guru-lyn-alden/

39 Russell, K., & Zhang, C. (2023, May 2). First Republic, Silicon Valley Bank and Signature: How banking Failures compare. The New York Times. https://www.nytimes.com/interactive/2023/business/bank-failures-svb-first-republic-signature.html

40 Frank, S. (n.d.). US Debt to GDP - 232 Year Chart | Longtermtrends. https://www.longtermtrends.net/us-debt-to-gdp/

41 Letters, F. (2020, July 21). Hirschmann Capital 1H 2020 Letter. Seeking Alpha. https://seekingalpha.com/article/4359674-hirschmann-capital-1h-2020-letter

42 TRADING ECONOMICS. (n.d.). United States Gross Federal Debt to GDP - 2023 Data - 2024 Forecast. https://tradingeconomics.com/united-states/government-debt-to-gdp

43 U.S. National Debt Clock : Real Time. (n.d.). https://www.usdebtclock.org/

44 Tech & Finance. (2023, May 5). Stanley Druckenmiller | May 2023 | Keynote at USC Marshall [Video]. YouTube. https://www.youtube.com/watch?v=SRPMHinrFKQ

45 U.S. National Debt Clock : Real Time. (n.d.). https://www.usdebtclock.org/

46 Recent balance sheet trends. (n.d.). https://www.federalreserve.gov/monetarypolicy/bst_recenttrends.htm

47 Monthly Budget Review: Summary for Fiscal Year 2022 | Congressional Budget Office. (n.d.). https://www.cbo.gov/publication/58592/html

48 USAFacts. (2023, March 20). 2023 Current State of the Union: US Federal Budget. https://usafacts.org/state-of-the-union/budget/

49 Canada Indicators. (n.d.). https://tradingeconomics.com/canada/indicators

50 FX Empire. (2022, July 26). Canada GDP Growth Rate 1961-2023 | FX Empire. https://www.fxempire.com/macro/canada/gdp-growth-rate

51 United Kingdom Indicators. (n.d.). https://tradingeconomics.com/united-kingdom/indicators.

52 Rabouin, D. (2021, February 18). Global debt soars to 356% of GDP. Axios. https://www.axios.com/2021/02/18/global-debt-gdp

53 @GameOfTrades_. (2023, August 6). World debt has rapidly increased since 1997. Twitter. https://twitter.com/GameofTrades_/status/1688188180619567104

54 What does 'global debt' mean and how high is it? (2022, November 24). World Economic Forum. https://www.weforum.org/agenda/2022/05/what-is-global-debt-why-high/

55 World GDP 1960-2023. (n.d.). MacroTrends. https://www.macrotrends.net/countries/WLD/world/gdp-gross-domestic-product

56   Estenssoro, A. (2021, December 9). A Decade after the Crisis, Has the Global Debt Burden Stabilized? St. Louis Fed. https://www.stlouisfed.org/publications/regional-economist/third-quarter-2019/decade-after-crisis-has-global-debt-burden-stabilized

57   Why does the Federal Reserve aim for inflation of 2 percent over the longer run? (n.d.). Board of Governors of the Federal Reserve System. https://www.federalreserve.gov/faqs/economy_14400.htm

58   Levine, M. (2018, September 6). Fed Rejects Bank for Being Too Safe. Bloomberg.com. https://www.bloomberg.com/opinion/articles/2018-09-06/fed-rejects-bank-for-being-too-safe#xj4y7vzkg

59   Ligon, C. (2023, January 27). Custodia Bank Denied Federal Reserve System Membership. CoinDesk. https://www.coindesk.com/policy/2023/01/27/custodia-bank-denied-federal-reserve-system-membership/

60   Custodia Wants Default Win In Fed Master Account Suit - Law360. (n.d.). https://www.law360.com/articles/1555065/custodia-wants-default-win-in-fed-master-account-suit

61   Neufeld, D. (2022). Mapped: Which Countries Have the Highest Inflation? Elements by Visual Capitalist. https://elements.visualcapitalist.com/mapped-countries-with-highest-inflation-rate/

62   Volatility & the Allegory of the Prisoner's Dilemma. (2015). Artemis Capital. http://csinvesting.org/wp-content/uploads/2015/10/Artemis-Q32015-Volatility-and-Prisoners-Dilemma.pdf

63   Quarterly Report. (2022). Federal Deposit Insurance Corporation. https://www.fdic.gov/analysis/quarterly-banking-profile/fdic-quarterly/2022-vol16-4/fdic-v16n4-3q2022.pdf

64   J, Haar. (2023). Fixed supply money does not lead to economic collapse. Swan Bitcoin. https://www.swanbitcoin.com/why-a-fixed-supply-money-does-not-lead-to-economic-catastrophe/

65   US Inflation Calculator. (2023, July 12). Inflation Calculator | Find US dollar's value from 1913-2023. US Inflation Calculator | Easily Calculate How the Buying Power of the U.S. Dollar Has Changed From 1913 to 2023. Get Inflation Rates and U.S. Inflation News. https://www.usinflationcalculator.com/

66   Federal Reserve Actions to Support the Flow of Credit to Households and Businesses. (n.d.). Board of Governors of the Federal Reserve System. https://www.federalreserve.gov/newsevents/pressreleases/monetary20200315b.htm

67   rezzsuperstar. (2020, May 18). Jerome Powell - we print money - 60 minutes interview [Video]. YouTube. https://www.youtube.com/watch?v=lK_rYS8L3kI

68   Hayes, A. (2021). Financial Repression Definition, Features, Consequences. Investopedia. https://www.investopedia.com/terms/f/financial-repression.asp

69   U.S. National Debt Clock : Real Time. (n.d.). https://www.usdebtclock.org/

70   United States Government Bonds - Yields Curve. (n.d.). World Government Bonds. http://www.worldgovernmentbonds.com/country/united-states/

71   TRADING ECONOMICS. (n.d.). United States Inflation Rate - June 2023 Data - 1914-2022 Historical - July Forecast. https://tradingeconomics.com/united-states/inflation-cpi

72   Pettis, Michael, Chandler, A. T (2014, September 2) The Great Rebalancing: Trade, Conflict, and the Perilous Road Ahead for the World Economy

73   World Bank Open Data. (n.d.). World Bank Open Data. https://data.worldbank.org/indicator/NY.GDP.MKTP.CD?locations=CN

74   Chancellor, E. (2022). The price of time: The Real Story of Interest. Atlantic Monthly Press.

75   Chancellor, E. (2022). The price of time: The Real Story of Interest. Atlantic Monthly Press.

76   10 Year Treasury Rate. (n.d.). YCharts. https://ycharts.com/indicators/10_year_treasury_rate

77   Iacurci, G. (2023, January 12). Here's the inflation breakdown for December 2022 — in one chart. CNBC. https://www.cnbc.com/2023/01/12/heres-the-inflation-breakdown-for-december-2022-in-one-chart.html

78   Steverman, B. (2019, June 12). World's Retirees Risk Running Out of Money a Decade Before Death. Bloomberg.com. https://www.bloomberg.com/news/articles/2019-06-13/world-s-retirees-risk-running-out-of-money-a-decade-before-death

79   Life Expectancy in the U.S. Dropped for the Second Year in a Row in 2021. (n.d.). https://www.cdc.gov/nchs/pressroom/nchs_press_releases/2022/20220831.htm

80   Why does the Federal Reserve aim for inflation of 2 percent over the longer run? (n.d.). Board of Governors of the Federal Reserve System. https://www.federalreserve.gov/faqs/economy_14400.htm

81   Barrett, B. (2022, June 23). Would a vacancy tax work in Whistler? It depends who you ask. Pique Newsmagazine. https://www.piquenewsmagazine.com/local-news/would-a-vacancy-tax-work-in-whistler-it-depends-who-you-ask-5508469

82   Peck, M. S. (2003). The Road Less Traveled, Timeless Edition: A New Psychology of Love, Traditional Values and Spiritual Growth. Touchstone.

83   Oxford Languages and Google - English | Oxford Languages. (2022, August 12). https://languages.oup.com/google-dictionary-en/

84   Booth, J. (2020). The Price of Tomorrow: Why Deflation is the Key to an Abundant Future. Stanley Press.

85   Dastin, J. (2023, January 20). Alphabet cuts 12,000 jobs after pandemic hiring spree, refocuses on AI. Reuters. https://www.reuters.com/business/google-parent-lay-off-12000-workers-memo-2023-01-20/

86   Booth, J. (2020). The Price of Tomorrow: Why Deflation is the Key to an Abundant Future. Stanley Press.

87   Eisenstein, C. (2011). Sacred Economics: Money, Gift, & Society in the Age of Transition. North Atlantic Books.

88   Welsh, B. L. (2022, November 2). Part IV: The Growth Imperative - Brianna Lee Welsh - Medium. Medium. https://briannasbites.medium.com/part-iv-the-growth-imperative-21f9180b49e6

89   Kopp, C. M. (2023). Creative Destruction: Out With the Old, in With the New. Investopedia. https://www.investopedia.com/terms/c/creativedestruction.asp

90   Academy, S. (2020). Winning the Customer Journey Battle: Netflix vs Blockbuster Case Study. THE STRATEGY JOURNEY. https://strategyjourney.com/winning-the-customer-journey-battle-netflix-vs-blockbuster-case-study/

91   Assets: Total Assets: Total Assets (Less Eliminations from Consolidation): Wednesday Level. (2023, July 20). https://fred.stlouisfed.org/series/WALCL

92   Stanton, E. (2022, March 9). Fed's Biggest-Ever Bond-Buying Binge Is Drawing to a Close. Bloomberg.com. https://www.bloomberg.com/news/articles/2022-03-09/fed-s-biggest-ever-bond-buying-binge-is-drawing-to-a-close

93   RSA. (2010, February 24). David Cameron in conversation with Nassim Taleb [Video]. YouTube. https://www.youtube.com/watch?v=QQAVDg4yqUU

94   Von Hayek, F. A. (2005). The Road to Serfdom, with The Intellectuals and Socialism: The Condensed Version of The Road to Serfdom by F.A. Hayek as it Appeared in the April 1945 Edition of Reader's Digest.

95   Bowman, R. (2021, November 29). Is value investing dead? – Why value stocks underperform growth stocks. LEHNER INVESTMENTS. https://www.lehnerinvestments.com/en/is-value-investing-dead-why-value-stocks-underperform-growth-stocks/

96   Siedle, E. (2022, October 6). UK Pension Fund Near-Collapse Is A Warning For America's Pensions. Forbes. https://www.forbes.com/sites/edwardsiedle/2022/10/06/uk-pension-fund-near-collapse-is-a-warning-for-americas-pensions/?sh=6704bcdb74fe

97   Throwing and catching. (2020, December 17). Seth's Blog. https://seths.blog/2018/07/throwingcatching/

98   Ponzi Scheme | Investor.gov. (n.d.). https://www.investor.gov/protect-your-investments/fraud/types-fraud/ponzi-scheme

99   Chancellor, E. (2022). The Price of Time: The Real Story of Interest. Atlantic Monthly Press.

100 Maté, G., MD. (2000). Scattered minds: The Origins and Healing of Attention Deficit Disorder. National Geographic Books.

101 Bradshaw, J. (1992). Homecoming: Reclaiming and Healing Your Inner Child. Bantam.

102 Navidad, A. E. (2023). Marshmallow Test Experiment and Delayed Gratification. Simply Psychology. https://www.simplypsychology.org/marshmallow-test.html

103 Mischel, W., Shoda, Y., & Peake, P. K. (1987). The nature of adolescent competencies predicted by preschool delay of gratification. Journal of Personality and Social Psychology, 54(4), 687–696. https://doi.org/10.1037/0022-3514.54.4.687

104 Mcleod, S., PhD. (2023). Maslow's Hierarchy of Needs. Simply Psychology. https://www.simplypsychology.org/maslow.html

105 Gierer, A. (1999). Evolution of Empathy as a Source of Human Altruism. Springer eBooks, 1036–1045. https://doi.org/10.1007/978-94-010-0870-9_65

106 The Evolution of Empathy. (n.d.). Greater Good. https://greatergood.berkeley.edu/article/item/the_evolution_of_empathy

107 Albom, M. (1997). Tuesdays with Morrie: An Old Man, a Young Man, and Life's Greatest Lesson, 25th Anniversary Edition. Crown.

108 Price, C. C. (2020, September 14). Trends in Income From 1975 to 2018. RAND. https://www.rand.org/pubs/working_papers/WRA516-1.html

109 Statista. (2023, April 28). Gross Domestic Product (GDP) in Africa 2010-2027. https://www.statista.com/statistics/1300858/total-gdp-value-in-africa/

110 How the Great Recession Changed American Workers - Knowledge at Wharton. (2018, September 10). Knowledge at Wharton. https://knowledge.wharton.upenn.edu/podcast/knowledge-at-wharton-podcast/great-recession-american-dream/

111 Shalby, C. (2018, September 15). The financial crisis hit 10 years ago. For some, it feels like yesterday - Los Angeles Times. Los Angeles Times. https://www.latimes.com/business/la-fi-financial-crisis-experiences-20180915-htmlstory.html

112 Lerner, M. (2018, October 4). 10 years later: How the housing market has changed since the crash. Washington Post. https://www.washingtonpost.com/news/business/wp/2018/10/04/feature/10-years-later-how-the-housing-market-has-changed-since-the-crash/

113 Ducharme, J. (2019, June 20). U.S. Suicide Rates Are the Highest They've Been Since World War II. Time. https://time.com/5609124/us-suicide-rate-increase/

114 Oxford Languages and Google - English | Oxford Languages. (2022, August 12). https://languages.oup.com/google-dictionary-en/

115 Why more young people are turning to nihilism. (2023, April 12). Huck. https://www.huckmag.com/article/why-more-young-people-are-turning-to-nihilism

116 Hanson, M. (2023, July 16). Student Loan Debt Statistics [2023]: Average + Total Debt. Education Data Initiative. https://educationdata.org/student-loan-debt-statistics

117 Rotter, J. (1966). Generalized expectancies for internal versus external control of reinforcement. American Psychological Association. https://psycnet.apa.org/record/2011-19211-001

118   Benassi, V., Sweeney, P. D., & Dufour, C. L. (1988). Is there a relation between locus of control orientation and depression? Journal of Abnormal Psychology, 97(3), 357–367. https://doi.org/10.1037/0021-843x.97.3.357

119   Shonkoff, J. P., & Phillips, D. A. (Eds.). (2000). From neurons to neighborhoods: The science of early childhood development. National Academy Press.

120   Kain, K. L., & Terrell, S. J. (2018). Nurturing resilience: Helping Clients Move Forward from Developmental Trauma--An Integrative Somatic Approach. North Atlantic Books.

121   Levine, P. A., PhD. (2010). In an Unspoken Voice: How the Body Releases Trauma and Restores Goodness. North Atlantic Books.

122   Adverse Childhood Experiences (ACEs). (n.d.). https://www.cdc.gov/violenceprevention/aces/index.html

123   O'Connor, T. G., Ben-Shlomo, Y., Heron, J., Golding, J., Adams, D., & Glover, V. (2005). Prenatal Anxiety Predicts Individual Differences in Cortisol in Pre-Adolescent Children. Biological Psychiatry, 58(3), 211–217. https://doi.org/10.1016/j.biopsych.2005.03.032

124   McGowan, P. O., & Matthews, S. G. (2017). Prenatal Stress, Glucocorticoids, and Developmental Programming of the Stress Response. Endocrinology, 159(1), 69–82. https://doi.org/10.1210/en.2017-00896

125   Bergman, K., Sarkar, P., Glover, V., & O'Connor, T. G. (2010). Maternal Prenatal Cortisol and Infant Cognitive Development: Moderation by Infant–Mother Attachment. Biological Psychiatry, 67(11), 1026–1032. https://doi.org/10.1016/j.biopsych.2010.01.002

126   Neufeld, G., & Maté, G., MD. (2006). Hold On to Your Kids: Why Parents Need to Matter More Than Peers. National Geographic Books.

127   Seth, A. K., & Baars, B. J. (2005). Neural Darwinism and consciousness. Consciousness and Cognition, 14(1), 140–168. https://doi.org/10.1016/j.concog.2004.08.008

128   Siegel, D. J. (2020). The developing mind: How Relationships and the Brain Interact to Shape Who We Are. Guilford Publications.

129   Neufeld, G., & Maté, G., MD. (2006). Hold On to Your Kids: Why Parents Need to Matter More Than Peers. National Geographic Books.

130   Surge in Child Loneliness From 2007 to Present, Coinciding with Advent of iPhone | Free-Range Kids. (n.d.). Free-Range Kids. https://www.freerangekids.com/surge-in-child-loneliness-from-2007-to-present-coinciding-with-advent-of-iphone/

131   Neufeld, G., & Maté, G., MD. (2006). Hold On to Your Kids: Why Parents Need to Matter More Than Peers. National Geographic Books.

132   Neufeld, G., & Maté, G., MD. (2006). Hold On to Your Kids: Why Parents Need to Matter More Than Peers. National Geographic Books.

133   Junger, S. (2017). Tribe: On Homecoming and Belonging. Harper Perennial.

134   Any Anxiety Disorder. (n.d.). National Institute of Mental Health (NIMH). https://www.nimh.nih.gov/health/statistics/any-anxiety-disorder#part_155096

135   The Wisdom Of Trauma. (2023, July 17). The Wisdom Of Trauma -. The Wisdom of Trauma -. https://thewisdomoftrauma.com/

136   Canada, F. (2022, June 7). Money is still the top source of stress for Canadians - and many feel less hopeful about their financial futures. Cision. https://www.newswire.ca/news-releases/money-is-still-the-top-source-of-stress-for-canadians-and-many-feel-less-hopeful-about-their-financial-futures-879224169.html

137   White, A. (2023, June 15). 73% of Americans rank their finances as the No. 1 stress in life, according to new Capital One CreditWise survey. CNBC. https://www.cnbc.com/select/73-percent-of-americans-rank-finances-as-the-number-one-stress-in-life/

138   Stelk, R. (2023, June 6). The 2nd Leading Cause of Divorce | Family Lawyer. The Law Offices of Roger W. Stelk. https://stelklaw.com/blog/divorce-financial-fights/

139   Hodge, S. (2023, February 8). America Has Become a Nation of Dual-Income Working Couples | Tax Foundation. Tax Foundation. https://taxfoundation.org/america-has-become-nation-dual-income-working-couples/

140   Traditional Families Account for Only 7 Percent of U.S. Households. (n.d.). PRB. https://www.prb.org/resources/traditional-families-account-for-only-7-percent-of-u-s-households/

141   LinkedIn. (n.d.). https://www.linkedin.com/pulse/nearly-half-mothers-work-take-break-again-why-still-stigma-fairchild/

142   Stahl, A. (2020, May 1). New Study: Millennial Women Are Delaying Having Children Due To Their Careers. Forbes. https://www.forbes.com/sites/ashleystahl/2020/05/01/new-study-millennial-women-are-delaying-having-children-due-to-their-careers/?sh=2041f0fb276a

143   Government of Canada, Statistics Canada. (2014, November 12). Fertility: Fewer children, older moms. https://www150.statcan.gc.ca/n1/pub/11-630-x/11-630-x2014002-eng.htm

144   L, Bridgestock. QS International. (2023). How much does it cost to study in the US? Top Universities. https://www.topuniversities.com/student-info/student-finance/how-much-does-it-cost-study-us

145   Shillan, J. (2022). Tuition Inflation - Finaid. Finaid. https://finaid.org/savings/tuition-inflation/

146   Average Hourly and Weekly Earnings, by Private Industry Group statistics - USA Census numbers. (n.d.). https://allcountries.org/uscensus/692_average_hourly_and_weekly_earnings_by.html

147   S&P 500 Historical Prices by Year. (n.d.). https://www.multpl.com/s-p-500-historical-prices/table/by-year

148   TRADING ECONOMICS. (n.d.). United States Average Hourly Earnings MoM - June 2023 Data - 2006-2022 Historical. https://tradingeconomics.com/united-states/average-hourly-earnings

149   Average Sales Price of Houses Sold for the United States. (2023, April 25). https://fred.stlouisfed.org/series/ASPUS

150   National Average Wage Index. (n.d.). https://www.ssa.gov/oact/cola/AWI.html

151   Market Report - Real Estate in Whistler. (2023, January 30). Real Estate in Whistler. https://www.realestateinwhistler.com/about/market-report/

152   Whistler Salary in Canada - Average Salary. (n.d.). Talent.com. https://ca.talent.com/salary?job=whistler

153   Clifford, L. (2020, July 17). This is what every generation thinks of real estate—and what each has spent on it. Fortune. https://fortune.com/2020/07/17/generational-differences-real-estate-wealth-gen-z-millennials-gen-x-boomers-housing-market/

154   Inflation Rate - Countries - List. (n.d.). https://tradingeconomics.com/country-list/inflation-rate

155   Robert Breedlove. (2021, November 23). The Ultimate Macro Framework with Raoul Pal (WiM078) [Video]. YouTube. https://www.youtube.com/watch?v=i9TXVjYBM3U

156   Pew Research Center. (2021, May 28). U.S. has world's highest rate of children living in single-parent households | Pew Research Center. https://www.pewresearch.org/short-reads/2019/12/12/u-s-children-more-likely-than-children-in-other-countries-to-live-with-just-one-parent/

157   Sharma, R. (2020, July 24). The Rescues Ruining Capitalism. WSJ. https://www.wsj.com/articles/the-rescues-ruining-capitalism-11595603720

158   r/wallstreetbets. (n.d.). Reddit. https://www.reddit.com/r/wallstreetbets/

159 Dowd, K. (2021, November 7). How Hertz Went From Bankrupt To Buying 100,000 Teslas. Forbes. https://www.forbes.com/sites/kevindowd/2021/11/07/how-hertz-went-from-bankrupt-to-buying-100000-teslas/?sh=29ffea96d8bb

160 Korosec, K. (2020, June 16). Forget the casino, bankrupt Hertz can now sell up to $1 billion in stock. TechCrunch. https://techcrunch.com/2020/06/12/forget-the-casino-bankrupt-hertz-can-now-sell-up-to-1-billion-in-stock/?guccounter=1

161 Dowd, K. (2021, November 7). How Hertz Went From Bankrupt To Buying 100,000 Teslas. Forbes. https://www.forbes.com/sites/kevindowd/2021/11/07/how-hertz-went-from-bankrupt-to-buying-100000-teslas/?sh=49229e6ed8bb

162 Chokshi, N. (2021, October 25). Hertz leaves bankruptcy, a year after the pandemic devastated the car rental business. The New York Times. https://www.nytimes.com/2021/06/30/business/hertz-bankrupcty.html

163 Bloomberg. (2020, June 8). Hertz is bankrupt. So why is everyone buying its stock? - Los Angeles Times. Los Angeles Times. https://www.latimes.com/business/story/2020-06-08/bankrupt-stock-hertz

164 Lee, A. (2015, July 17). Welcome To The Unicorn Club: Learning From Billion-Dollar Startups. TechCrunch. https://techcrunch.com/2013/11/02/welcome-to-the-unicorn-club/

165 Lee, A. (2023). $1B+ Market Map: The world's 1,206 unicorn companies in one infographic. CB Insights Research. https://www.cbinsights.com/research/unicorn-startup-market-map/

166 Dempsey, M. (2015). Two Years Of Unicorns: Every Post We've Done On Unicorns Since The Term Was Coined. CB Insights Research. https://www.cbinsights.com/research/cb-insights-unicorn-history/

167 Statista. (2022, October 14). Global unicorns 2022, by year founded. https://www.statista.com/statistics/955973/unicorn-companies-foundation-year/

168 Howarth, J. (2023, March 16). Startup Failure Rate Statistics (2023). Exploding Topics. https://explodingtopics.com/blog/startup-failure-stats

169 Tun, Z. T. (2023). Theranos: A Fallen Unicorn. Investopedia. https://www.investopedia.com/articles/investing/020116/theranos-fallen-unicorn.asp

170 EQS Integrity Line. (2023, April 17). Elizabeth Holmes & the Theranos case: History of a fraud scandal. https://www.integrityline.com/expertise/blog/elizabeth-holmes-theranos/

171 Boudette, N. E. (2021, January 27). Tesla Has First Profitable Year, but Competition Is Growing. The New York Times. https://www.nytimes.com/2021/01/27/business/tesla-earnings.html

172 Johnston, M. (2022). Biggest Companies in the World by Market Cap. Investopedia. https://www.investopedia.com/biggest-companies-in-the-world-by-market-cap-5212784

173 Cain, T., & Cain, T. (2020). Tesla Inc Sales Figures - US Market | GCBC. GCBC. https://www.goodcarbadcar.net/tesla-inc-us-sales-figures/

174 Tesla Market Cap 2010-2023 | TSLA. (n.d.). MacroTrends. https://www.macrotrends.net/stocks/charts/TSLA/tesla/market-cap

175 Zlatev, D. (2022, March 23). Tesla disclosed government credits profit only after the SEC mandated it, new documents show. Notebookcheck. https://www.notebookcheck.net/Tesla-disclosed-government-credits-profit-only-after-the-SEC-mandated-it-new-documents-show.609779.0.html

176 Statista. (2023, March 17). Wholesale vehicle sales of the Ford Motor Company 2009-2022. https://www.statista.com/statistics/297315/ford-vehicle-sales/

177 Ford Motor Net Income 2010-2023 | F. (n.d.). MacroTrends. https://www.macrotrends.net/stocks/charts/F/ford-motor/net-income

178 Ford Motor Market Cap. (n.d.). YCharts. https://ycharts.com/companies/F/market_
     cap
179 Richter, F. (2022, December 20). Tesla's Market Cap Drop Is Bigger Than the
     Legacy Car Industry. Statista Daily Data. https://www.statista.com/chart/29002/
     tesla-market-capitalization/
180 Tesla (TSLA) PE Ratio. (n.d.). Tesla Inc. https://www.gurufocus.com/term/pettm/
     TSLA/PE-Ratio/Tesla
181 Bryant, C. (2021, March 24). Is $9 Billion WeWork Ready for the Stock Market
     Now Via BOWX SPAC? Bloomberg.com. https://www.bloomberg.com/opinion/
     articles/2021-03-24/is-9-billion-wework-ready-for-the-stock-market-now-via-
     bowx-spac
182 Chancellor, E. (2022). The price of time: The Real Story of Interest. Atlantic Monthly
     Press.
183 Citi will have almost 30,000 employees in compliance by year-end. (2014, July 14).
     MarketWatch. https://www.marketwatch.com/story/citi-will-have-almost-30-000-
     employees-in-compliance-by-year-end-1405371366
184 Arnn, L. P. (2022). Education as a Battleground. Imprimis. https://imprimis.hillsdale.
     edu/education-as-a-battleground/
185 Chambers, Dustin, Collins, Courtney and Krause, Alan (2019) How do Federal
     Regulations affect Consumer Prices? An Analysis of the Regressive Effects of
     Regulation. https://core.ac.uk/download/pdf/111216976.pdf
186 Cost of Compliance: State Regulations Increase Health Care Costs. (n.d.). https://
     oahhs.org/press-releases/cost-of-compliance--state-regulations-increase-health-
     care-costs/
187 Brenne, P. (n.d.). US companies poised to prop up EPS with share buybacks in 2023.
     S&P Global Market Intelligence. https://www.spglobal.com/marketintelligence/en/
     news-insights/latest-news-headlines/us-companies-poised-to-prop-up-eps-with-
     share-buybacks-in-2023-72955469
188 Ibrahim, R. (2016, August 8). The number of publicly-traded US companies is
     down 46% in the past two decades. Yahoo Finance. https://finance.yahoo.com/
     news/jp-startup-public-companies-fewer-000000709.html?guccounter=1
189 Thomas, K. (2018, February 24). Patients eagerly awaited a generic drug. then they
     saw the price. The New York Times. https://www.nytimes.com/2018/02/23/health/
     valeant-drug-price-syprine.html
190 Pollack, A. (2015, September 20). Drug goes from $13.50 a tablet to $750, overnight.
     The New York Times. https://www.nytimes.com/2015/09/21/business/a-huge-
     overnight-increase-in-a-drugs-price-raises-protests.html
191 Reis, R. A. (2009). The Empire State Building. Facts On File.
192 Wikipedia contributors. (2023). The One (Toronto). Wikipedia. https://en.wikipedia.
     org/wiki/The_One_(Toronto)
193 Polmar, N., & Moore, K. J. (2005). Cold War submarines: The Design and Construction
     of U.S. and Soviet Submarines.
194 Wikipedia contributors. (2023). USS Gerald R. Ford. Wikipedia. https://en.wikipedia.
     org/wiki/USS_Gerald_R._Ford
195 Construction - Bridge Construction | Golden Gate. (n.d.). https://www.goldengate.
     org/bridge/history-research/bridge-construction/construction/
196 Martinez, C. (2022, December 30). Golden Gate Bridge "suicide net" could cost
     $400 million - Los Angeles Times. Los Angeles Times. https://www.latimes.com/
     california/story/2022-12-04/golden-gate-bridge-suicide-net-could-cost-400-million
197 Malo, E. G. (2022, September 23). gato's postulate. By El Gato Malo - Bad Cattitude.
     https://boriquagato.substack.com/p/gatos-postulate?utm_source=substack&utm_
     medium=email

198 Research Page: Lord Acton Quote Archive. (2023, July 22). Acton Institute. https://www.acton.org/research/lord-acton-quote-archive

199 Hülsmann, J. G. (n.d.). The Cultural and Political Consequences of Fiat Money. Mises Institute. https://mises.org/library/cultural-and-political-consequences-fiat-money-0

200 Dickler, J. (2022, March 8). As inflation heats up, 64% of Americans are now living paycheck to paycheck. CNBC. https://www.cnbc.com/2022/03/08/as-prices-rise-64-percent-of-americans-live-paycheck-to-paycheck.html

201 Wikipedia contributors. (2023). Perverse incentive. Wikipedia. https://en.wikipedia.org/wiki/Perverse_incentive

202 Prins, N. (2009). It Takes a Pillage: An Epic Tale of Power, Deceit, and Untold Trillions. Wiley. https://nomiprins.com/. https://amzn.to/3KeltlW.

203 Summers, L. H. (2009). Responding to an Historic Economic Crisis. Brookings Institution, Washington, DC, United States of America. https://www.brookings.edu/wp-content/uploads/2012/04/0313_summers_remarks.pdf

204 401(k)s, Retirement Savings and the Financial Crisis. (2008, December 6). https://www.washingtonpost.com/wp-dyn/content/graphic/2008/12/06/GR2008120600089.html

205 Kalleberg, A. L., & Von Wachter, T. M. (2016). The U.S. Labor Market During and After the Great Recession: Continuities and Transformations. RSF: The Russell Sage Foundation Journal of the Social Sciences, 3(3), 1. https://doi.org/10.7758/rsf.2017.3.3.01

206 Stempel, J. (2009, August 24). SEC, BofA plead for Merrill bonus settlement. U.S. https://www.reuters.com/article/us-bankofamerica-merrill-bonuses-idUSN2416081220090824

207 FRB: Mortgage Debt Outstanding, First Quarter 2009. (n.d.). https://www.federalreserve.gov/econresdata/releases/mortoutstand/mortoutstand20090331.htm

208 Parlapiano, A., Solomon, D. B., Ngo, M., & Cowley, S. (2022, March 12). Where $5 Trillion in Pandemic Stimulus Money Went. The New York Times. https://www.nytimes.com/interactive/2022/03/11/us/how-covid-stimulus-money-was-spent.html

209 Smialek, J. (2021, June 2). The Fed announces plans to sell off its corporate bond holdings. The New York Times. https://www.nytimes.com/2021/06/02/business/fed-sells-corporate-bond-holdings.html

210 Ottawa has spent $240B fighting COVID-19. Here's where the money went. (1970, January 19). CBC News. https://newsinteractives.cbc.ca/features/2020/thebigspend/

211 Government of Canada, Statistics Canada. (2023, July 11). Tax filers and dependants with income by total income, sex and age. https://www150.statcan.gc.ca/t1/tbl1/en/tv.action?pid=1110000801

212 Alini, E. (2021, December 3). CERB poses back-to-work dilemma: 'We're being incentivized to make just under $1,000' Global News. https://globalnews.ca/news/7092281/cerb-back-to-work-dilemma/

213 Express Employment Professionals. (2022, March 23). Labour Shortages Forcing Canadian Companies to Scrap Job Requirements. GlobeNewswire News Room. https://www.globenewswire.com/en/news-release/2022/03/23/2408622/0/en/Labour-Shortages-Forcing-Canadian-Companies-to-Scrap-Job-Requirements.html

214 Sky News. (2023, January 23). Record number of Britons receiving benefits that amount to more than they pay in tax, study finds. Sky News. https://news.sky.com/story/record-number-of-britons-receiving-benefits-that-amount-to-more-than-they-pay-in-tax-study-finds-12793349

215 Karimov, S. R. (2005). International Trade Distorting Agricultural Subsidies: Legal and Policy Analysis. In Maurer School of Law. https://www.repository.law.indiana.edu/cgi/viewcontent.cgi?article=1114&context=etd

216   Nestle, M. FAO Archives - Food Politics by Marion Nestle. (n.d.). Food. https://www.foodpolitics.com/tag/fao/

217   4 Facts on Big Food. (n.d.). https://us6.campaign-archive.com/?e=6b8df24d6a&u=a60af0e1a541ec26cf4658f45&id=05b2c57afd

218   Deering, K. (2015). How to heal your metabolism: Learn How the Right Foods, Sleep, the Right Amount of Exercise, and Happiness Can Increase Your Metabolic Rate and Help Heal Your Broken Metabolism. Createspace Independent Publishing Platform.

219   Brown, S. (2022, March 28). Most Dietary Guideline Advisors Have Ties to Food and Pharma Industries, Study Finds. Verywell Health. https://www.verywellhealth.com/dietary-guidelines-committee-conflicts-of-interest-5223556

220   Heid, M. (2016, January 8). Experts Say Lobbying Skewed the U.S. Dietary Guidelines. Time. https://time.com/4130043/lobbying-politics-dietary-guidelines/

221   Bratskeir, K. (2016). 8 Times Food Companies Funded Studies to Prove Their Product Was "Healthy." Mic. https://www.mic.com/articles/145634/nutrition-science-is-whack-food-studies-lies

222   Domonoske, C. (2016, September 13). 50 Years Ago, Sugar Industry Quietly Paid Scientists To Point Blame At Fat. NPR. https://www.npr.org/sections/thetwo-way/2016/09/13/493739074/50-years-ago-sugar-industry-quietly-paid-scientists-to-point-blame-at-fat

223   Mercola, J. (2023, March 22). Conflicts of Interest: Pfizer's Secret Collusion With the NIH. www.theepochtimes.com. https://www.theepochtimes.com/health/conflicts-of-interest-pfizers-secret-collusion-with-the-nih-5138161

224   Clark, J. (2023, February 21). Russell Brand interviews Coca-Cola whistleblower on Big Food, diabetes drugs: "Your obesity is their profit." Fox News. https://www.foxnews.com/media/russell-brand-interviews-coca-cola-whistleblower-big-food-diabetes-drugs-your-obesity-their-profit

225   Nsw, R. (2023). Shared Equity Home Buyer Helper. NSW Government. https://www.nsw.gov.au/housing-and-construction/home-buying-assistance/shared-equity

226   Zeller, P. (2021, August 18). Government, Not Wall Street, Caused Financial Crisis - American Experiment. American Experiment. https://www.americanexperiment.org/government-not-wall-street-caused-financial-crisis/

227   Loan-Level Price Adjustment Matrix. (2023). Fannie Mae. https://singlefamily.fanniemae.com/media/9391/display

228   Barrabi, T. (2023, April 20). How the US is subsidizing high-risk homebuyers -- at the cost of those with good credit. New York Post. https://nypost.com/2023/04/16/how-the-us-is-subsidizing-high-risk-homebuyers-at-the-cost-of-those-with-good-credit/?utm_medium=social&utm_source=twitter&utm_campaign=nypost

229   7 Things You Need to Know About Fannie Mae and Freddie Mac. (2012, September 6). Center for American Progress. https://www.americanprogress.org/article/7-things-you-need-to-know-about-fannie-mae-and-freddie-mac/

230   BrokerLink. (2021, October 17). Average monthly car insurance rates in Alberta. BrokerLink. https://www.brokerlink.ca/blog/average-monthly-car-insurance-rates-in-alberta

231   Fiscal Data Explains the National Deficit. (n.d.). https://fiscaldata.treasury.gov/americas-finance-guide/national-deficit/

232   Morgan, G. (2022). The Greedy Ones: Comparing Public and Private Sector Compensation in Canada. C2C Journal. https://c2cjournal.ca/2022/09/the-greedy-ones-comparing-public-and-private-sector-compensation-in-canada/

233   The Fraser Institute. (2022, September 1). Comparing Government and Private Sector Job Growth in the COVID-19 Era. Fraser Institute. https://www.fraserinstitute.org/studies/comparing-government-and-private-sector-job-growth-in-the-covid-19-era

234 Chancellor, E. (2022). The price of time: The Real Story of Interest. Atlantic Monthly Press.

235 Dragomir, M. (2017). Control the money, control the media: How government uses funding to keep media in line. Journalism: Theory, Practice & Criticism, 19(8), 1131–1148. https://doi.org/10.1177/1464884917724621

236 Dragomir, M. (2017). Control the money, control the media: How government uses funding to keep media in line. Journalism: Theory, Practice & Criticism, 19(8), 1131–1148. https://doi.org/10.1177/1464884917724621

237 Fildebrandt, D. (2020, October 10). How Trudeau bought the media. Western Standard. https://www.westernstandard.news/features/how-trudeau-bought-the-media/article_58fdf7e6-39b9-5e78-a174-4a132b58a767.html

238 Chung, E. (2010, September 29). Government accused of manipulating science news. CBC. https://www.cbc.ca/news/science/government-accused-of-manipulating-science-news-1.965777

239 Westphal, D. (2009, November 29). American government: It's always subsidized commercial media. Online Journalism Review. https://www.ojr.org/american-government-its-always-subsidized-commercial-media/index.html

240 Nava, V. (2022, December 21). FBI paid Twitter $3.4M for doing its dirty work on users, damning email shows. New York Post. https://nypost.com/2022/12/19/fbi-reimbursed-twitter-for-doing-its-dirty-work-on-users/

241 Baron, E. (2018). Google, Tesla, Apple, Facebook rake in massive subsidies: report. The Mercury News. https://www.mercurynews.com/2018/07/03/google-tesla-apple-facebook-rake-in-massive-subsidies-report/

242 Solon, O., & Levin, S. (2017, February 21). How Google's search algorithm spreads false information with a rightwing bias. The Guardian. https://www.theguardian.com/technology/2016/dec/16/google-autocomplete-rightwing-bias-algorithm-political-propaganda

243 York, J. K. a. J. C. (2018, January 2). Seven Times Journalists Were Censored: 2017 in Review. Electronic Frontier Foundation. https://www.eff.org/deeplinks/2017/12/seven-times-2017-journalists-were-censored

244 Museum of communism | Nearly 1,500 m2 of an authentic feel of the era. (n.d.). https://muzeumkomunismu.cz/en/

245 Schäpe, B. (2022, May 24). Opinion: China's crucial role in decarbonising the global steel sector. China Dialogue. https://chinadialogue.net/en/climate/opinion-chinas-crucial-role-in-decarbonising-the-global-steel-sector/

246 Rickter, W. China's Steel Industry Bleeds, Prices Collapse, Losses Mount, and Now the Government Gets Gloomy | Wolf Street. (2015, December 9). https://wolfstreet.com/2015/12/09/chinas-steel-industry-teeters-prices-collapse-losses-mount-and-even-the-government-gets-gloomy/

247 European Central Bank. (2023, June 13). Targeted longer-term refinancing operations (TLTROs). https://www.ecb.europa.eu/mopo/implement/omo/tltro/html/index.en.html

248 European Central Bank. (2015, January 21). ECB announces expanded asset purchase programme. https://www.ecb.europa.eu/press/pr/date/2015/html/pr150122_1.en.html

249 Jackson, G. (2016, September 12). Apple and McDonald's on BoE's bond-buying list. Financial Times. https://www.ft.com/content/9915ff32-7909-11e6-97ae-647294649b28

250 Dittli, M. (2022, October 13). Russell Napier: The world will experience a capex boom. The Market. https://themarket.ch/interview/russell-napier-the-world-will-experience-a-capex-boom-ld.7606

251 Ghosh, I. (2020, July 22). How Much Do Countries Spend on Healthcare Compared to the Military? Visual Capitalist. https://www.visualcapitalist.com/what-do-countries-spend-on-healthcare-versus-military/

252 Thompson, L. (2011, March 28). The Real Cost Of U.S. In Libya? Two Billion Dollars Per Day. Forbes. https://www.forbes.com/sites/beltway/2011/03/28/the-real-cost-of-u-s-in-libya-two-billion-dollars-per-day/?sh=55053e697b5f

253 Kroll, A. (2023). Unwarranted Influence, Twenty-First-Century-Style. TomDispatch.com. https://tomdispatch.com/unwarranted-influence-twenty-first-century-style/

254 State, M. (2019, June 5). Gold Dinar: the Real Reason Behind Gaddafi's Murder - Millenium State blog. Millenium State Blog. https://millenium-state.com/blog/2019/05/03/the-dinar-gold-the-real-reason-for-gaddafis-murder/

255 Statista. (2023, March 15). Proved crude oil reserves in Africa by main countries 2021. https://www.statista.com/statistics/1178147/crude-oil-reserves-in-africa-by-country/

256 Oil Reserves by Country - Worldometer. (n.d.). https://www.worldometers.info/oil/oil-reserves-by-country/

257 Sherwood, H. (2017, November 26). Libya rebels to get $25m of US military equipment under Pentagon proposal. The Guardian. https://www.theguardian.com/world/2011/apr/20/libya-rebels-us-military-equipment-non-lethal

258 Thompson, L. (2011, March 28). The Real Cost Of U.S. In Libya? Two Billion Dollars Per Day. Forbes. https://www.forbes.com/sites/beltway/2011/03/28/the-real-cost-of-u-s-in-libya-two-billion-dollars-per-day/?sh=55053e697b5f

259 RT. (2011, May 5). Gaddafi gold-for-oil, dollar-doom plans behind Libya "mission"? [Video]. YouTube. https://www.youtube.com/watch?v=GuqZfaj34nc

260 Cockburn, P. (2011, June 23). Amnesty questions claim that Gaddafi ordered rape as weapon of war | The Independent. The Independent. https://www.independent.co.uk/news/world/africa/amnesty-questions-claim-that-gaddafi-ordered-rape-as-weapon-of-war-2302037.html

261 Brown, E. (2017, November 17). Why Qaddafi had to go: African gold, oil and the challenge to monetary imperialism. The Ecologist. https://theecologist.org/2016/mar/14/why-qaddafi-had-go-african-gold-oil-and-challenge-monetary-imperialism

262 Oil Reserves by Country - Worldometer. (n.d.). https://www.worldometers.info/oil/oil-reserves-by-country/

263 Gladstein, A. (2021, September 21). Uncovering The Hidden Costs Of The Petrodollar. Bitcoin Magazine - Bitcoin News, Articles and Expert Insights. https://bitcoinmagazine.com/culture/the-hidden-costs-of-the-petrodollar

264 Kessler, G. (2021, December 6). The Cheneys' claim of a 'deep, longstanding, far-reaching relationship' between al-Qaeda and Saddam. Washington Post. https://www.washingtonpost.com/news/fact-checker/wp/2014/07/17/the-cheneys-claims-of-a-deep-longstanding-far-reaching-relationship-between-al-qaeda-and-saddam/

265 Azam, M. (2020). Does military spending stifle economic growth? The empirical evidence from non-OECD countries. Heliyon, 6(12), e05853. https://doi.org/10.1016/j.heliyon.2020.e05853

266 Kitco.com | KITCO. (n.d.). https://www.kitco.com/ind/VanEeden/feb242006.html.

267 Bryan, M. F. (1997, October 14). On the Origin and Evolution of the Word Inflation. https://www.clevelandfed.org/en/publications/economic-commentary/1997/ec-19971015-on-the-origin-and-evolution-of-the-word-inflation

268 Muresianu, A. (2023, April 13). IRS Strategic Operating Plan Shows Promise, but Concerns Remain. Tax Foundation. https://taxfoundation.org/irs-funding-plan-inflation-reduction-act/

269   S.Amdt.438 to S.Amdt.935 to S.2226 - 118th Congress (2023-2024). (n.d.). Congress. gov | Library of Congress. https://www.congress.gov/amendment/118th-congress/ senate-amendment/438

270   Masters, J. (2023, July 10). How Much Aid Has the U.S. Sent Ukraine? Here Are Six Charts. Council on Foreign Relations. https://www.cfr.org/article/how-much-aid-has-us-sent-ukraine-here-are-six-charts

271   Rummel, R. J. (1994). Death by government. Transaction Pub.

272   Joe Rogan Experience. (2023, June 14). #1999 - Robert Kennedy, Jr. Spotify. https:// open.spotify.com/episode/3DQfcTY4viyXsIXQ89NXvg

273   Homo sapiens. (2021, January 22). The Smithsonian Institution's Human Origins Program. https://humanorigins.si.edu/evidence/human-fossils/species/homo-sapiens

274   Robinson, D. (2023). 15 Biggest Environmental Problems of 2023 | Earth.Org. Earth. Org. https://earth.org/the-biggest-environmental-problems-of-our-lifetime/

275   Igini, M. (2023). 10 Concerning Fast Fashion Waste Statistics. Earth.Org. https:// earth.org/statistics-about-fast-fashion-waste/

276   CEICdata.com. (2018). United States Private Consumption: % of GDP. www.ceicdata. com. https://www.ceicdata.com/en/indicator/united-states/private-consumption--of-nominal-gdp

277   Blockworks Macro. (2023, February 23). Energy Security And The Green New Deal | Doomberg & Steve Keen [Video]. YouTube. https://www.youtube.com/ watch?v=SiWlWSHylHw

278   Grabish, B. United Nations. (n.d.). Dry Tears of the Aral | United Nations. https:// www.un.org/en/chronicle/article/dry-tears-aral

279   Gaybullaev, B., Chen, S., & Gaybullaev, D. (2012). Changes in water volume of the Aral Sea after 1960. Applied Water Science, 2(4), 285–291. https://doi.org/10.1007/ s13201-012-0048-z

280   Hurst, E. &. S. F. (2004). Home Is Where the Equity Is: Mortgage Refinancing and Household Consumption. ideas.repec.org. https://ideas.repec.org/a/mcb/jmoncb/ v36y2004i6p985-1014.html

281   Parker, J. A., Souleles, N. S., Johnson, D. S., & McClelland, R. (2013). Consumer Spending and the Economic Stimulus Payments of 2008. The American Economic Review, 103(6), 2530–2553. https://doi.org/10.1257/aer.103.6.2530

282   Valentina Bruno et al. Vol. 108, MAY 2018 of AEA Papers and Proceedings on JSTOR. (n.d.). https://www.jstor.org/stable/e26452693

283   Chancellor, E. (2022). The price of time: The Real Story of Interest. Atlantic Monthly Press.

284   Weissman, R. (2020, April 14). ISM: Lead times are up 200% or more across the world. Supply Chain Dive. https://www.supplychaindive.com/news/coronavirus-ism-lead-times-supply-chains/576070/

285   AFP (2021, July 4). Pandemic drives freight prices to record high with disrupted logistics. The Economic Times. https://economictimes.indiatimes.com/small-biz/trade/exports/insights/pandemic-drives-freight-prices-to-record-high-with-disrupted-logistics/bad-news-for-shipping-lines/slideshow/84132727.cms

286   Kutukwa, K. (2022, December 18). Bitcoin vs The Petrodollar - The Looking Glass Education. The Looking Glass Education. https://lookingglasseducation.com/ bitcoin-vs-the-petrodollar/

287   Manson, M. (2016c). The Subtle Art of Not Giving a F*ck: A Counterintuitive Approach to Living a Good Life. HarperOne.

288   Desmet, M. (2022). The psychology of totalitarianism. Chelsea Green Publishing.

289   Goldberg, N. (2021, July 29). The legend of Kitty Genovese and those who ignored her screams - Los Angeles Times. Los Angeles Times. https://www.latimes.com/ opinion/story/2020-09-10/urban-legend-kitty-genovese-38-people

290   Byrka, K., Cantarero, K., Dolinski, D., & Van Tilburg, W. A. (2021). Consequences of Sisyphean Efforts: Meaningless Effort Decreases Motivation to Engage in Subsequent Conservation Behaviors through Disappointment. Sustainability, 13(10), 5716. https://doi.org/10.3390/su13105716

291   Baras, S., Lekka, D., Bokari, M., Orlandou, K., Arachoviti, V., Roubi, A., Tsaraklis, A., Pachi, A., & Douzenis, A. (2021). Investigation of the Relationship Between Aggression and Adult Attachment in Healthcare Professionals. Cureus. https://doi.org/10.7759/cureus.19360

292   Azrin, N. H., Rubin, H. B., & Hutchinson, R. R. (1968). BITING ATTACK BY RATS IN RESPONSE TO AVERSIVE SHOCK1. Journal of the Experimental Analysis of Behavior, 11(5), 633–639. https://doi.org/10.1901/jeab.1968.11-633

293   Brosnan, S. F., & De Waal, F. B. M. (2003). Monkeys reject unequal pay. Nature, 425(6955), 297–299. https://doi.org/10.1038/nature01963

294   Hyperinflation. (n.d.). https://www.johndclare.net/Weimar_hyperinflation.htm

295   Ryu, S., & Fan, L. (2022). The Relationship Between Financial Worries and Psychological Distress Among U.S. Adults. Journal of Family and Economic Issues, 44(1), 16–33. https://doi.org/10.1007/s10834-022-09820-9

296   Mahaffey, J. (2010). Atomic Awakening: A new look at the history and future of nuclear power. Pegasus Books.

297   Albaugh, G., & Albaugh, G. (2022). From 100% to 20%: Video Shows Radically Shifting Narrative Of Vaccine Effectiveness - Citizens Journal. Citizens Journal. https://www.citizensjournal.us/from-100-to-20-video-shows-radically-shifting-narrative-of-vaccine-effectiveness/

298   Wikipedia contributors. (2023). Great Leap Forward. Wikipedia. https://en.wikipedia.org/wiki/Great_Leap_Forward

299   The Sunk Cost Fallacy - Biases & Heuristics | The Decision Lab. (2022, December 17). The Decision Lab. https://thedecisionlab.com/biases/the-sunk-cost-fallacy

300   Fellows, N. (2022). Stalin's Terror. In Hodder & Stoughton. https://www.hoddereducation.co.uk/media/Documents/magazine-extras/Modern History Review/MHR Vol 4 No 4/HistoryReview24_4_Stalin.pdf

301   "Nudge Unit" | Institute for Government. (2020, March 11). Institute for Government. https://www.instituteforgovernment.org.uk/article/explainer/nudge-unit

302   Dodsworth, L. (2021). A state of fear: How the UK Government Weaponised Fear During the COVID-19 Pandemic.

303   Diver, B. T. (2022, January 28). Government 'used grossly unethical tactics to scare public into Covid compliance.' The Telegraph. https://www.telegraph.co.uk/politics/2022/01/28/grossly-unethical-downing-street-nudge-unit-accused-scaring/

304   Mianecki, J. (2011, June 22). 378 Years Ago Today: Galileo Forced to Recant. Smithsonian Magazine. https://www.smithsonianmag.com/smithsonian-institution/378-years-ago-today-galileo-forced-to-recant-18323485/

305   The drama of the Gifted Child: The Search for the True Self. (1997). Basic Books.

306   Denyer, S. (2021, January 8). N. Korea's Kim calls U.S. 'our biggest enemy,' says its hostile policies never change. Washington Post. https://www.washingtonpost.com/world/northkorea-kim-us-enemy/2021/01/08/666ba97a-5216-11eb-b2e8-3339e73d9da2_story.html

307   Festival de Cannes. (2023, March 25). THE POWER OF NIGHTMARES - Festival de Cannes. Festival De Cannes. https://www.festival-cannes.com/en/f/the-power-of-nightmares/

308   Inflation Rate - Countries - List. (n.d.). https://tradingeconomics.com/country-list/inflation-rate

309   CEICdata.com. (2023). Argentina Monetary Base: Currency in Circulation. Economic Indicators | CEIC. https://www.ceicdata.com/en/argentina/monetary-base/monetary-base-currency-in-circulation

310   Statista. (2023, May 4). Inflation rate in Argentina 2028. https://www.statista.com/statistics/316750/inflation-rate-in-argentina/

311   M2. (2023, July 25). https://fred.stlouisfed.org/series/M2SL

312   Melore, C. (2021, April 29). Lonely nation: 2 in 3 Americans feel more alone than ever before, many admit to crying for first time in years. Study Finds. https://studyfinds.org/lonely-nation-two-thirds-feel-more-alone-than-ever-many-cry-first-time/

313   Statista. (2022, November 28). Feeling of loneliness among adults 2021, by country. https://www.statista.com/statistics/1222815/loneliness-among-adults-by-country/

314   Thompson, D. (2018, December 18). Three-quarters of people in U.S. struggling with loneliness - UPI.com. UPI. https://www.upi.com/Health_News/2018/12/18/Three-quarters-of-people-in-US-struggling-with-loneliness/3691545170724/

315   Twenge, J. M., Haidt, J., Blake, A. B., McAllister, C., Lemon, H., & Roy, A. L. (2021). Worldwide increases in adolescent loneliness. Journal of Adolescence, 93(1), 257–269. https://doi.org/10.1016/j.adolescence.2021.06.006

316   Friedman, V. (2023, July 26). Poll: 9 in 10 Young Britons Believe Their Lives Have No Purpose. Breitbart. https://www.breitbart.com/europe/2019/08/02/poll-9-10-young-britons-believe-their-lives-have-no-purpose/

317   Commisso, D. (2021, October 19). As Job Satisfaction Declines, Workers Across Industries Turn to Job Searching - CivicScience. CivicScience. https://civicscience.com/as-job-satisfaction-declines-workers-across-industries-turn-to-job-searching/

318   United States of America - Place Explorer - Data Commons. (n.d.). https://datacommons.org/place/country/USA/?utm_medium=explore&mprop=count&popt=Person&hl=en

319   Real Personal Consumption Expenditures. (2023, June 30). https://fred.stlouisfed.org/series/PCEC96

320   U.S. Census Bureau. (2022, April 13). Vaccinated Adults Report Symptoms of Anxiety or Depression Less Frequently Than the Unvaccinated. Census.gov. https://www.census.gov/library/stories/2022/02/frontline-workers-more-likely-to-report-symptoms-of-anxiety-depressive-disorder.html

321   Hargreaves, D. (n.d.). Minds matter: time to take action on children and young people's mental health. Nuffield Trust. https://www.nuffieldtrust.org.uk/news-item/minds-matter-time-to-take-action-on-children-and-young-people-s-mental-health

322   Kevin, A. (2020, November 30). US Social Trust Has Fallen 23 Points Since 1964. https://www.kevinvallier.com/reconciled/new-finding-us-social-trust-has-fallen-23-points-since-1964/

323   Dimock, M. Pew Research Center. (2022, October 26). America is exceptional in the nature of its political divide | Pew Research Center. https://www.pewresearch.org/short-reads/2020/11/13/america-is-exceptional-in-the-nature-of-its-political-divide/

324   Bishop, B. (2020, December 16). For Most Americans, the Local Presidential Vote Was a Landslide. The Daily Yonder. https://dailyyonder.com/for-most-americans-the-local-presidential-vote-was-a-landslide/2020/12/17/

325   Lukianoff, G., & Haidt, J. (2019). The coddling of the American mind: How Good Intentions and Bad Ideas Are Setting Up a Generation for Failure. Penguin.

326   Gun Deaths in America, 2021 - Data Details - Injury Facts. (2023, February 14). Injury Facts. https://injuryfacts.nsc.org/home-and-community/safety-topics/guns/data-details/

327   Cools, S. (2020, June 16). Op sociale media ging het er nog nooit zo ranzig aan toe. De Standaard. https://www.standaard.be/cnt/dmf20200616_04992948

328 Hülsmann, J. G. (n.d.). The Cultural and Political Consequences of Fiat Money. Mises Institute. https://mises.org/library/cultural-and-political-consequences-fiat-money-0

329 OHCHR. (n.d.). A/HRC/47/40: Arbitrary detention relating to drug policies Study of the Working Group on Arbitrary Detention. https://www.ohchr.org/en/documents/thematic-reports/ahrc4740-arbitrary-detention-relating-drug-policies-study-working-group

330 Lopez, G. (2016, October 11). Mass incarceration in America, explained in 22 maps and charts. Vox. https://www.vox.com/2015/7/13/8913297/mass-incarceration-maps-charts

331 Monazzam, K. M. B. P. a. N. (2023). Private Prisons in the United States. The Sentencing Project. https://www.sentencingproject.org/reports/private-prisons-in-the-united-states/

332 USAFacts. (2023). How much do states spend on prisons? - USAFacts. USAFacts. https://usafacts.org/articles/how-much-do-states-spend-on-prisons/

333 Alden, L. (2023). Broken Money: Why Our Financial System is Failing Us and How We Can Make It Better.

334 OHCHR. (n.d.). End 'war on drugs' and promote policies rooted in human rights: UN experts. https://www.ohchr.org/en/statements/2022/06/end-war-drugs-and-promote-policies-rooted-human-rights-un-experts

335 Jackson, R. (2023, July 20). War on terrorism | Summary & Facts. Encyclopedia Britannica. https://www.britannica.com/topic/war-on-terrorism

336 Chomsky, N. (2016, August 22). Noam Chomsky: The Cost of Violence in the War on Terror. BillMoyers.com. https://billmoyers.com/story/chomsky-the-cost-of-violence/

337 Duignan, B. (2023, July 6). USA PATRIOT Act | Facts, History, Acronym, & Controversy. Encyclopedia Britannica. https://www.britannica.com/topic/USA-PATRIOT-Act

338 Gopnik, A., Zelinsky, W., Pole, J., Beeman, R. R., Lewis, P. F., Pessen, E., Bradley, H. W., Winther, O. O., Flaum, T. K., Wallace, W. M., Oehser, P. H., Harris, J. T., Schmidt, K. P., Naisbitt, J., Weisberger, B. A., Hassler, W. W., Economist Intelligence Unit, Freidel, F., O'Neill, W. L., . . . Donald, D. H. (2023, July 25). United States | History, Map, Flag, & Population. Encyclopedia Britannica. https://www.britannica.com/place/United-States

339 Marshall, P. (2012). The Big Bamboozle: 9/11 and the War on Terror.

340 Kotlikoff, L. (2019, January 9). Holding U.S. Treasurys? Beware: Uncle Sam Can't Account For $21 Trillion. Forbes. https://www.forbes.com/sites/kotlikoff/2019/01/09/holding-u-s-treasuries-beware-uncle-sam-cant-account-for-21-trillion/?sh=445eac037644

341 American Medical Association & American Medical Association. (2023, March 20). Trends in health care spending. American Medical Association. https://www.ama-assn.org/about/research/trends-health-care-spending

342 Ray, M. (2023, June 16). Edward Snowden | Education, Biography, Russia, & Facts. Encyclopedia Britannica. https://www.britannica.com/biography/Edward-Snowden

343 Hayes, A. (2023). Dodd-Frank Act: What It Does, Major Components, Criticisms. Investopedia. https://www.investopedia.com/terms/d/dodd-frank-financial-regulatory-reform-bill.asp

344 Zeller, P. (2021, August 18). Government, Not Wall Street, Caused Financial Crisis - American Experiment. American Experiment. https://www.americanexperiment.org/government-not-wall-street-caused-financial-crisis/

345   Wion. (2022, August 29). A glance at countries that have approved Vaccine Passport. WION. https://www.wionews.com/photos/a-glance-at-countries-that-have-approved-vaccine-passport-388251#israel-388241

346   Office of the Privacy Commissioner of Canada. (2021, October 7). Privacy and COVID-19 Vaccine Passports. https://www.priv.gc.ca/en/opc-news/speeches/2021/s-d_20210519/

347   Covid-19 Triggers Wave of Free Speech Abuse. (2021, March 29). Human Rights Watch. https://www.hrw.org/news/2021/02/11/covid-19-triggers-wave-free-speech-abuse

348   Nelson, S. (2021, July 15). White House "flagging" posts for Facebook to censor over COVID "misinformation." New York Post. https://nypost.com/2021/07/15/white-house-flagging-posts-for-facebook-to-censor-due-to-covid-19-misinformation/

349   Cleveland, M. (2023). The U.S. Government Is Building A Vast Surveillance And Speech Suppression Web Around Every American. The Federalist. https://thefederalist.com/2023/03/21/grants-reveal-federal-governments-horrific-plans-to-censor-all-americans-speech/

350   Wong, Q. (2021, August 18). Facebook removed more than 20 million posts for COVID-19 misinformation. CNET. https://www.cnet.com/news/social-media/facebook-removed-more-than-20-million-posts-for-covid-19-misinformation/

351   Bell, K. (2021). Facebook has banned 3,000 accounts for COVID-19 and vaccine misinformation. Engadget. https://www.engadget.com/facebook-removed-3000-accounts-covid-vaccine-misinformation-184254103.html

352   Bokhari, A. (2023, July 26). Facebook Admits in Court That "Fact Checks" Are Just Opinion. Breitbart. https://www.breitbart.com/tech/2021/12/13/facebook-admits-in-court-that-fact-checks-are-just-opinion/

353   Mason, E. (2022, October 27). After PayPal Revokes Controversial Misinformation Policy, Major Concerns Remain Over $2,500 Fine. Forbes. https://www.forbes.com/sites/emilymason/2022/10/27/after-paypal-revokes-controversial-misinformation-policy-major-concerns-remain-over-2500-fine/?sh=6f4eaa9130c4

354   Bumsted, R., Gillies, R., & Ring, W. (2022, February 18). Ottawa crackdown: police arrest 100 after 3-week protest | AP News. AP News. https://apnews.com/article/canada-truck-blockade-protest-coronavirus-police-1f2c87b2c31fef9cdce65449a0035334

355   Nardi, C., & Lévesque, C. (2022, November 17). Bureaucrats who froze bank accounts of Freedom Convoy leaders weren't trying to "get at the family." Nationalpost. https://nationalpost.com/news/politics/bureaucrats-who-froze-bank-accounts-of-freedom-convoy-leaders-werent-trying-to-get-at-the-family

356   Wikipedia contributors. (2023). Nuremberg Code. Wikipedia. https://en.m.wikipedia.org/wiki/Nuremberg_Code

357   Bill S. 686. (2023). In Authenticated US Government Information. https://t.co/U9zdn2guCy

358   Communications Legislation Amendment (Combatting Misinformation and Disinformation) Bill 2023. (2023). In The Parliament of the Commonwealth of Australia. https://www.infrastructure.gov.au/sites/default/files/documents/communications-legislation-amendment-combatting-misinformation-and-disinformation-bill2023-june2023.pdf

359   Beaumont, R. (2019, February 24). Mastercard and Doconomy Launch the Future of Sustainable Payments. Mastercard Newsroom. https://www.mastercard.com/news/press/2019/february/mastercard-and-doconomy-launch-the-future-of-sustainable-payments/

360   United Nations. (n.d.). Net Zero Coalition | United Nations. https://www.un.org/en/climatechange/net-zero-coalition

361 Sahakian, T. (2022, May 18). ESG scores similar to China's social credit system, designed to transform society, think tank director says. Fox Business. https://www.foxbusiness.com/economy/esg-scores-similar-china-social-credit-system-designed-to-transform-society-think-tank-director-says

362 Johnson, B. S. (2023, July 23). SNP plans to effectively ban sale of homes with gas boilers. The Telegraph. https://www.telegraph.co.uk/news/2023/07/23/scotland-homes-sale-ban-swap-gas-boilers-heat-pumps-snp/

363 Jones, W. (2023, July 31). Major Heat Pump Supplier Attacks Plans to Replace Gas Boilers With Heat Pumps Saying They "Don't Work" in the Cold – The Daily Sceptic. The Daily Sceptic. https://dailysceptic.org/2023/07/31/major-heat-pump-supplier-attacks-plans-to-replace-gas-boilers-with-heat-pumps-saying-they-dont-work-in-the-cold/

364 Wikipedia contributors. (2023). Economy of Scotland. Wikipedia. https://en.wikipedia.org/wiki/Economy_of_Scotland

365 Statista. (2023, July 20). Number of school pupils in Scotland 2013-2022. https://www.statista.com/statistics/715853/number-of-pupils-in-scotland-by-school-type/

366 BBC News. (2021, October 21). Scottish schools spending "is highest per pupil in UK." BBC News. https://www.bbc.com/news/uk-scotland-59000077

367 Wipulasena, A., & Mashal, M. (2021, December 7). Sri Lanka's Plunge Into Organic Farming Brings Disaster. The New York Times. https://www.nytimes.com/2021/12/07/world/asia/sri-lanka-organic-farming-fertilizer.html

368 Abrahams, B. J. (2023, June 3). Irish farmers revolt over plan for cattle cull to meet green target. The Telegraph. https://www.telegraph.co.uk/world-news/2023/06/03/ireland-farmers-revolt-cattle-cull-plan-climate-change-targ/?utm_source=substack&utm_medium=email

369 McCullough, C. (2022, December 9). Food control: Dutch farming on the verge of a disaster as government pushes to close 3,000 farms. Tri-State Livestock News | Food Control: Dutch Farming on the Verge of a Disaster as Government Pushes to Close 3,000 Farms. https://www.tsln.com/news/food-control-dutch-farming-on-the-verge-of-a-disaster-as-government-pushes-to-close-3000-farms/

370 Statista. (2022, September 20). Number of arable farms in the Netherlands 2008-2021. https://www.statista.com/statistics/647393/total-number-of-arable-farms-in-the-netherlands/

371 Wikipedia contributors. (2023). Nuclear power phase-out. Wikipedia. https://en.wikipedia.org/wiki/Nuclear_power_phase-out

372 Wilke, S. (n.d.). Energieverbrauch nach Energieträgern und Sektoren. Umweltbundesamt. https://www.umweltbundesamt.de/daten/energie/energieverbrauch-nach-energietraegern-sektoren#entwicklung-des-endenergieverbrauchs-nach-sektoren-und-energietragern

373 Oltermann, P. (2022, September 5). How reliant is Germany – and the rest of Europe – on Russian gas? The Guardian. https://www.theguardian.com/world/2022/jul/21/how-reliant-is-germany-and-europe-russian-gas-nord-stream

374 Grieshaber, K. (2022, July 27). Russia cuts gas through Nord Stream 1 to 20% of capacity | AP News. AP News. https://apnews.com/article/russia-ukraine-germany-d040fce8b07abc2ab6bb2cbf31a0df47

375 Elbein, S. (2019, March 4). Europe's renewable energy policy is built on burning American trees. Vox. https://www.vox.com/science-and-health/2019/3/4/18216045/renewable-energy-wood-pellets-biomass

376 Brief on biomass for energy in the EU. (2016). In European Commission. https://ourworldindata.org/energy-mixhttp://publications.jrc.ec.europa.eu/repository/bitstream/JRC109354/biomass_4_energy_brief_online_1.pdf

377   Ritchie, H. (2022, October 27). Energy. Our World in Data. https://ourworldindata.
       org/energy-mix
378   Frost, L. (2023, May 29). Not Dark Yet, But It's Getting There. Frontier Centre For
       Public Policy. https://fcpp.org/2023/05/29/not-dark-yet-but-its-getting-there/
379   Plimer, I. R. (2009). Heaven and earth: Global Warming, the Missing Science. Taylor
       Trade Publishing.
380   Tremoglie, C. (2022, March 21). Washington Examiner. Washington Examiner.
       https://www.washingtonexaminer.com/opinion/on-this-date-51-years-ago-climate-
       scientists-predicted-a-new-ice-age-was-coming
381   Spielmann, P. J. (1989, June 29). U.N. Predicts Disaster if Global Warming Not
       Checked. AP NEWS. https://web.archive.org/web/20200924233458mp_/https://
       apnews.com/article/bd45c372caf118ec99964ea547880cd0
382   Frederick, K. (n.d.). Sleepwalking Into a China-Style Social Credit System |
       The Heritage Foundation. The Heritage Foundation. https://www.heritage.org/
       technology/commentary/sleepwalking-china-style-social-credit-system
383   Reiff, N. (2023). The Collapse of FTX: What Went Wrong with the Crypto Exchange?
       Investopedia. https://www.investopedia.com/what-went-wrong-with-ftx-6828447
384   Agrawal, N. (2022, December 14). The Digital Asset Anti-Money Laundering
       Act is an opportunistic, unconstitutional assault on cryptocurrency self custody,
       developers, and node operators. Coin Center. https://www.coincenter.org/the-
       digital-asset-anti-money-laundering-act-is-an-opportunistic-unconstitutional-
       assault-on-cryptocurrency-self-custody-developers-and-node-operators/
385   Frederick, K. (n.d.). Sleepwalking Into a China-Style Social Credit System |
       The Heritage Foundation. The Heritage Foundation. https://www.heritage.org/
       technology/commentary/sleepwalking-china-style-social-credit-system
386   National Strategy for Countering Terrorism. (2021). In National Security Council.
       http://www.whitehouse.gov/wp-content/uploads/2021/06/National-Strategy-for-
       Countering-Domestic-Terrorism.pdf
387   Tunney, C. (2022, February 14). Federal government invokes Emergencies Act for
       first time ever in response to protests, blockades. CBC. https://www.cbc.ca/news/
       politics/trudeau-premiers-cabinet-1.6350734
388   Manley, C. (2022, February 1). Covid Misinformation That Turned Out to Be True -
       Point of View. Point of View. https://pointofview.net/articles/covid-misinformation-
       that-turned-out-to-be-true/
389   Fox News. (2023, February 14). Face masks made 'little to no difference' in preventing
       spread of COVID: study. New York Post. https://nypost.com/2023/02/14/face-masks-
       made-little-to-no-difference-in-preventing-covid-study/
390   Stein, C., Nassereldine, H., Sorensen, R. J. D., Amlag, J. O., Bisignano, C., Byrne,
       S., Castro, E., Coberly, K., Collins, J. K., Dalos, J., Daoud, F., Deen, A., Gakidou, E.,
       Giles, J. R., Hulland, E. N., Huntley, B. M., Kinzel, K. E., Lozano, R., Mokdad, A. H.,
       ... Lim, S. S. (2023). Past SARS-CoV-2 infection protection against re-infection: a
       systematic review and meta-analysis. The Lancet, 401(10379), 833–842. https://doi.
       org/10.1016/s0140-6736(22)02465-5
391   Grunwald, M. (2009, December 16). Person of the Year 2009 - TIME.
       TIME.com. https://content.time.com/time/specials/packages/
       article/0,28804,1946375_1947251_1947520,00.html
392   Gladstein, A. (2023, March 11). Structural Adjustment: How The IMF And World
       Bank Repress Poor Countries And Funnel Their Resources To Rich Ones. Bitcoin
       Magazine - Bitcoin News, Articles and Expert Insights. https://bitcoinmagazine.
       com/culture/imf-world-bank-repress-poor-countries

393 Masters, J. (2021, September 8). The IMF: The World's Controversial Financial Firefighter. Council on Foreign Relations. https://www.cfr.org/backgrounder/imf-worlds-controversial-financial-firefighter

394 Toussaint, E., & Millet, D. (2010). Debt, the IMF, and the World Bank: Sixty Questions, Sixty Answers. NYU Press.

395 Jason Hickel, Dylan Sullivan & Huzaifa Zoomkawala (2021) Plunder in the Post-Colonial Era: Quantifying Drain from the Global South Through Unequal Exchange, 1960–2018, New Political Economy, 26:6, 1030-1047, DOI: 10.1080/13563467.2021.1899153 https://www.tandfonline.com/doi/abs/10.1080/13563467.2021.1899153?journalCode=cnpe20

396 Hickel, J. (2021, October 24). Aid in reverse: how poor countries develop rich countries. The Guardian. https://www.theguardian.com/global-development-professionals-network/2017/jan/14/aid-in-reverse-how-poor-countries-develop-rich-countries

397 Hancock, G. (1989). Lords of poverty: The Power, Prestige, and Corruption of the International Aid Business. Atlantic Monthly Press.

398 Singh, T. (2022, July 21). Ghana's unions and left reject bailout talks with the IMF as economic crisis spirals. The Real News Network. https://therealnews.com/ghanas-unions-and-left-reject-bailout-talks-with-the-imf-as-economic-crisis-spirals

399 (Above) Hancock, G. (1989). Lords of poverty: The Power, Prestige, and Corruption of the International Aid Business. Atlantic Monthly Press.

400 History of Lending Commitments: Brazil. (2013, August 30). https://www.imf.org/external/np/fin/tad/extarr2.aspx?memberKey1=90&date1key=2013-08-31

401 George, S. (1990). A fate worse than debt. Grove Press.

402 Danaher, K. (1994b). 50 Years is Enough: The Case Against the World Bank and the International Monetary Fund. South End Press.

403 Study links 35 percent of Chinese Belt and Road Initiative projects to scandals involving corruption, environmental problems, labour violations - Business & Human Rights Resource Centre. (n.d.). Business & Human Rights Resource Centre. https://www.business-humanrights.org/en/latest-news/study-links-35-percent-of-chinese-belt-and-road-initiative-projects-to-scandals-involving-corruption-environmental-problems-labour-violations/

404 Wooley, A. (n.d.). AidData's new dataset of 13,427 Chinese development projects worth $843 billion reveals major increase in 'hidden debt' and Belt and Road Initiative implementation problems. https://www.aiddata.org/blog/aiddatas-new-dataset-of-13-427-chinese-development-projects-worth-843-billion-reveals-major-increase-in-hidden-debt-and-belt-and-road-initiative-implementation-problems

405 George, S. (1990). A fate worse than debt. Grove Press.

406 CFA Franc | History and information | BCEAO. (2016, June 1). https://www.bceao.int/en/content/history-cfa-franc

407 (Above) Oxford Languages and Google - English | Oxford Languages. (2022, August 12). https://languages.oup.com/google-dictionary-en/

408 Gladstein, A. (2023, April 25). Fighting Monetary Colonialism With Open-Source Code. Bitcoin Magazine - Bitcoin News, Articles and Expert Insights. https://bitcoinmagazine.com/culture/bitcoin-a-currency-of-decolonization

409 Sylla, N. S. (2020, January 6). The Franc Zone, a Tool of French Neocolonialism in Africa. https://jacobin.com/2020/01/franc-zone-french-neocolonialism-africa

410 LeBor, A. (2014). Tower of Basel: The Shadowy History of the Secret Bank that Runs the World. PublicAffairs.

411 Mehta, S. (2023). Halogen vs LED bulbs (Switch to LEDs & Save $253 a Year). LiquidLEDs. https://www.liquidleds.com.au/blogs/news/halogen-vs-led-bulbs

412   Dittmar, H., Bond, R., Hurst, M., & Kasser, T. (2014). The relationship between materialism and personal well-being: A meta-analysis. Journal of Personality and Social Psychology, 107(5), 879–924. https://doi.org/10.1037/a0037409

413   O'Donnell, G., & Oswald, A. J. (2015). National well-being policy and a weighted approach to human feelings. Ecological Economics, 120, 59–70. https://doi.org/10.1016/j.ecolecon.2015.09.021

414   Tonga Remittances, percent of GDP - data, chart | TheGlobalEconomy.com. (n.d.). TheGlobalEconomy.com. https://www.theglobaleconomy.com/Tonga/remittances_percent_GDP/

415   This is the Fee Table. (n.d.). Western Union. https://www.westernunion.com/content/dam/wu/EU/EN/feeTableRetailEN-ES.PDF

416   Tonga - Place Explorer - Data Commons. (n.d.). https://datacommons.org/place/country/TON/?utm_medium=explore&mprop=amount&popt=Economic Activity&cpv=activitySource,GrossDomesticProduction&hl=en

417   Nowicki, S., & Strickland, B. R. (1973). A locus of control scale for children. Journal of Consulting and Clinical Psychology, 40(1), 148–154. https://doi.org/10.1037/h0033978

418   Lefcourt, H. M. (1982). Locus of control: Current Trends in Theory and Research. Psychology Press.

419   Judge, T. A., & Bono, J. E. (2001). Relationship of core self-evaluations traits—self-esteem, generalized self-efficacy, locus of control, and emotional stability—with job satisfaction and job performance: A meta-analysis. Journal of Applied Psychology, 86(1), 80–92. https://doi.org/10.1037/0021-9010.86.1.80

420   Pressman, S. D., Matthews, K. A., Cohen, S., Martire, L. M., Scheier, M. F., Baum, A., & Schulz, R. (2009). Association of Enjoyable Leisure Activities With Psychological and Physical Well-Being. Psychosomatic Medicine, 71(7), 725–732. https://doi.org/10.1097/psy.0b013e3181ad7978

421   Hawkins, E. (2022). London home to £41bn empty properties despite soaring buyer demand. CityAM. https://www.cityam.com/london-home-to-41bn-empty-properties-despite-soaring-buyer-demand/

422   Government of Canada, Statistics Canada. (2019, June 17). Census Profile, 2016 Census - Whistler [Population centre], British Columbia and Saskatchewan [Province]. https://www12.statcan.gc.ca/census-recensement/2016/dp-pd/prof/details/page.cfm?Lang=E&Geo1=POPC&Code1=1309&sGeo2=PR&Code2=47&Data=Count&SearchText=Whistler&SearchType=Begins&SearchPR=01&B1=All&GeoLevel=PR&GeoCode=1309&TABID=1&utm_source=pique%20newsmagazine&utm_campaign=pique%20newsmagazine%3A%20outbound&utm_medium=referral

423   Hopkins, E. (2022, March 31). How Many Vacant Homes Are There Across New York State? 101.5 WPDH. https://wpdh.com/housing-market-in-new-york/

424   Miettinen, D. (2022). How brutal is NYC's rental market? Just ask this producer. Marketplace. https://www.marketplace.org/2022/09/28/how-brutal-is-nycs-rental-market-just-ask-this-producer/

425   Steele, G. (2020, November 23). The New Money Trust: How Large Money Managers Control Our Economy and What We Can Do About It - American Economic Liberties Project. American Economic Liberties Project. https://www.economicliberties.us/our-work/new-money-trust/

426   Fragnito, A. (2023, June 30). What's The Average ROI On Real Estate Investments In 2023? Peoples Capital Group. https://www.peoplescapitalgroup.com/average-roi-real-estate/

427   S&P 500 Returns since 1957. (n.d.). https://www.officialdata.org/us/stocks/s-p-500/1957?amount=100&endYear=2022/

428   AcreTrader, I. (n.d.). Average U.S. Farmland Investment Returns | AcreTrader. AcreTrader. https://acretrader.com/resources/farmland-values/farmland-returns

429   Joe Rogan Experience. (2022, December 21). #1914 - Siddharth Kara. Spotify. https://open.spotify.com/episode/3ZBdeZLitzqNPBbvv9QIEz?si=d79b7a2a52fd41ca&nd=1

430   Paycor. (n.d.). The Biggest Cost of Doing Business: A Closer Look at Labor Costs. https://www.paycor.com/resource-center/articles/closer-look-at-labor-costs/

431   Jamasmie, C. (2022, May 17). Electric vehicles surpass phones as top driver of cobalt demand. MINING.COM. https://www.mining.com/electric-vehicles-surpass-phones-as-top-driver-of-cobalt-demand/

432   WHD by the Numbers 2022. (n.d.). DOL. https://www.dol.gov/agencies/whd/data

433   Business and Employee Supports | OCC. (n.d.). OCC. https://occ.ca/covid19-supportforbusinesses/

434   Record-high corporate profits behind inflation. (2022, December 8). Canadian Union of Public Employees. https://cupe.ca/record-high-corporate-profits-behind-inflation

435   Lévesque, C. (2022, October 17). Initial ArriveCAN costs were $80,000. Here's how it got to $54M. Nationalpost. https://nationalpost.com/news/the-initial-cost-of-arrivecan-was-80000-what-about-the-other-54m

436   Defense Acquisitions annual Assessment. (2020). In United States Government Accountability Office. https://www.gao.gov/assets/gao-20-439.pdf

437   Reducing Health Care Costs: Decreasing Administrative Spending. (2018, July 31). Testimony for Senate Committee on Health, Education, Labor and Pensions Hearing, United States of America. https://www.help.senate.gov/imo/media/doc/Cutler.pdf

438   Must, E. (2017, July 21). Toronto tears down elderly man's $550 staircase, promises to build new one for $10K. Nationalpost. https://nationalpost.com/news/toronto/toronto-tears-down-elderly-mans-550-staircase-promises-to-build-new-ones-for-10000

439   Hulsmann, J. G. (2018). The ethics of money production.

440   Szabo, N. (n.d.). Shelling Out: The Origins of Money | Satoshi Nakamoto Institute. https://nakamotoinstitute.org/shelling-out/

441   Environmental & Social Footprint - Patagonia. (n.d.). https://www.patagonia.com/our-footprint/

442   Arc'teryx Equipment. (n.d.). Sustainability: The Long Run | Arc'teryx | Arc'teryx. https://arcteryx.com/ca/en/explore/sustainability/

443   Sustainability. (n.d.). https://www.tentree.ca/pages/sustainability

444   Svanholm, K. (2022). Bitcoin: Everything Divided by 21 Million. Konsensus Network.

445   CEICdata.com. (2018). United States Private Consumption: % of GDP. www.ceicdata.com. https://www.ceicdata.com/en/indicator/united-states/private-consumption--of-nominal-gdp

446   Gold standard. (n.d.). https://www.cs.mcgill.ca/~rwest/wikispeedia/wpcd/wp/g/Gold_standard.htm

447   Chart: How Much Gold is in the World? (2021, November 16). Visual Capitalist. https://www.visualcapitalist.com/sp/chart-how-much-gold-is-in-the-world/

448   Ronayne, M. (2017, October 5). Jeffrey Snider: Eurodollar University Part 2. https://www.macrovoices.com/310-jeffrey-snider-eurodollar-university-part-2

449   Central bank swaps then and now: swaps and dollar liquidity in the 1960s. (2020). In BIS Working Papers. https://www.bis.org/publ/work851.pdf

450   Snider, J. P. (2013, May 28). Sunday Gold Fix - The Basics of Leasing. Alhambra Investments. https://alhambrapartners.com/2013/05/28/sunday-gold-fix-the-basics-of-leasing/

451 Cable: 1974LONDON16154_b. (n.d.). https://wikileaks.org/plusd/cables/1974LONDON16154_b.html?ref=the-qi-of-self-sovereignty

452 Atlantic Council. (2023, July 14). Central Bank Digital Currency Tracker - Atlantic Council. https://www.atlanticcouncil.org/cbdctracker/

453 CBUAE launches a Financial Infrastructure Transformation Programme to accelerate the digital transformation of the financial services sector. (2023). In Central Bank of UAE. https://www.centralbank.ae/media/mdupathy/cbuae-launches-a-financial-infrastructure-transformation-programme-to-accelerate-the-digital-transformation-of-the-financial-services-sector-en.pdf

454 Havenstein, R. (2023, March 23). "The central bank will have absolute control." SubStack. https://rudy.substack.com/p/the-central-bank-will-have-absolute

455 Bfsi, E. (2021, April 13). Digital Currency: Yuan comes with an expiry date: Spend or it will vanish. ETBFSI.com. https://bfsi.economictimes.indiatimes.com/news/policy/digital-currency-yuan-comes-with-an-expiry-date-spend-or-it-will-vanish/82059471

456 Hinchliffe, T. (2022, October 17). IMF Exec Touts CBDC Programmability, CCP Style Credit Scoring. The Sociable. https://sociable.co/government-and-policy/imf-cbdc-programmability-ccp-credit-scoring/

457 Willis, M. (2023). Plandemic Series | Official Home of The Great Awakening. Plandemic Series Official. https://plandemicseries.com/

458 Stevens, S. (2020). Shareholder Letter. In Stone Ridge Asset Management. https://www.microstrategy.com/content/dam/website-assets/collateral/bitcoin-downloads/Stone-Ridge-2020-Shareholder-Letter.pdf

459 BitBaggins. Tweet / Twitter. (n.d.). Twitter. https://twitter.com/bitbaggins/status/1619901047132282881?s=46&t=FH7Drfo7gUkKs1UR6udvew

460 The Nantucket Project. (2014, October 3). Julian Assange: Bitcoin is Much More Than Just a Currency [Video]. YouTube. https://www.youtube.com/watch?v=MaB3Zw5_p9c

461 Orwell, G. (2009). 1984: A Novel.

462 Sigalos, M., & Kharpal, A. (2022, October 13). El Salvador's bitcoin experiment: $60 million lost, $375 million spent, little to show so far. CNBC. https://www.cnbc.com/2022/10/13/el-salvadors-bitcoin-holdings-down-60percent-to-60-million-one-year-later.html

463 Morris, D. Z. (2023, May 11). 1 Year of Bitcoin in El Salvador: The Bad, the Good and the Ugly. Coindesk. https://www.coindesk.com/layer2/2022/09/15/one-year-of-bitcoin-in-el-salvador-the-bad-the-good-and-the-ugly/

464 Exchange. (2022). The state of cryptocurrency adoption in Africa per country. FurtherAfrica. https://furtherafrica.com/2022/07/14/the-state-of-cryptocurrency-adoption-in-africa-per-country/

465 Hall, J. (2022, October 24). The Madeira Bitcoin adoption experiment takes flight. Cointelegraph. https://cointelegraph.com/news/the-madeira-bitcoin-adoption-experiment-takes-flight

466 White, L. H. (2023). Better money: Gold, Fiat, or Bitcoin? Cambridge University Press.

467 Lowrey, A. (2020, May 15). Millennials Are the New Lost Generation. The Atlantic. https://www.theatlantic.com/ideas/archive/2020/04/millennials-are-new-lost-generation/609832/

468 Mitchell, T. (2020, August 17). Trends in U.S. income and wealth inequality | Pew Research Center. Pew Research Center's Social & Demographic Trends Project. https://www.pewresearch.org/social-trends/2020/01/09/trends-in-income-and-wealth-inequality/

469 2020 Poll | Victims of Communism. (2022, November 18). Victims of Communism. https://victimsofcommunism.org/annual-poll/2020-annual-poll/

470   Who Killed More: Hitler, Stalin, or Mao? (2018, February 28). ChinaFile. https://
      www.chinafile.com/library/nyrb-china-archive/who-killed-more-hitler-stalin-or-
      mao
471   How Did the North Korean Famine Happen? (n.d.). Wilson Center. https://www.
      wilsoncenter.org/article/how-did-the-north-korean-famine-happen
472   Taylor & Francis Ltd. (n.d.). The Demography of Genocide in Southeast Asia: The
      Death Tolls in Cambodia, 1975-79, and East Timor, 1975-80. Taylor & Francis.
      https://www.tandfonline.com/doi/abs/10.1080/1467271032000147041
473   South African History Online. (n.d.). https://www.sahistory.org.za/sites/default/files/
      file%20uploads%20/peter_gill_famine_and_foreigners_ethiopia_sin%20cebook4you.
      pdf
474   Minsky, H. (2008). Stabilizing an unstable economy. McGraw Hill Professional.
475   Ranasinghe, D. (2021, September 14). Global debt is fast approaching record
      $300 trillion - IIF. Reuters. https://www.reuters.com/business/global-debt-is-fast-
      approaching-record-300-trillion-iif-2021-09-14/
476   Hosking, G. (n.d.). Trust and Distrust in the USSR: An Overview on JSTOR. https://
      www.jstor.org/stable/10.5699/slaveasteurorev2.91.1.0001
477   Cox, J. (2015, April 15). 5 biggest banks now own almost half the industry. CNBC.
      https://www.cnbc.com/2015/04/15/5-biggest-banks-now-own-almost-half-the-
      industry.html
478   CBS News. (2023, March 16). Treasury Secretary Janet Yellen tells Congress nation's
      banking system remains "sound" | full video [Video]. YouTube. https://www.youtube.
      com/watch?v=CX6O--sk48A
479   Who Pays Income Taxes? (n.d.). National Taxpayers Union. https://www.ntu.org/
      foundation/tax-page/who-pays-income-taxes
480   Expert, A. T. (2022). States with the Lowest Taxes and the Highest Taxes. Copyright
      1997-2022 Intuit, Inc. All Rights Reserved. https://turbotax.intuit.com/tax-tips/
      fun-facts/states-with-the-highest-and-lowest-taxes/L6HPAVqSF
481   Passy, J. (2019, September 29). Nearly half of the U.S.'s homeless people live in one
      state: California. MarketWatch. https://www.marketwatch.com/story/this-state-
      is-home-to-nearly-half-of-all-people-living-on-the-streets-in-the-us-2019-09-18
482   Oil & Gas. (2020). Green California Has the Nation's Worst Power Grid. Oil & Gas
      360. https://www.oilandgas360.com/green-california-has-the-nations-worst-power-
      grid/
483   Casiano, L. (2022, November 17). California faces budget deficit despite nearly $100
      billion surplus last fiscal year. Fox News. https://www.foxnews.com/us/california-
      faces-budget-deficit-nearly-100-billion-surplus-last-fiscal-year
484   Abadi, M. (2018, March 1). California has the worst quality of life in the 50 US
      states, and some conservatives are celebrating. Business Insider. https://www.
      businessinsider.com/california-worst-quality-of-life-2018-3
485   Biermeier, D. (2023, July 4). 10 States People Are Fleeing And 10 States People Are
      Moving To. Forbes Home. https://www.forbes.com/home-improvement/features/
      states-move-to-from/9o
486   Wikipedia contributors. (2023). List of countries by GDP (nominal). Wikipedia.
      https://en.wikipedia.org/wiki/List_of_countries_by_GDP_(nominal)
487   IBISWorld - Industry Market Research, Reports, and Statistics. (n.d.). https://www.
      ibisworld.com/industry-statistics/market-size/tax-preparation-services-united-
      states/
488   Griffith, J. (2016). FREEDOM: The End Of The Human Condition.
489   Nickerson, C. (2023). Learned Helplessness Theory in Psychology (seligman):
      Examples & Coping. Simply Psychology. https://www.simplypsychology.org/
      learned-helplessness.html

Made in United States
Troutdale, OR
04/05/2024

18965001R00246